Faulkner and War
FAULKNER AND YOKNAPATAWPHA,
2001

Faulkner and War

FAULKNER AND YOKNAPATAWPHA, 2001

EDITED BY
NOEL POLK
AND
ANN J. ABADIE

UNIVERSITY PRESS OF MISSISSIPPI
JACKSON

www.upress.state.ms.us

The University Press of Mississippi is a member of the Association of
American University Presses.

Copyright © 2004 by University Press of Mississippi
All rights reserved
Manufactured in the United States of America

Illustrations courtesy of Special Collections, University of Mississippi Libraries
Library of Congress Cataloging-in-Publication Data
Faulkner and Yoknapatawpha Conference (28th : 2001 : University of Mississippi)
Faulkner and war : Faulkner and Yoknapatawpha, 2001 / edited by
Noel Polk and Ann J. Abadie.
p. cm.
"The Twenty-Eighth Annual Faulkner and Yoknapatawpha Conference sponsored by the
University of Mississippi in Oxford took place July 22–27, 2001"—Introd.
Includes bibliographical references and index.
ISBN: 978-1-60473-851-3
1. Faulkner, William, 1897–1962—Criticism and interpretation—Congresses.
2. Faulkner, William, 1897–1962—Knowledge—Military art and science—Congresses.
3. Faulkner, William, 1897–1962—Knowledge—War—Congresses.
4. War stories, American—History and criticism—Congresses.
5. Military art and science in literature—Congresses.
6. War in literature—Congresses.
I. Polk, Noel. II. Abadie, Ann J. III. Title.

PS3511.A86Z7832117   2004
813'.52—dc22   2003017444

British Library Cataloging-in-Publication Data available

Contents

Introduction: Faulkner and War and Peace NOEL POLK	vii
A Note on the Conference	xv
Faulkner's Civil War in Fiction, History, and Memory DON H. DOYLE	3
William Faulkner and Theater of War JAMES G. WATSON	20
Addie in No-Man's-Land JOHN LIMAN	36
Daughters of Necessity, Mothers of Resource: White Women and the War in *Absalom, Absalom!* PAULA ELYSEU MESQUITA	55
Fraternal Fury: Faulkner, World War I, and Myths of Masculinity JOHN LOWE	70
Quentin, Listen! DAVID MADDEN	102
Imagining the Abstract: Faulkner's Treatment of War and Values in *A Fable* LOTHAR HÖNNIGHAUSEN	120
Scar NOEL POLK	138
Contributors	160
Index	163

Introduction:
Faulkner and War and Peace

NOEL POLK

Fighting is more important than truth. . . . So we must restrict the prestiges and privileges of it to the few so that it will not lose popularity with the many who have to die.
—Ad Astra 409[1]

Defeat will be good for us. Defeat iss good for art; victory, it iss not good.
— 413

Along with race and gender, war is one of the touchstones triumvirate, lodestones even, central to William Faulkner's works and to the combustible age which he chronicled so intensely. His life was framed by war—by the cultural memory and the still-regnant physical scars of the Civil War on the one end and by the gathering storms of the civil wars Vietnam and the civil rights movement would cause on the other—and punctuated throughout by military irruptions and their bitter residues. The twentieth was a century studded with those residues: sunbleached skeletons and dank memorial ossuaries, corpses stacked like bricks, their blood the mortar holding the twentieth century together, if indeed one may say that it did hold together; it was a century suffocated by the sanctimony of high idealism and of naked aggression, often identical; by language refracted to meaninglessness by the screaming of howitzers and the weeping of children; by human displacement and turmoil, by ceaseless fragmentation and despair.

And yet, having acknowledged that, it is worth noting how little of battle actually appears in his fiction, narrated directly by the author or by one of the characters, although to be sure few are the characters who have not been affected by war in one way or another. In fact, Faulkner seems more concerned with the gaps between the battles, the interims between wars, when warriors military and civil must figure out how to deal with peace: with the repercussions in home life rather than with corpse-strewn battlegrounds and the fury of combat. Even in *A Fable*, his novel most directly engaged with conditions of the battle, he is more concerned with war not as a temporary aberration from peace but rather as a condition of civilization, one of its basic, sustaining behaviors. Though set during World War I, *A Fable* is really a meditation on the state of the world following World War II—it is a Cold War novel which dramatizes the inextricability of the military hierarchy from the political and economic and cultural hierarchies that run the world's nations, hierarchies that know no political boundaries and often connive with each other to insure their own survival, no matter the cost in blood to the expendable grunts who form the teeming masses of those whose lives are in their control. In *A Fable*, Faulkner is interested in the mechanisms of power which hold those masses in place during and between wars.

The characters in an early story, "Ad Astra," find themselves dumped unceremoniously into one of those gaps by the Armistice of November 11, 1918. The story is about the war that follows war, since in Faulkner there never is really any such thing as peace; peace is only an extenuating circumstance between battles, a kind of furious, shapeless enigma with which people must grapple instead with war's more comprehensible and graspable shapes of honor and courage and simple escape, in comparison with which quotidian life means, can mean, less than nothing. Indeed, for many of Faulkner's characters, war is attractive precisely because it offers escape from the routine of the daily, in the deadening routine of the middle-class life to which the Armistice condemns these survivors. The narrator of "All the Dead Pilots"—probably the same narrator as "Ad Astra," certainly the same voice—describes these men thirteen years later:

> . . . they are dead, all the old pilots, dead on the eleventh of November, 1918. . . . They are thick men now, a little thick about the waist from sitting behind desks, and maybe not so good at it, with wives and children in suburban homes almost paid out, with gardens in which they putter in the long evenings after the 5:15 is in, and perhaps not so good at that either: the hard, lean men who swaggered hard and drank hard because they had found that being dead was not as quiet as they had heard it would be. (511–12)

Almost certainly the same narrator as him of "All the Dead Pilots," "Ad Astra"'s narrator remembers the immediate, local aftermath of the Armistice: the disorientation of a group of friends as they try to come to terms with a life without an enemy to kill, a bomb to throw, or a no-man's-land to cross. Without war, they have lost definition, national and personal; "I dont know what we were" during the war, he remembers. "With the exception of Comyn, we had started out Americans, but after three years, in our British tunics and British wings and here and there a ribbon, I dont suppose we had even bothered in three years to wonder what we were, to think or to remember" (407).

On that "day, that evening," November 11, 1918, they were "even less than that, or more than that" (407). Presumably *that* means their national identities—the Americans are in British uniform, so that presumably after Armistice those sorts of distinctions, nationalisms, are meaningless, or at best confusing. They are between national boundaries, "either beneath or beyond the knowledge that we had not even wondered in three years." The subadar suggests that they were "like men trying to move in water, with held breath watching our terrific and infinitesimal limbs, watching one another's terrific stasis without touch, without contact, robbed of all save the impotence and the need" (407). But the narrator takes the subadar's metaphor a step or two further: "I think of us as bugs in the surface of the water, isolant and aimless and unflagging. Not on the surface; in it, within that line of demarcation not air and not water, sometimes submerged, sometimes not. You have watched an unbreaking groundswell in a cove," he continues, elaborating,

> the water shallow, the cove quiet, a little sinister with satiate familiarity, while beyond the darkling horizon the dying storm has raged on. That was the water, we the flotsam. Even after twelve years it is no clearer than that. It had no beginning and no ending. Out of nothing we howled, unwitting the storm which we had escaped and the foreign strand which we could not escape; that in the interval between two surges of the swell we died who had been too young to have ever lived. (408)

The extended metaphor is an arresting one, if not completely clear. They, the dead pilots, are flotsam carried helplessly by a tide over which they have no control into a cove, usually a safeplace, a harbor—peace—but disturbing nevertheless, because it is only a momentary lull between "the storm which we had escaped and the foreign strand which we could not escape." It is a "little sinister with satiate familiarity"—too familiar, that is, too regular and predictable and dulling to the sensibilities.

A good bit of Faulkner's fiction is set in such a cove, with conflicts behind and ahead, always part of the landscape even if over the horizon in a "foreign strand," but always present; war is a central structure of Yoknapatawpha's collective unconscious and consciousness too.

The fliers of "Ad Astra" turn their intended celebration of the Armistice into a mourning for the war's end. They who lived through the war are destroyed by the peace: "Those who have been four years rotting out yonder," says the subadar, "are not more dead than we" (421). They dread the sameness of peace and turn against each other, shouting "at one another, speaking in foreign tongues out of our inescapable isolations, reiterant, unlistened to by one another" (413). They also turn on the French, their former allies, provoking them by bringing with them into a bistro a

German prisoner. The French, offended, order them to leave and a barroom brawl ensues, after which they eject the new alignment of forces. In war, men bond against a common enemy; lacking war, the only enemy is themselves; they revert to their "inescapable isolations" where national alignments, brotherhood, means nothing, and where they will have to live the rest of their lives: "What is your destiny except to be dead?" the subadar says: "It is unfortunate that your generation had to be the one. It is unfortunate that for the better part of your days you will walk the earth a spirit. But that was your destiny" (428).

In Faulkner, then, war and peace are inextricable, the domestic and the battlefield always hand in hand in profound reciprocation. The papers delivered at the 2001 Faulkner and Yoknapatawpha Conference at the University of Mississippi all address this relationship in Faulkner's work in diverse and interesting ways. Don Doyle's "Faulkner's Civil War in Fiction, History, and Memory" provides an opening comprehensive overview of the historical aspects of Faulkner's treatment of the Civil War—not the written record so much as that record transmitted by regional memory and by the tales of those combatants of both genders who survived into Faulkner's own life. Though there's no evidence that Faulkner "ever did much historical research," Doyle notes, it would have been difficult for him not to have absorbed "the ever-present legacy of the Civil War. As a boy and well into his adult life Faulkner surrounded himself with people who were obsessed with and often quite knowledgeable about the Civil War, particularly the war as it affected northern Mississippi." Doyle's purpose is not to uncover how much factual Civil War history Faulkner knew, but rather to explore his "fictional treatment of the war and demonstrate how it squares with the historical evidence." In successive sections on Yankees, Slaves, Women, and Memory, Doyle leads us to understand how in some ways Faulkner was "decades ahead of historians" precisely because he eschewed factual history in favor of his region's memories. Particularly in *The Unvanquished*, Doyle argues, Faulkner's presentation of the war is an "insightful and prescient reading of the Civil War with fresh and subtle treatments of Yankee soldiers, slaves, white women, and Southern bushwhackers, all groups that had been mostly ignored in the fictional and historical treatments of the war."

James Watson's "William Faulkner and the Theater of War" is also a wide-ranging overview of "the scope of the war matter and its modes of representation in [Faulkner's] early life and art." He argues that World War I was a significant source for his writing, though not at all a "source" in the traditional meaning of that term: "Initially a *subject* of his writing, by which he might measure and when necessary revise and reconstitute images of himself and his circumstances in the actual world, the Great

War also modeled for him a *means* of written expression." The "theater" of war becomes, in effect, Faulkner's theater for representing himself to the world during his young manhood, during which time he presented himself and his writings as evidence that he, too, had been an actor in that war, though to be sure he was not. Watson's discussion of this aspect of Faulkner's life as it appears in his fiction offers us many insights into Faulkner's work, and an especially rewarding reading of Dalton Ames's place in *The Sound and the Fury*.

John Liman's "Addie in No-Man's-Land" focuses on the mud rampant in the Great War's trenches and in *As I Lay Dying*, on the peculiar combination of dirt, symbolizing death, and water, symbolizing cleansing and rebirth, that make mud such a potent symbol of both the Great War and Faulkner's novel: "What seems to fascinate Faulkner most concerning mud is its yellow impurity, or better say its nonelementality. About Jewel's ankle swirls 'a runnel of yellow neither water nor earth'; it curves with the 'yellow road neither of earth nor water'; it dissolves 'into a streaming mass of dark green neither of earth nor sky.' . . . What mud means to Faulkner is that the world is nauseating . . . because it cannot be contained, categorized, and idealized." Mud represents, then, both the modernist's interest in the breakdown of boundaries and Faulkner's own inability to think of war as heroic. He thus understands, according to Liman, that "to join the twentieth century he will have to come to terms with the trenches. This confrontation alone will allow him to put to rest his dreams of a redeemed Civil War"—that is, of war as a heroic undertaking.

Paula Mesquita, in "Daughters of Necessity, Mothers of Resource: White Women and the War in *Absalom, Absalom!*," demonstrates how the Civil War in *Absalom* gives agency to white women, if only because the absence of men forces them into new relationships with their home circumstances. Mesquita sees this as an entirely positive condition, however, noting how many women "eventually began to realize that in the midst of catastrophe and misfortune a blessing in disguise had been lurking. A new source of political power was made available to them as they inadvertently became the champions of Southern liberties on the home front. Still," Mesquita asks, "what did it mean, this new power? Going to war pretty much summed up for men what it meant to be a man. But what were women to think of the new position in which political developments they were never consulted about had landed them?" This is the question Mesquita explores, paying especial attention to Rosa Coldfield and Judith Sutpen, but concluding with an especially rewarding discussion of the white women's developing relationship with *Absalom's* perhaps most enigmatic figure, certainly its most enigmatic woman, Clytie.

In "Fraternal Fury: Faulkner, World War I, and Myths of Masculinity," John Lowe discusses Faulkner's competition with his brothers Jack and John. He believes that "many of the narratives he created during these turbulent years [of his youth and early career] . . . led Faulkner into much more than biographical fiction, for in his quarrel with Jack and John Faulkner he found a metaphor for war, regional animosities, finance capitalism, the split consciousness of literary modernism, and, finally, the tragic racial history of the region and nation"; as well, war became for Faulkner "a central pole of masculine identity." In the first part of his paper, Lowe reads Faulkner's relationship with these brothers—Jack, who became the war hero Faulkner wanted to be; John, who stayed home too and became a writer—through Blotner's and other biographical accounts as well as through family photographs. In the remaining pages, he shows how these curious relationships make their way into Faulkner's fiction about World War I; he gives us interesting readings of *Soldiers' Pay*, *Flags in the Dust*, and short stories "Victory," "Crevasse," and "Turnabout."

Novelist and Civil War historian David Madden brings these skills to bear on his contribution, "Quentin! Listen!" Madden argues that Quentin Compson, not Thomas Sutpen, is the major character in *Absalom, Absalom!* Indeed, Madden has found "nothing in all fiction as fascinatingly complex as Quentin's shifting role in the works of Faulkner," and he "would claim for Quentin a significant uniqueness in all world literature, while lamenting that he is one of its most neglected characters." Madden believes that the Civil War is a "catalyst for Faulkner personally and for his characters, especially Quentin Compson, whose consciousness is at the center of Faulkner's creative consciousness." His paper thus argues that the power of the Civil War in Faulkner lies obviously not in its vivid depiction of battle, but in "the ways in which the war is more alluded to and its effects implied rather than dramatized." With emphasis on the novel's methods of narration, Madden discusses *Absalom*'s narrative power in its "pervasive use of the technique of context and implication, what is more important [than the battles themselves]—the war's effect on Americans, especially Southerners," and especially on Quentin.

Lothar Hönnighausen brings us to Faulkner's most complex treatment of war, *A Fable*, in "Imagining the Abstract: Faulkner's Treatment of War and Values in *A Fable*." Hönnighausen suggests that "what distinguishes the treatment of war in both *Soldiers' Pay* and *Flags in the Dust* from that in *A Fable* is that, in the early novels, war appears primarily as an arena of psychological projections," whereas *A Fable*, "although dealing with war, does so by making it the subject of far-ranging moral reflections: on power and order, on war and peace, on hierarchical authority and the freedom of the individual, and on death and life as moral goods." Faulkner doesn't present these themes *in abstracto* in the novel, but "embodies them through plotting and character drawing," but avoiding "wooden allegories and cheap moral propaganda" through a "peculiar mode of *metaphorical thinking*, indigenous to *A Fable* but also to some of the great writing in *Absalom, Absalom!* and *The Hamlet*" that his titular phrase "Imagining the Abstract" draws attention to. Hönnighausen's essay, full of rich readings of individual passages, offers convincing evidence why *A Fable* should be taken more seriously than it usually is by the Faulkner community.

My own contribution also deals with *A Fable*. "Scar" investigates first those low in the military hierarchy, those expendables whom any nation expects to die or suffer for the nation's survival as a nation; these are the ones who bear the scars of battle and to whom a nation builds its tombs—also "scars," though of another type, since they constantly sermonize the citizenry on the meaning of heroic death: sitting monumentally in marble, such tombs disguise the wound, cover the ugly death with a beautiful memory, a hope for the future. "Scar" then looks at the various hierarchies in *A Fable*, at how they work from the top down to manipulate and control those who must die for the sake of the nation into patriotic self-sacrifice.

NOTE

1. William Faulkner, *Collected Stories* (New York: Random House, 1950). Hereafter cited in parenthesis.

A Note on the Conference

The Twenty-Eighth Annual Faulkner and Yoknapatawpha Conference sponsored by the University of Mississippi in Oxford took place July 22–27, 2001, with nearly two hundred of the author's admirers from around the world in attendance. Eight presentations at the conference are collected in this volume. Brief mention is made here of other conference activities and details about special groups in attendance.

In addition to eight formal papers presented by scholars from the United States, Germany, and Portugal, the Rivendell Theatre Ensemble of Chicago presented the play *Faulkner's Bicycle*. The play is set in Oxford in 1962 and concerns a fictional family that finds itself intimately involved with the famous writer a few months before his death. Among other program events were presentations by members of Faulkner's family and friends; *Voices from Yoknapatawpha*, readings from Faulkner's fiction selected and arranged by actor George Kehoe and Betty Harrington, widow of former conference director Evans Harrington; and "Teaching Faulkner" sessions conducted by James B. Carothers, Robert W. Hamblin, Arlie E. Herron, and Charles A. Peek.

The conference opened on Sunday with a reception at the University Museums for an exhibition of photographs entitled *River Walk* and two displays from the Museums' collections relating to the theme of the conference, one of Civil War memorabilia and the other of World War I posters. The afternoon program included readings from Faulkner; a performance by the Rising Star Fife and Drum Band, with Othar Turner; and Allan Kilsky's reading of his winning entry for the twelfth Faux Faulkner Contest, sponsored by *Hemispheres* magazine of United Airlines, the University of Mississippi, and Yoknapatawpha Press. Donald M. Kartiganer, director of the conference, presented the fourteenth annual Eudora Welty Awards in Creative Writing. Angela D. Fortner, a student at Callaway High School in Jackson, won first prize, $500, and Sarah Wheat, of Central Hinds Academy in Raymond, won second prize, $250. Frances Patterson, of Tupelo, established and endowed the awards, which are selected through a competition held in high schools throughout Mississippi. Following a buffet supper, at the home of Dr. and Mrs. M. B. Howorth Jr., James Watson gave the first lecture of the conference.

Monday's program included three lectures and the presentation of "Knowing William Faulkner," slides and commentary by the writer's nephew, J. M. Faulkner, and Meg Faulkner DuChaine. The Center for the Study of Southern Culture then hosted a reception for *After Reading*

Faulkner: His Myriad World, a selection of photographs Arlie Herron made during Faulkner and Yoknapatawpha Conferences over the years. The day ended as Colby Kullman moderated the third "Faulkner on the Fringe" open-mike session at Milly Moorhead's Southside Gallery. Tuesday offered daylong tours of North Mississippi, followed by a party at Tyler Place hosted by Charles Noyes, Sarah and Allie Smith, and Colby Kullman. On Wednesday, "Faulkner in Oxford" assembled local residents Will Lewis Jr. and Harter Crutcher as panelists for a discussion moderated by M. C. "Chooky" Faulkner, another of the writer's nephews. Other events included a picnic at Faulkner's home, Rowan Oak; a party at Square Books; and a closing reception at Betty Jane Gary's home, in which Faulkners lived when he and his family moved to Oxford in 1902. The University Press of Mississippi hosted a display of Faulkner books published by university presses throughout the country, and the University's John Davis Williams Library mounted an exhibition of Faulkner books, manuscripts, photographs, and memorabilia.

For the third year, high school teachers from five Southern states, the recipients of fellowships funded by a grant from Saks Incorporated Foundation, on behalf of McRae's, Proffitt's, and Parisian Department Stores, attended the conference. Also attending were an Elderhostel group led by Carolyn Vance Smith and Joan Popernik.

On Monday of conference week, we learned of the death, at the age of ninety-two, of Eudora Welty. Wednesday morning, conference registrants and members of the University and Oxford communities gathered at the Education Auditorium for an impromptu series of readings and comments on the life and work of Miss Welty. Although indeed a sad and unexpected event, it seemed appropriate that the annual celebration of one great Mississippi writer became the occasion to acknowledge the magnificent career of another, one who, born in 1909, was the last of Faulkner's great literary contemporaries.

The conference planners are grateful to all the individuals and organizations who support the Faulkner and Yoknapatawpha Conference annually. In addition to those mentioned above, we wish to thank Mr. Richard Howorth of Square Books, St. Peter's Episcopal Church, the City of Oxford, and the Oxford Tourism Council.

Faulkner and War
FAULKNER AND YOKNAPATAWPHA,
2001

Faulkner's Civil War in Fiction, History, and Memory

Don H. Doyle

For William Faulkner the Civil War was the major crisis in the history of his fictional Yoknapatawpha County, as it was in the nation's history. The war was the central theme of *Sartoris*, his first Yoknapatawpha novel, and it was a subject that continued to engage him as a writer. *Light in August, Absalom, Absalom!, The Unvanquished*, and *Requiem for a Nun* all dealt with the Civil War, not with the military events of the war itself, but with the war as the disaster that determined what followed. It is the legacy of the war, the burned courthouse and town square, the violent demand of white supremacy after emancipation, and the depressed economy of cotton sharecropping that shaped postwar society. There is a psychological repercussion as well, the humiliating experience of defeat, the determined campaigns to honor the veterans, the statue of the armed soldier standing before the courthouse, his back to the North, defiant, unbowed, paying honor to a "just and holy cause." Like Quentin Compson, many of the people of Faulkner's county are "a barracks filled with stubborn back-looking ghosts" who know that history has dealt them a painful and humiliating defeat. In a nation that otherwise celebrates its prosperity and success, the postwar South became scarred by poverty and defeat. Douglas Miller, writing on Faulkner and the Civil War in 1963, observed: "In the broadest sense most of Faulkner's fiction is concerned with the defeat of the South or the effects of that defeat."[1]

There is little evidence that Faulkner ever did much historical research on the Civil War, but coming of age in Mississippi in the early twentieth century, it would be difficult *not* to absorb the ever-present legacy of the Civil War. As a boy and well into his adult life Faulkner surrounded himself with people who were obsessed with and often quite knowledgeable about the Civil War, particularly the war as it affected northern Mississippi. In 1910 the local newspaper began a Confederate column filled with reminiscences of the war. The fiftieth anniversary of the war brought a flood of local newspaper accounts and commemorations that must have left a powerful impression on young Bill Falkner. His school teacher at that time took special care to teach the history of the Civil War, and an otherwise indifferent student may have turned his gaze from the window to listen to her stories. Maybe Faulkner had himself in mind when he wrote of that day at Gettysburg that "every Southern boy fourteen years old" can recall, that "instant when it's still not yet two o clock on that July afternoon in 1863, the brigades are in position behind the rail fence, the guns are laid and ready in the woods and the furled flags are already loosened to break out and Pickett ... looking up the hill waiting for Longstreet to give the word and it's all in the balance, it hasn't happened yet."[2]

As a young boy Bill Falkner spent countless hours down at the courthouse square listening enraptured to war tales of the veterans, and more hours with Caroline Barr (Mammy Callie) and other black house servants who told stories of "secesh times" from their experience as slaves. Phil Stone, Faulkner's friend and mentor, spent hours talking about the military aspects of the war, especially the role of Faulkner's great-grandfather, William C. Falkner, known to the family as the "Old Colonel." Maud Morrow Brown, a neighbor and good friend, wrote a deeply researched and well-crafted history of Lafayette County during the war. Her family's Quaker heritage and her feminine perspective on the home front probably did not appeal to the market for Civil War history at the time; her manuscript was never published, but her influence on Faulkner is evident in *The Unvanquished*.

Historians are usually distrustful of fictional accounts of the past. They expend a good deal of energy trying to undo the influence of novels, movies, and other popular influences on the historical consciousness of the American public. Hollywood's historical productions have generated a cottage industry among historians who review the inaccuracies and try to set things straight in the public memory. It was with this jaundiced historian's eye that I approached Faulkner's interpretation of the past. But what I found in Faulkner was a remarkably astute historian, not as a factually accurate researcher, but as an intuitive interpreter of his people and their past.

In his treatment of the Civil War, particularly as depicted in *The Unvanquished*, William Faulkner was decades ahead of the historians. With few exceptions, the main focus of historians working on the Civil War was the military leadership and strategies and political leaders and politics. One of the underlying themes had to do with whether the war was avoidable; implicit in this question was the notion that it was a war that might not have been necessary to fight, that it was the product of ideological fanaticism and political failure. Arthur Cole's *The Irrepressible Conflict* (1934) became the point of departure for this debate. For the next three decades Cole's thesis was attacked by revisionists who argued essentially that the war was an unnecessary blunder by inept politicians over issues that ought to have been compromised. Not until the 1960s during what some call the Second Reconstruction would such historians as Kenneth Stampp, Eric Foner, and James McPherson begin to revisit the Civil War as a massive conflict over slavery and race.

During the time Faulkner was writing there was some work was being done on the role of slaves, rank and file soldiers, and dissenters within the South. W. E. B. Du Bois's *Black Reconstruction* was a discerning study of the vital role of slaves in seizing their own emancipation and undermining the Confederacy from within. Herbert Aptheker also emphasized the important role of rebellious slaves in shaping the South. Bell Irvin Wiley did pioneering studies of slaves and the common soldier in the Civil War. Here at the University of Mississippi, Charles S. Sydnor did a fine study of *Slavery in Mississippi* that in many ways countered the views of the historian U. B. Phillips, who emphasized the paternalistic features of slavery and the general contentment of slaves. But most historians of the Civil War era dwelt almost exclusively on military and political leaders. The social history of the home front and combatants was only beginning to be discovered by historians in the 1930s; novelists were already exploring that terrain.[3]

Faulkner was one of dozens of writers who sought to cash in on the brisk trade in fiction on the Civil War, a market most famously exploited by Margaret Mitchell in *Gone with the Wind* (1936). Four chapters of *The Unvanquished* had been published originally in the *Saturday Evening Post* and *Scribner's Magazine*, both popular publications that aimed to entertain their readers. The book was published in 1938 with two additional chapters dealing with Reconstruction. Most literary scholars would probably not rank this book among Faulkner's greatest achievements, but it is the book I always recommend to those wanting to wade into Faulkner for the first time. It is a good read, accessible, with a straightforward plot and characters. It is also an insightful and prescient reading of the history of the Civil War with fresh and subtle treatments of Yankee soldiers, slaves, white women, and Southern bushwhackers, all groups that had been mostly ignored in the fictional and historical interpretations of the war.

What I want to do here is explore his fictional treatment of the war and to demonstrate how it squares with the historical evidence. Historians are not just concerned with telling *what* happened; they want to know *why* it happened and what it *means*. Faulkner was never very careful about such details as chronology and many of his "facts" are inconsistent with what we know happened. But what interests us here is not just the comparison of the actual and the apocryphal, but what Faulkner was making of all this, what his views were on the Civil War, why it was fought, and what it meant.

The Yankees' War

Let us turn first to the Yankees and their invasion of the South. Union soldiers invaded Mississippi beginning after the Battle of Shiloh, just north of the Tennessee line, in April 1862, and the fall of Memphis in June; then Corinth, Mississippi, which fell after a long and painful siege in October. Under the leadership of General Ulysses S. Grant and General William Tecumseh Sherman, the Union Army in the West was moving south into the interior of Mississippi intent on gaining control of the Mississippi River. With Memphis and New Orleans in Union hands, it remained to knock out Confederate defenses at Vicksburg to win control of the entire river and cut the Confederacy in two in the process.

At the beginning of the war Union policy was guided by the assumption that a selfish, willful slave-holding aristocracy led the rebellion, and that it had thin popular support among the population in the South. Secession was very controversial throughout the South, and it remained so during the war. Some of the wealthiest slave owners, such as the Natchez Whigs in Mississippi, adamantly opposed secession. These were men of great wealth and large slaveholdings who felt that the Union protected slavery more than it threatened it. They opposed the fire-eating secessionists who were more prominent in the smaller plantation districts of northern Mississippi. The opponents of secession believed that secession would bring war and destruction to the South and that it would hasten the abolition of slavery. They were right.

A large majority of Southern whites had no stake in slavery as property. Three in four white families in the slave-holding states owned no slaves in 1860, and half of those who owned slaves owned less than five. Slave ownership was higher in northern Mississippi where about 40 percent of white families owned slaves, but they were still in the minority.[4]

Lincoln and his advisors believed that an appropriate show of force, combined with a conciliatory treatment of civilians, would bring the South back into the Union and win support for the Republican Party, which had come to office in 1861 with no support from the Deep South. This was the thinking behind the so-called rose water policy that was in operation until late in 1862.[5] Civilians in the South were assumed to be loyal citizens of the United States, unless they demonstrated otherwise. If civilian property was confiscated or destroyed, vouchers would be issued with the understanding that loyal citizens would have their property or its value restored to them once hostilities were over. Even slaves who ran to Union lines at this point were treated as "contraband of war," with the understanding that they would be returned to their masters. The Union Army even kept track of the labor they extracted from these contraband slaves, with the expectation that their masters would be compensated after the war.

Faulkner captures this rose water policy in Colonel Dick, the kindly Union officer who graciously allows Granny Millard to hide Ringo and Bayard, the two boys who have shot a Union horse out from under one of his men. Colonel Dick even offers to help Granny get back her silver and mules after her disloyal slave, Loosh, has betrayed their whereabouts to the Yankees. Granny has a son serving as Colonel in the Confederate Army and there is no reason why such a person would be treated as a loyal Union citizen, but if this stretches historical accuracy some, it illustrates the conciliatory strategy of the early Union policy. Throughout the novel, and I would say throughout Faulkner's entire body of work, one does not find the vindictive Yankee fiend bent on punishing the South, unless one tries to put the Burden family in that category.

Colonel Dick was apparently based on an actual Union Colonel named Lyle Dickey. He led the cavalry invasion of Lafayette County in December 1862 and was remembered fondly by some civilians. Mary Smither recalled the day Colonel Dickey and his troops descended on them: "The whole hillside was covered with men and horses. . . . We were so helpless and frightened." But she remembered Dickey as "an elegant gentleman" with "fine men" on his staff. Dickey assured her "he could not fight and starve out women and children."[6]

Union policy toward civilians would turn away from conciliation and toward "total war" not all at once, but during the invasion of northern Mississippi in late 1862 one could definitely see the turn. The failure of this conciliatory policy stemmed from two misunderstandings of the South. One was that a slave was simply a species of property concentrated in the hands of a wealthy minority. Slavery was also a means of racial control, the cornerstone of white supremacy, the destruction of which threatened racial chaos. A second source of white solidarity was generated by the war itself; whatever divided white Southerners, they found a source of unity in the presence of an invading army. Confederate nationalism found unexpected strength as the war progressed, and the North's turn toward total war would in some respects give it a new tenacity.

Perhaps the term "total war" exaggerates the nature of war as practiced in the 1860s, but we use it to refer to a method of war that goes beyond military conflict between armies to an assault on civilian society. The decisions to emancipate slaves, to enlist slaves in the Union Army, to subsist the invading army on the civilian food supply, and to destroy civilian property were all parts of a cruel new practice of war that evolved in the American Civil War. As General Sherman explained, it was not enough to contest the Confederate military: the people of the South must feel the "hard hand of war" before they would realize their cause was lost.[7]

Grant and Sherman were chief among the architects of the new policy, and their experience in Lafayette County was critical to the turn they and the Union military strategy took late in 1862.[8] Grant had set up headquarters in Oxford and was prepared to stay the winter before continuing the drive south to Vicksburg. He invited his wife, Julia, to Oxford, apparently to help appease the Mississippi civilians who Grant thought were ready to surrender. The Grants were astonished at the belligerence of the Southern women she met. Julia, after all, was a native of the South who came attended by one of her slaves and expected to be welcomed by her people. Instead, a delegation of Holly Springs ladies treated her to a concert of rebel songs and berated her about the unconstitutional nature of the Union's war against them.[9]

When Confederate General Van Dorn raided the Union supply depot at Holly Springs and upset the entire invasion plan, the civilians in Oxford were ecstatic. Grant remembered the Oxford citizens who gathered outside his headquarters to gloat: "They came with broad smiles on their faces to ask what I was going to do now without anything for my soldiers to eat." When Grant told them that his army was going to confiscate all the food and forage they could find on their farms "the smiles soon turned to dismay." Now they asked: "What are *we* to do?" Grant must have been furious with the people of Oxford that day. One soldier's diary indicates that Grant considered burning the whole town of Oxford, but thought better of it and rescinded his order.[10]

Conciliation was turning rapidly to punishment in the Yankee treatment of Lafayette County that December. "For 15 miles east and west of the Railroad, from Coffeeville to La Grange, nearly everything for the subsistence of man or beast has been appropriated for the use of our army," Grant boasted to his superiors in Washington. "I was amazed at the quantity of supplies the country afforded," he later recorded in his memoirs. "It showed that we could have subsisted off the country for two months instead of two weeks. . . . This taught me a lesson which was taken advantage of later in the campaign."[11] In Faulkner's images of burned plantation houses with whites living in the cabins of their escaped slaves, Faulkner captured the essence of this cruel new form of war. His own home county had provided a dress rehearsal for total war that would find its fullest expression in Sherman's March to the Sea.

The Slaves

In *The Unvanquished* Faulkner also captured the central role of slaves in shaping the outcome of the war, a subject that was largely left out of both fictional and historical treatments of the war at this time. In September

1862 President Lincoln took the first major step away from the policy of reconciliation and toward total war by issuing the Emancipation Proclamation. The terms of this initial proclamation still guaranteed federal protection of slavery if the states or parts of states in rebellion simply put down their arms and returned to the Union. They had until January 1, 1863, to decide; after that all slaves in rebellious states would be forever free. This was the Day of Jubilee still celebrated in the African American community. Through the "grapevine telegraph" the slaves learned that the "blue men" were coming to free the slaves. They fled by the thousands to Union lines in an exodus that astonished their masters and perplexed the Union soldiers who were suddenly transformed into an army of liberation.

Faulkner captured vividly this moment in the war with the variety of slave responses to freedom, their cruel treatment at the hands of Union soldiers, and the confusion of white rebels, slave masters, confronted with rebelious slaves.

Faulkner's Loosh, a slave of John Sartoris, anticipates the invasion with dreams of freedom, and he seems to know more than the Confederate military officers do about the course of the war as it comes nearer to his home in Yoknapatawpha County. "Watch Loosh, because he knows," John Sartoris advises his family. What Loosh knows is that "Ginral Sherman gonter sweep the earth and the Race gonter all be free!"[12]

Slaves like Loosh take flight with a firm notion of the meaning of freedom as something God wants for his people. "I going," Loosh announces in a forceful summary of the meaning of emancipation. "I done been freed; God's own angel proclamated me free and gonter general me to Jordan. I don't belong to John Sartoris now; I belongs to me and God."[13] Playing off the stereotype of the faithful darkie who refuses to betray the hidden silver of the master's family, Faulkner has Loosh deliberately tell the Yankees where to dig to find the box of silver Granny has buried. She confronts Loosh: "Who are you" to give the family silver to the Yankees? "You ax me that?" Loosh answers defiantly. "Where John Sartoris? Whyn't he come and ax me that? Let God ax John Sartoris who the man name that give me to him. Let the man that buried me in the black dark ax that of the man what dug me free."[14] Loosh's speech is a powerful indictment of slavery and an extraordinary celebration of self-emancipation.

As the Union Army drove south, word went out ahead of them and large groups of refugee slaves came north to the advancing line of blue coats. "They seem to be intoxicated with the idea of careless freedom held out to them," one slave owner complained that fall.[15] Slave masters were faced with a constant threat of rebellion or flight. In early November, above Holly Springs, one Illinois soldier wrote in his diary: "nothing to day worth note only occasionally we see a drove of female negroes fleeing from Bondage." Again, the next day, "we see large groups of negroes."[16] Another described a scene near Corinth in late September: "Negroes old and young crowded both sides of the road and hung screaming and crying upon the rear of our retreating forces." He found two slave children "whom their mother had dropped in her scared and hasty flight and left to the tender mercies of the forest and the rebellion." "We moved in a cloud of dust" toward the Union lines, this soldier wrote.[17] Those familiar with *The Unvanquished* know how close these scenes are to the ones Faulkner describes in his fiction. It is as though he had read the same documents or heard these stories; he probably had.

Listen to the words of John Eaton, the young chaplain whom General Grant had assigned to supervise the contraband camp set up in Grand Junction, Tennessee, just above the Mississippi line, the birthplace of what became the Freedman's Bureau. Eaton witnessed the massive exodus out of slavery with a mix of awe and exasperation:

> Imagine, if you will, a slave population, springing from antecedent bondage, forsaking its local traditions and all the associations and attractions of the old plantation life, coming garbed in rags or in silks, with feet shod or bleeding, individually or in families, and larger groups—an army of slaves and fugitives, pushing its way irresistibly toward an army of fighting men. . . . The arrival among us of these hordes was like the oncoming of cities. There was no plan to this exodus, no Moses to lead it. Unlettered reason or the mere inarticulate decision of instinct brought them to us . . . a blind terror stung them, an equally blind hope allured them, and to us they came. There were men, women, and children in every stage of disease or decrepitude, often nearly naked, with flesh torn by the terrible experiences of their escapes.

Now let us turn to Faulkner's depiction of the exodus of slaves out of Mississippi. In *The Unvanquished* Granny Millard, Bayard Sartoris, and his slave friend Ringo at first see the fleeing slaves from a distance, signified only by huge clouds of dust moving north. They are drawn by religious faith to a river they call Jordan across which is a promised land of something called freedom. Bayard Sartoris, a young white boy whose family owns slaves, is amazed at "the motion, the impulse to move which had already seethed to a head among his [Ringo's] people, darker than themselves, reasonless, following and seeking a delusion, a dream, a bright shape which they could not know since there was nothing in their heritage, nothing in the memory even of the old men to tell the others." This yearning for freedom, Faulkner tells us, is something that transcends memory and race; it is a basic human instinct: "one of those impulses inexplicable yet invincible which appear among races of people at intervals and drive them to pick up and leave all security and familiarity of earth and home and start out, they dont know where, empty handed, blind to everything but a hope and a doom."[18]

Slave owners were not prepared for the sudden defection of their slaves. One woman told of how a Union officer had turned her house into a camp for "straggling negroes that come to him for protection." The soldiers fraternized with her slaves, and she had reason to suspect they might run off sooner or later. But her slaves reassured her they would remain loyal to her and not leave. Then, after Van Dorn's raid, the Yankees suddenly left, and she was astonished to find "they took *all* of my negroes even *Hester* and Bet and Chapman an orphan boy in the kitchen." What bothered her was not so much that the soldiers "took" the slaves but that her slaves, her trusted servants, had betrayed her. They "were so deceitful ... they talked against the Yankees.... Old Harry assured me that they were none of them going to the yankees and they all deceived me very well." That morning she rang her bell to call her servants: "I kept thinking they would come in directly."[19] There is something poignant about that image of her ringing the bell that morning, thinking she was summoning her slaves from their slumber to serve her, and only slowly realizing the bell was tolling her own reveille to their betrayal.

The Women

The ordeal of white women, like her, left to fend for themselves at the Confederate home front has recently become a subject of major interest among historians. George Rable's *Civil Wars*, Drew Faust's *Mothers of Invention*, along with LeeAnn Whites, Catherine Clinton, and Nina Silber have revealed the important role of women in what formerly had been the most masculine strongholds of history.[20] Faulkner took particular interest in the role of women in the war. Drusilla Hawk's loss of her fiancé in the war opens an opportunity for her to escape the confining role of Southern belle, to dress like a man, to ride horseback, and to fight with the men; she joins Colonel Sartoris in a scandalous and romantic adventure that takes her outside the conventional roles assigned to Southern women.

Rosa Millard, "Granny," is Drusilla's aunt and John Sartoris's mother-in-law; she also finds in the war an opportunity to enlarge upon her already formidable role as plantation mistress. Together with Ringo, the slave boy who rises into his own new role during the war, Granny organizes a thriving operation in which mules acquired from the U.S. army by forged vouchers are sold back to them. They share their profits with the poor hill country white people, who were left destitute by the war.

There were many Granny Millards at work in the Confederacy, at least many white Southerners whose loyalties became more flexible in the heat of war. Much of the trade with the enemy came out of sheer desperation as much as out of war profiteering. During the entire last three years of the war northern Mississippi was pillaged not only by invading Union forces who scoured the countryside for food and livestock, but also by Confederate raiding parties and bushwhackers. Furthermore, prices for cotton had risen to $2.50 a pound and higher, up from 10 cents, and cotton traders flocked to Memphis to buy up any cotton they could from Southerners willing to run the blockade.

At night, along roads leading toward Memphis, with wagons and mules loaded with cotton, blockade runners made their way to Union lines in a clandestine trade of growing magnitude. One Southern cotton trader in Memphis had a fleet of boats plying the Tallahatchie when the water was up.[21] Faulkner's great-grandfather, Colonel William C. Falkner, having resigned his command of the Partisan Rangers in the fall of 1862, turned to blockade running, smuggling cotton to Memphis or across the river to Arkansas. With the money earned from cotton, he and other traders bought essential food supplies, such as salt, to sell in Mississippi, often at inflated wartime prices.[22] Like Granny and her business associates, their willingness to do business with the enemy became a useful virtue in a war-torn society where the objective was to survive.

But Confederate officials considered these blockade runners traitors to the Confederacy, and they came down hard on those they caught. Marthy Cragin, a hapless counterpart to Granny Millard, headed north from Oxford in 1863 with an ox wagon full of cotton, which she hoped to trade for salt and other necessities. But after crossing the Tallahatchie River, she explained in a letter to the governor, a group of Confederate pickets overtook them, "burned our cotton, confiscated our drivers, wagons and teams. . . . I never would have attempted it if necessity had not have drove me to it, having been deprived of the necessaries of life for the last three years with a large and helpless family of girls, with no husband or son to assist in making them a support, and all but one old and decrepid servant, the one they confiscated." General Chalmers returned her elderly servant, but her pleas to give back her oxen and wagon fell on deaf ears. My oxen, she begged, are too "poor to eat for food," but they would help "alleviate the sufferings of a poor widow and helpless family. . . . I do not see where we are to get salt and cards," she added, "but we could better do without them then our team."[23]

Women at the home front suffered more than want of salt and food; they were losing their men, their husbands, sons, and brothers. The men died not defending their homeland in Mississippi, which was being invaded and pillaged, but in distant battlefields in Virginia and at Gettysburg.

More than two thousand men enlisted from Lafayette County, and despite many draft dodgers, shirkers, and deserters, this was an impressive show of support. Women had played a vital role in the mobilization of these men. Young women, dressed in white with sashes representing each state of the new nation, presented flags to the companies going off to war. This flag, one young Southern belle told the young men, is a "memorial of our confidence and our approval. . . . As you gaze upon it you must remember that our eyes are upon you." Then she neatly summarized the exchange between masculine chivalry and feminine devotion that was being performed: "As man can not love and cherish woman bereft of honor, so woman can not reverence and honor man devoid of courage."[24] There was not a young man in the audience who could have missed the more carnal implications that lay behind this prim pronouncement.

Beginning in April 1862 many of those young men who had gone off to war the previous spring so full of courage were coming back in caskets or on stretchers with bodies mangled and limbs crudely amputated. The university campus was converted to a hospital for some 1500 wounded soldiers; about half died. The magnetic observatory's "dead room" took on macabre new meaning by serving as a morgue. Initially the bodies were buried in pine coffins, but as the numbers of dead grew, a slave woman who worked at the hospital recalled, "they just buried them in bunches like dead chickens."[25] Most were not even identified before they were interred in their anonymous graves in a cemetery on campus, which can be found not far from the football field. Above ground were hundreds more who lost limbs or were otherwise maimed for life.

Those who survived the hospital were placed in homes of local citizens to convalesce. Women who tended them now saw the horrifying face of a war to which they had sent their own sons, husbands, and brothers. Like Faulkner's Judith Sutpen, they served "in the improvised hospital where (the nurtured virgin, the supremely and traditionally idle) they cleaned and dressed the self-fouled bodies of strange injured and dead and made lint of the window curtains and sheets and linen of the houses in which they had been born."[26]

It was only beginning. Each letter between the home front and the battle front reported disaster at home and death at far away battles. Margery Clark sent two sons and a husband off to fight; their letters home were full of depressing stories of starvation diets and shoddily dressed, often barefoot soldiers. But nothing had prepared her for the news that came from Gettysburg in July 1863. All three of the Clarks wound up in Pickett's charge on the third day of battle. All three were shot dead in the wheat field they crossed in that hopeless charge. When the news reached home Margery Clark wailed and prayed aloud all night long. The rest of her life she would say to her surviving family that they "did not know what sorrow was."[27]

Many would learn sorrow before this cruel war was over. Over one third of Mississippi's enlisted men were killed or died of disease. An estimated 770 of the approximately 2,200 men who served from Lafayette County died from wounds or disease. Countless others returned with missing limbs or scarred and mutilated bodies.[28] In a predominantly agricultural economy these disabilities often meant they could no longer farm. Their families had to rely on the paltry welfare of the county. Men who had taken up arms to defend hearth and home now saw their women and children left to the uncertain fate of public charity.[29]

The final desecration came in August 1864 with the burning of Oxford. Though Faulkner and other local historians have often incorrectly blamed Grant for this, it did not take place until August 1864. Union forces under the command of General Andrew Jackson Smith, "Whiskey" Smith, as he is known locally, advanced on Oxford because it served as the headquarters for Nathan Bedford Forrest's forces. There was no strategic military reason to destroy the town; it was done apparently out of irritation with Forrest and to punish the civilian population for supporting his presence. After learning that Forrest had deceived him and raided Memphis, Smith ordered his troops to burn the courthouse and all the buildings surrounding the Oxford town square. He also ordered that the homes of several prominent Confederate sympathizers, all wealthy citizens, be ransacked and razed. Chief among the targets was the home of Jacob Thompson. One Union soldier wrote home to Iowa: "The splendid mansion of Jacob Thompson, rebel Secretary of the Interior, with its gorgeous furniture, went up in crackling flames, a costly burnt offering to the 'Moloch of treason.'"[30]

The destruction that took place that afternoon left the Oxford town square a scorched field of rubble. One surviving photograph of the ruins shows nothing but a few jagged brick chimneys and remnants of walls surviving in a scene of utter desolation. Some thirty-four stores and business houses, along with the courthouse, Masonic Hall, two large hotels, and other businesses were all laid waste. Five dwellings, all of prominent Confederate supporters, were also sacked and burned. General Smith, acting "brutal in the extreme" and "mad with whiskey for the occasion . . . refused to allow the citizens to remove anything of value from their burning dwellings."[31]

William Faulkner's great-grandmother, Burlina Butler, widowed proprietor of the Oxford Inn, begged General Smith to spare her only means of livelihood. But he "replied very sneeringly and insultingly and went on with the burning." Mrs. Butler was "not permitted to move anything out of her house but her clothing, one bed and some little furniture out of her private room. All was consumed."[32]

Belle Edmondson recorded in her diary that August: "God grant the days may brighten for our poor bleeding Confederacy. . . . Oh! God we have suffered, we have endured patiently thy chastenings . . . let thy smile brighten the Sunny South with peace, soften the hearts of our enemies."[33] We are "a subjugated people," Rebecca Pegues recorded in her diary, "humiliated to the dust."[34]

For the remainder of the war, between August 1864 and the surrender at Appomattox in April 1865, the civilian population of Lafayette County did what they could to survive. There were no more major military engagements in the area, and little left for foraging parties to pillage. Soon the soldiers were straggling back home, as Faulkner imagined, "afoot like tramps or on crowbait horses, in faded and patched (and at times obviously stolen) clothing, preceded by no flags nor drums and followed not even by two men to keep step with one another, in coats bearing no glitter of golden braid and with scabbards in which no sword reposed."[35] They returned to a home front that had already surrendered "so that in the almost faded twilight of that land, the knell of Appomattox made no sound."[36]

Memory

For more than seven years Oxford's courthouse, former symbol of civic pride, remained an ugly reminder of that day of humiliation and desecration, as Faulkner wrote, with its "blackened jagged topless jumbles of brick wall enclosing like a ruined jaw the blackened shell of the courthouse."[37] All but one of the stores and offices that faced the square were in the same ruined state. Oxford, visitors noted, "is the most completely demolished town they [had] seen anywhere."[38] Some suggested erecting a Confederate memorial on the site of the courthouse. For a time, the county considered turning the property over to the town for use as a park.[39]

What saved the courthouse was the federal government. Oxford was designated the new site of the U. S. Federal District Court for northern Mississippi. Local town boosters sent Robert Hill, a Republican Judge, to secure congressional funding to rebuild the courthouse.[40] The reincarnated courthouse was grander than the one Smith's troops burned, topped with a magnificent clock tower. "Our people are indebted to General A. J. Smith for the brilliant illumination, during the 'late unpleasantness,' of the old courthouse and almost the entire town of Oxford," the local newspaper noted wryly.[41]

In 1907 in front of the courthouse a Confederate monument was unveiled, an armed soldier standing at rest atop a high pedestal overlooking the south side of the square. There had been a furious debate over this memorial. The United Daughters of the Confederacy, Albert Sidney Johnston Chapter, voted to place a monument on the university campus as a special tribute to the University Greys who had fallen in Pickett's Charge at Gettysburg. Sally Murry Falkner, Faulkner's grandmother, led the dissenting faction that wanted to memorialize all the county's Confederates with a monument on the square. Sally Falkner resigned from the UDC chapter and led a fund-raising campaign on behalf of the United Confederate Veterans, Camp 752, to erect a second monument that stood in front of the courthouse.

But which side and facing which way? There was another battle. Sally Falkner and her faction insisted that the marble Confederate soldier stand at the south side of the courthouse, armed, with his back defiantly to the North, and there it stands today.

Sally's grandson enjoyed vindicating her by taking the statue the UDC put on campus in front of the courthouse where she wanted it. There the carved soldier stood with his hand shading his eyes, looking, Faulkner noted impishly, not toward the approaching enemy from the North, but toward the South "for reinforcements; or perhaps not a combat soldier at all, but a provost marshal's man looking for deserters, or perhaps himself for a safe place to run to." Now that the war was thirty-five years in the past, Faulkner imagined, people could joke about it "because that old war was dead." The monument was merely its "epilogue and epitaph" and "at last even the last old sapless indomitable unvanquished widow or maiden aunt had died and the old deathless Lost Cause had become a faded . . . social club or caste, or form of behavior when you remember to observe it."

For a time, it seemed that the memory of the Civil War, of the town's whole past, was dying out with the last veterans, except for the "women, the ladies, the unsurrendered, the irreconcilable, who even after another thirty-five years would still get up and stalk out of picture houses showing *Gone with the Wind*." But as he wrote in 1951, he noted, "something curious was happening or had happened here: that instead of dying off as they should as time passed, it was as though these old irreconcilables were actually increasing in number."

He imagines an outlander, a relative or friend who happens to drop by Jefferson on a trip South, and winds up listening to one of the volunteer guides. It is one of the resurrected old guard who answers the stranger's questions "out of the town's composite heritage of remembering."[42]

Of course, the history and memory of the Civil War, Reconstruction, and the entire history of the South involved much more than stubborn, irreconcilable old women or men clinging to the past out of romantic nostalgia. David Blight's recent book, *Race and Reunion*, examines the politics of memory.[43] He tells us how, in the interest of sectional reconciliation following Reconstruction, the Civil War came to be remembered as a romantic though tragic conflict between Americans who allowed political and moral zeal to tear them apart. Both sides fought heroically for what they thought was right, according to the new orthodoxy that emerged in this "culture of reunion." Men fought valiantly and women sacrificed nobly for their cause; now their quarrel could be forgotten. It was in this spirit that the Confederate memorial on the Oxford town square honored a "just and holy cause."

What was not remembered, what was in fact deliberately forgotten in such memorials, in school textbooks, and in the entire public memory of the past, was that this was a war caused by conflict over slavery and one in which African Americans played a crucial role. Also forgotten was the decade-long struggle known as Reconstruction, an ongoing contest over the status of blacks in America. It was that unresolved war, that "unfinished revolution," that was forgotten or revised in such a way as to minimize sectional and racial differences. It was that war and those unsettled issues that William Faulkner probed in his fiction, and it was his imagined war that encompassed the experience of slaves, and women, and others behind the front lines who shaped the outcome of the war. It was a past seen through Faulkner's imagination, one that enabled historians to see what they had so long ignored as they set about revisiting the war and the issues of race that it left unresolved.

NOTES

Abbreviation: MDAH – Mississippi Department of Archives and History, Jackson, Mississippi

1. Douglas T. Miller, "Faulkner and the Civil War: Myth and Reality," *American Quarterly* 15 (1963): 200. A fuller discussion of the Civil War and Reconstruction era as it relates to Faulkner's fiction can be found in Don H. Doyle, *Faulkner's County: The Historical Roots of Yoknapatawpha* (Chapel Hill: University of North Carolina Press, 2001), from which much of this essay is drawn.

2. Faulkner, *Intruder in the Dust* (1948; New York: Vintage, 1991), 190.

3. Du Bois, *Black Reconstruction: An Essay Toward a History of the Part Which Black Folk Played in the Attempt to Reconstruct Democracy in America, 1860–1880* (1935; New York: S. A. Russell, 1956); Bell Irvin Wiley, *The Life of Johnny Reb, the Common Soldier of the Confederacy* (Indianapolis, New York: The Bobbs-Merrill Company, 1943); Wiley, *Southern Negroes, 1861–1865* (New Haven: Yale University Press, 1938); Charles S. Sydnor, *Slavery in Mississippi* (1933; Gloucester, Mass.: Peter Smith, 1965); Ulrich Bonnell Phillips, *American Negro Slavery: A Survey of the Supply, Employment and Control of Negro Labor as Determined by the Plantation Regime*, 2d ed. (1918; Baton Rouge: Louisiana State University Press, 1969).

4. Kenneth M. Stampp, *The Peculiar Institution: Slavery in the Ante-Bellum South* (1956; New York: Vintage, 1989), 29–30.

5. Stephen V. Ash, *When the Yankees Came: Conflict and Chaos in the Occupied South, 1861–1865* (Chapel Hill: University of North Carolina Press, 1995), chs. 1, 2.

6. Mary L. Smither, "Reminiscences of Mary L. Smither," 19, typescript, Skipwith Historical and Genealogical Society Collection, Oxford-Lafayette County Public Library. Smither says Dickey resigned after the northern Mississippi campaign, apparently because of his disgust with the Union treatment of civilians.

7. Mark Grimsley, *The Hard Hand of War: Union Military Policy toward Southern Civilians, 1861–1865* (Cambridge: Cambridge University Press, 1995).

8. On the importance of the western theater of war, see William L. Barney, *Flawed Victory: A New Perspective on the Civil War* (New York: Praeger, 1975); Ash, *Yankees*.

9. Julia Dent Grant, *The Personal Memoirs of Julia Dent Grant* (New York: G. P. Putnam's Sons, 1975), 104–9; Ash, *Yankees*, ch. 2.

10. Ulysses S. Grant, *Personal Memoirs of U. S. Grant*, 2 vols. (New York, 1885–86), 1:435; J. V. Frederick, ed., "An Illinois Soldier in North Mississippi: Diary of John Wilson, February 15–December 30, 1862," *Journal of Mississippi History* 1 (1939): 193. Wilson's diary entry for Dec. 21, 1862, reports: "Gen. Grant orders the town burned but reconsiders the thing and counter mands [sic] the order."

11. U. S. Grant to Col. J. C. Kelton, Holly Springs, Miss., Dec. 25, 1862, in Official Records, *The War of the Rebellion: A Compilation of the Official Records of the Union and Confederate Armies* (Washington: Government Printing Office, 1886) ser 1, vol. 27, part 1, 478; ibid., 480; Ulysses S. Grant, *Personal Memoirs of U. S. Grant*, 2 vols. (New York, 1885–86), 1:435–36, 432. See also, James W. Silver, ed., *Mississippi in the Confederacy as Seen in Retrospect* (Baton Rouge: Louisiana State University Press, 1961), 267; Mildred Throne, ed., *The Civil War Diary of Cyrus F. Boyd, Fifteenth Iowa Infantry, 1861–1863* (Iowa City: State Historical Society of Iowa), 95–96.

12. Faulkner, *The Unvanquished* (1938; New York: Vintage International: 1991), 23. Armstead Robinson, "Day of Jubilo: Civil War and the Demise of Slavery in the Mississippi Valley, 1861–1865" (Ph.D. dissertation, University of Rochester, 1976).

13. Faulkner, *The Unvanquished*, 24–25, 26, 74–75.

14. Ibid.

15. S. G. Miller to George Miller, Pontotoc, Mississippi, October 31, 1862, Miller Family Papers, University of Mississippi, John Davis Williams Library, Special Collections.

16. Frederick, "An Illinois Soldier," 92, Nov. 7, 8, 1862.

17. C. Carpenter to Emmett, Sept. 20, 1862, quoted in Robinson, "Jubilo," 470.

18. Faulkner, *The Unvanquished*, 81.

19. Unsigned letter to sister Dona, Oxford, Miss., Jan. 27, 1863, H. W. Walters Papers, University of Mississippi, John Davis Williams Library, Special Collections.

20. George Rable, *Civil Wars: Women and the Crisis of Southern Nationalism* (Urbana: University of Illinois Press, 1989); Drew Faust, *Mothers of Invention: Women of the Slaveholding South in the American Civil War* (Chapel Hill: University of North Carolina Press, 1996); LeeAnn Whites, *The Civil War as a Crisis in Gender: Augusta, Georgia, 1860–1890* (Athens: University of Georgia Press, 1995); Catherine Clinton and Nina Silber, eds., *Divided Houses: Gender and the Civil War* (New York: Oxford University Press, 1992).

21. Harold D. Woodman, *King Cotton and His Retainers: Financing and Marketing the Cotton Crop of the South, 1800–1925* (1968; Columbia: University of South Carolina Press, 1990), 221, 217–24.

22. Joel Williamson, *William Faulkner and Southern History* (New York: Oxford University Press, 1993), 44–45.

23. John K. Bettersworth, *Confederate Mississippi: The People and Policies of a Cotton State in Wartime* (Baton Rouge: Louisiana State University Press, 1943), 176–77; Marthy [Martha?] Cragin to Governor Clark, Oxford, Miss., Nov. 28, 1863, and Chalmer's response, Jan. 11, 1864, Governor's Records, Administration of Governor Charles Clark, vol. 56, RG 27, Mississippi Department of Archives and History (MDAH).

24. *Mercury* (Oxford), Mar. 9, 1861, reprinted in *Lamar Rifles: A History of Company G, Eleventh Mississippi Regiment, C. S. A.* (1901; Topeka, Kansas: Bonnie Blue Press, 1992), 52–57; *Oxford Intelligencer*, Mar. 20, 1861. Transcripts of the speech differ slightly in the two accounts.

25. Maud Morrow Brown, "At Home in Lafayette County, Mississippi, 1860–1865," 54, Maud Morrow (Mrs. Calvin S.) Brown Papers, MDAH.

26. Faulkner, *Absalom, Absalom!* (1936; New York: Vintage International, 1990), 155–56; Matthew C. O'Brien, "William Faulkner and the Civil War in Oxford, Mississippi," *Journal of Mississippi History* 35 (May, 1973): 167–74. *Oxford Eagle*, Mar. 27, 1969; Ella F. Pegues, "Recollections of the Civil War in Lafayette County," Maud Morrow (Mrs. Calvin S.) Brown Papers, MDAH; Brown, "At Home in Lafayette County," 54–57. See also: Johnson, "The University War Hospital," *Publications of the Mississippi Historical Society* 7 (1912): 94–106. On Confederate women as nurses, see George C. Rable, *Civil Wars: Women and the Crisis of Southern Nationalism* (Urbana: University of Illinois Press, 1991), 121–28.

27. Kate Barnes, obituary of Mrs. Margery Rogers Clark, n.d., newspaper clipping in Thomas G. Clark Civil War Letters, UMSC. See also, Brown, "Lafayette County at Home," 141–42.

28. Estimates of Mississippi casualties are found in Dunbar Rowland, *Encyclopedia of Mississippi History* 1 (Madison, Wis.: S.A. Brant, 1907): 141. On maimed soldiers in Lafayette County, see "List of names of Destitute families of Soldiers in Lafayette Co., Mississippi," in Confederate Records, Indigent and Disabled Soldiers and Dependents, 1863–1868, RG151, MDAH.

29. On public support of destitute after the war, see "Minutes of the Board of Police, beginning Oct. 10, 1859 through 1863," Apr. 3, 1865,Works Progress Administration typescript, vol. 3, 243, RG 60, vol. 583, MDAH. The estimate of 2,220 Lafayette County soldiers is made in William Delay, Clerk, to A. J. Gillespie, Oxford, Miss., telegram, May 30, 1864, in Confederate Records, Indigent and Disabled Soldiers and Dependents, MDAH.

30. Correspondent of the *Dubuque Times*, in *New York Times*, September 10, 1864, quoted in Garner, *Reconstruction in Mississippi*, 17.

31. Charles T. Biser to General S. Cooper, Oxford, Miss., Aug. 31, 1864, Official Records, *The War of the Rebellion: A Compilation of the Official Records of the Union and Confederate Armies* (Washington: Government Printing Office, 1886), series 1, vol. 39, part 1, 400–1.

32. *Oxford Falcon*, Nov. 23, 1865, reprinted in *Lafayette County Heritage News* 11 (Fall, 1988): 5–6.

33. Belle Edmondson Diary, Aug. 25, June 17, 1864, in Loretta and William Galraith, *A Lost Heroine of the Confederacy: The Diaries and Letters of Belle Edmondson* (Jackson: University Press of Mississippi, 1990), 172, 145.

34. "Diary of Rebecca Ann Evans Pegues, 1840–1882," June 17, 1865, Pegues Diaries and Letters, typescript, in possession of Guy Turnbow, Oxford, Mississippi.

35. Faulkner, *The Unvanquished*, 95.

36. Faulkner, *Requiem for a Nun* (1951; New York: Vintage Books, 1975), 201.

37. Ibid., 200, 40.

38. *Oxford Falcon*, Nov. 23, 1865.

39. Aug. 10, 1867.

40. *Oxford Falcon*, June 19, 1869; Aug. 10, 1867; Aug. 2, Oct. 18, 1866; Oct. 12, 1867; Jan. 23, Mar. 20, Apr. 17, 1869; Apr. 30, 1870; May 24, June 14, Dec. 15, 1866; Jan. 15, 1867; Apr. 10, 1869.

41. Aug. 18, 1871.

42. Faulkner, *Requiem*, 206–7, 212, 217, 220.

43. David W. Blight, *Race and Reunion: The Civil War in American Memory* (Cambridge: Harvard University Press, 2001).

William Faulkner and Theater of War
For Joseph Blotner

JAMES G. WATSON

There is hardly a book about the war that at some point does not avail itself of a theatrical figure.
—PAUL FUSSELL

A quarter century ago, in an introduction to Faulkner's brief, early essay "Literature and War," Michael Millgate noted the "extraordinary persistence with which the First World War pervades Faulkner's work both as subject matter and as theme—as a point of reference, a gauge of morale, a phenomenon at once physical and psychical with which his characters must come to terms." To this I would add the pervasively theatrical modes of expression that he found to derive from World War I. His lifelong protestations to the contrary, Faulkner had no direct military experience beyond his ground school training with the Royal Air Force in Toronto in July–December 1918. His war was "borrowed," to use Professor Millgate's phrase. What Millgate finds remarkable in this "is not the borrowing but the marvelous absorption and transmutation of the borrowed"[1] in the resulting art, to which I again would add that his borrowing was also, and from the very beginning, self-consciously performative.

It may be helpful here, at the beginning of a conference on "Faulkner and War," to review the scope of the war matter and its modes of representation in his early life and art and to suggest some of its sources. Recall, to begin with, that he spent his childhood in a time and place still thick with Civil War history in which his own family had been intimately involved. He knew and venerated veterans of that war—his grandfather, J. W. T. Falkner periodically sponsored reunions of his great-grandfather's Partisan Rangers;[2] later on, a uniformed portrait of the Old Colonel would hang in the living room at Rowan Oak—and it was still possible in Oxford in the early years of the century for a boy to discover in Bailey's Woods an actual Confederate cap-and-ball horse pistol, and actually fire it.[3] He was seventeen when the war in Europe began, nineteen on April 1, 1917, when America entered the war. His parents denied him permission to join the Red Cross Ambulance Corps,[4] and legend has it that he was turned down for service as a pilot by the U.S. Signal Corps (MBB 134). But the longing for military service persisted. In New York and New Haven in the spring of 1918 he found himself surrounded by military men, either just returned from service or just departing, including even a troop of black veterans of the Grand Army of the Republic who marched in New Haven on Decoration Day (TofH 61–62). In July he enlisted in the Royal Air Force, served six months as a ground school cadet in Canada, and returned home in December wearing the uniform of a commissioned officer. Drawings of soldiers, sailors, airmen, and their airplanes appear regularly in the pages of his letters from Toronto, his RAF notebook, and the 1920 University of Mississippi yearbook, for which he also had himself photographed, fraudulently, with veterans of the American Expeditionary Forces. Invented military adventures in the letters, and in his accounts of his service when he returned home, carried directly into his poetry and fiction. Well before he wrote *Soldiers' Pay* in Spring 1925, he was writing poems such as "Lilacs," about a dying pilot, flying stories such as his first published story, "Landing in Luck," and the review essay "Literature and War," with its long opening sentence that self-consciously begins, "Siegfried Sassoon moves one who has himself slogged up to Arras or its corresponding objective, who has trod duck-boards and heard and felt them sqush [sic] and suck in the mud."[5] Among the New Orleans newspaper pieces he wrote at about the same time is a sketch called "Home," about a wounded French combat veteran turned safe-cracker, who learned his trade in a munitions factory like the Winchester Plant where Faulkner worked in New Haven in 1918.[6] Sherwood Anderson believed his new friend to be a wounded pilot who drank to ease his pain, and wrote a story about him for the *Dial*.[7]

It was not about life in the Vieux Carré that Faulkner immediately wrote his mother when he arrived in New Orleans in January 1925, but about British cruisers in the harbor, one of which he toured and described to Maud Falkner in detail, even to the full name and rank of the commanding officer, "Vice Admiral Sir J. Ferguson, K.C.M.G., C.B." The city was full of British sailors, whom the old R.A.F. man dutifully saluted with "God save King George" (TofH 171). He began wearing the veteran aviator's insignia of the Quiet Birdmen; frequented the British Service Club that spring wearing an R.A.F. necktie sent him by Sherwood Anderson;[8] and sailed Lake Ponchartrain with Anderson and a British marine colonel named Glen Collins who, he claimed, had commanded a battalion at Gallipoli (TofH 201–2). Col. Collins would shortly become Major Ayers of *Mosquitoes*. In Europe that fall Faulkner wrote the poem "On Seeing the Winged Victory for the First Time,"[9] wrote stories about the war, including probably "The Leg,"[10] and started a loosely autobiographical novel he called "Elmer" in which the protagonist sustains a hand-grenade wound and is hospitalized in England as Jack Falkner was in Paris after his wounding at the Argonne Forest in November 1918.[11] Faulkner toured the battlefields at Amiens and Soissons in September 1925, and wrote home about the scattered detritus of war he found there—not the rare Confederate pistol, now, but "rolls of wire and shell cases and 'duds' piled along the hedge-rows, and an occasional tank rusting in a farm yard" (SLWF 26). In January, within a month of his return to Oxford, he gave Helen Baird a handmade manuscript book about another kind of soldier, a medieval knight named Sir Galwyn of Arthgyl. The title *Mayday* was the same as the working title of *Soldiers' Pay*, written the year before, evoking both the rites of spring that both books ironically celebrate and the international military distress signal *m'aidez*, help me. Thirty years later, a Japanese interviewer, who assumed that Faulkner had seen military service in World War I, asked if the war had made a deep impression on his mind. The Nobel laureate replied with a straight face: "When I went to that war I was more or less a child, and anything that happens to the mind of a child impresses it. And war is very likely to make an impression on any mind. But I don't know that it made an uncommon impression. I don't know that it altered very much what I might have gone into otherwise.... I prefer to think that it would not have, that I would have been more or less what I am now, with war or without it."[12]

This is pure theater, of course, opposite to but ironically of a kind with the theatrics that commonly evolved from the hazards of actual World War I military situations as Paul Fussell describes them in *The Great War and Modern Memory*. "The whole thing," Fussel writes of battle,

> is too grossly farcical, perverse, cruel, and absurd to be credited as a form of "real life." Seeing warfare as theater provides a psychic escape for the participant: with a sufficient sense of theater, he can perform his duties without implicating his "real" self and without impairing his innermost conviction that the world is still a rational place.[13]

In William Faulkner's case, alternatively, *invented* service provided him a role by which to keep at a distance the cruel perversity that he had *not* been shot down "raiding over Mannheim," as he wrote in "Lilacs" in 1920 (AGB 9). Perhaps he was thinking of that poem in 1943 when he wrote to his nephew Jimmy Faulkner, who was then a marine pilot, "I would have liked for you to have had my dog-tag, R.A.F., but I lost it in Europe, in Germany. I think the Gestapo has it; I am very likely on their records right now as a dead British flying officer-spy" (SLWF 170). Such role-playing typifies combat soldiers' accounts of World War I, as Fussell says, extending to their sense of the battlefield as a theater, in which boy actors were costumed in uniforms and battles were scripted performances at which the audience was sometimes the Allies, sometimes the Germans. The "not real" of the Front became a "theater of war" that included "fraud, illusion, misrepresentation.... [and] melodramatic self-casting" (Great War 195). In the 1920 poem and the 1943 letter, writing itself filled the vacuum in Faulkner's personal experience of the major event in his young manhood. The written to him was real, a World in the Word, and written performances in the context of the Great War validated not only his manhood but also his artistic genius. He ironically said as much himself in 1946 when he said of Malcolm Cowley's introduction to *The Portable Faulkner*, "The only point a war reference or anecdote could serve would be to reveal me a hero, or (2) to account for the whereabouts of a male my age on Nov. 11, 1918" (SLWF 219).[14]

William Faulkner went for a soldier in July 1918, not to France but to the peaceful lake shore city of Toronto, Canada. He went with all the theatricality he could muster, including fictional status as a second year Yale man and invented English antecedents scripted by a New Haven high school principal, a Yale Classics professor, and an itinerant Englishman named Bernard Reed (TofH 64). He even took a stage name—*Faulkner*, spelled with a "u". His head was full of the Lafayette Escadrille that spring, whose heroic feats he romanticized for his mother when Raoul Lufbery was shot down in May (TofH 56). Yet he appears to have joined the Royal Air Force almost by accident, having asked and received his parents' blessing to enlist in the "English Army," which he characterized in a letter of June 7, 1918, as the safest service in the world. "The English officers are the best yet," he wrote, "take better care of their men and weigh all chances for them. So I shall learn war in the best of schools, where the elimination of risk is taught above every thing" (TofH 63). He told his mother that "The chances of advancement in the English army are very good" (TofH 63), and he looked forward to being promoted to major at the end of the year's service. If he knew the mortality figures for British officers at the front, he did not share them with Maud Falkner. Fussel points out that in October 1914, alone, the British had 30,000 casualties. The minimum height for enlistment was reduced from five feet eight inches to five feet five and then five feet three. The volunteer system having proved insufficient, the Military Service Act was passed early in 1916, but that proved insufficient, as well. Of the 110,000 men involved in the first day's attack on the Somme in June 1916, 60,000 were killed or wounded. Less than a year later, there were 160,000 British casualties in five days of fighting at the Ypres Salient. In March 1918, three months before Faulkner wrote his mother about "elimination of risk" and "chances of advancement in the English Army," the British lost another 300,000 men at the Somme and by early summer the Germans were advancing successfully near the rivers of Lys and Marne (Great War 8–18). By the time it was all over, the Central Powers had lost three and a half million men; the Allies had lost five million. William Faulkner was not among them.

Whatever of ignorance or naiveté or bravado it contains, Faulkner's letter is primarily theater, a conscious performance by a young man released by his parents into the uniformed, hierarchic arena of heroic possibility—even though, as it immediately turned out, that was not precisely the arena he had described. For it was not, of course, to an English *Army* recruiter that William Faulkner went on June 14 with his forged papers and his new name, but to the Royal Air Force Cadet Recruiting Office at 220 West 42nd Street in New York, Lord Wellesley commanding (TofH 64). Faulkner's fellow cadet, Bostonian Ted Tebbetts, has written that by that summer,

> the Americans and Canadians had reached an agreement to the effect that neither country would enlist the other's nationals. In the RAF this was circumvented by claiming birth in Alberta, where apparently there were no birth certificates issued before 1900. So the outfit was full of boys with Southern drawls and New England twangs.[15]

Tebbetts remembered Faulkner as a serious cadet, "retiring, overly-introspective, a 'loner,' keeping mostly to himself," adding that "I always thought Faulkner had a tough time separating reality from reverie."[16] In Canada he played the part of a serious soldier: he passed the test for Class A: Cadet for Pilot, passed the ground school physical training program, and on November 18, a week after the Armistice, he passed the examinations for flight school. To cadets who remarked his strange accent, the "loner" sometimes presented himself as a French Canadian (TofH 115); to Canadian civilians, on occasion, as "a flying officer in mufti" (TofH 130). Tebbetts himself thought of him as the son of a decaying antebellum Southern aristocracy, "poling or canoeing down the bayous, with banjos strumming, a crock of white mule on hand, and for the diversion of youth, some high-spirited female mulattoes."[17]

The training in Toronto in the fall of 1918 soon generated more needful impostures. According to Tebbetts, "There were too many cadets going through at that time and too few planes to take care of them."[18] Their frustration was exacerbated in late September by the Spanish Influenza quarantine that further limited training (TofH 109). In this situation, theatrical artifice was elevated to a near necessity. The longer cadets went without flight training, the closer they came to being demobilized without a commission. For young men such as Faulkner, with so much of himself invested in the idea of flying, imaginary performances filled the vacuum. He turned to poetry, writing of the pilot in "The Ace,"

> The sun light
> Paints him as he stalks, huge through the morning
> In his fleece and leather, and gilds his bright
> Hair. The first lark hovers, singing, where
> He flashes through the shining gates of day. (TofH 99)

In his letters during the last weeks in Toronto, he claimed to be flying the planes he in fact was assigned to dismantle. Demobilized in December, he purchased a discounted officer's rig from a Toronto tailor and arrived home dressed in the hot-pilot hat, belted tunic and jodhpurs he had drawn pictures of in his letters to his parents.[19] He completed the costume with a swagger stick, a little mustache, and a story he would tell for years to come of cracking up training planes.

Such impostures were a matter of greater moment than Ted Tebbetts understood. Intensified by his forestalled military ambitions, the theatrical artifice inherent to war became a staple of the written world Faulkner set about making; theatrical performance became a strategy fundamental to its realization.[20] Literally, he was writing himself into being then. His imaginative subjectivity was such that real and invented experiences tangled inextricably together in writing of every kind—in personal letters as well as in novels, in essays as well as in stories and poems. Driven though it was by personal imperatives and private needs, his art never was self-seeking but rather self-pleasuring and assertive, often violent and chaotic but ecstatic and, above all, controlled. He apparently kept no journals or notebooks, wrote no outlines except the famous one for *A Fable* on the wall of his study; at any rate, none survive. From the outset, his approach was self-presentational and performative, capitalizing on his experience as a man and a writer, including especially the performative experience. He chose heightened modes of linguistic expression to represent that self and all the other selves, situations and events of his books. If self-presentation was a *record* of the life and time that he lived and imagined, performance was the *act* of its recording. Clearly, the image of war as theater was congenial to this work: the theatric conventions of military life complemented and reinforced his imaginative preoccupation with a Southern literary tradition he associated with "ceremony" and "spectacle."[21] Initially a *subject* of his writing, by which he might measure and when necessary revise and reconstitute images of himself and his circumstances in the actual world, the Great War also modeled for him a *means* of written expression. Writing for Faulkner, as his fastidiously crafted manuscripts show, "always was a deed, an event at least as much as a record of events, a compulsively individual act, at once self-disruptive and self-affirming. By writing he reconstructed the World in the Word, and in the World-as-Word, anything and everything were put in the service of art. Anything there is possible, everything is real"[22]—including even the demobilized R.A.F. cadet he rejected in 1918 and the wounded commissioned officer he pretended to be.

To an extent Faulkner's challenge in *Soldiers' Pay* was to capture and represent everything he knew, remembered, believed, and had written about the months immediately preceding and following his peripheral experience of the Great War. His longest literary production to that time was the forty published pages of *The Marble Faun* (1924). Before that he had reprised his early military impostures in the comic story "Landing in Luck" (1919), where Cadet Thompson crashes and hangs face down in the cockpit of his wrecked plane as Faulkner claimed to have done;[23] he investigated the psychological wound of his not having flown in the 1920 poem "Lilacs," where the war experience of the shattered pilot is represented as a composite memory of multiple personalities.[24] Now he wrote the two elements of his 1918 masquerade into the paired characters of Cadet Julian Lowe and the wounded Lieutenant Donald Mahon. In dismissing the low-ranking Lowe from Mahon's homecoming and from the novel, Faulkner effectively exorcised him from his own emotional biography as he was rescripting it. Lowe is supplanted at the homecoming by the figure of the wounded soldier that Faulkner introduced in a four-line epigraph to the novel from his 1924 poem "November 11":

> The hushed plaint of wind in stricken trees
> Shivers the grass in path and lane
> And Grief and Time are tideless golden seas—
> Hush, hush! He's home again. (SP n.p.; AGB Poem XXX, 53)

As "Landing in Luck" looks forward to Lowe, so "Lilacs" looks forward to Mahon, whose return to Charleston in his aviator's "belt and wings" (SP 25) rewrites the cadet as a combat officer and validates the reality of Faulkner's 1918 homecoming masquerade. Drawing on his own composite memory, Faulkner has Mahon abandoned by Cecily Saunders as he had been abandoned himself the previous spring when Estelle married Cornell Franklin. Cecily, like Estelle then, is a popular flapper whose given name and elopement Faulkner took from Jack Falkner's first wife, Cecile Hargis, who eloped with Jack in 1922. Jack's experience as a marine in France may also have contributed to the portrait of Donald Mahon: like him, Jack was wounded late in the war, was feared dead, and returned home in the spring after a long hospitalization.[25]

In *Soldiers' Pay* for the first time, Faulkner attempted to accommodate several images of himself at once, not only the cadet and the wounded pilot but also the nonmilitary characters whom he set in ironic counterpoint to them. The satyrlike Januarius Jones quotes from Faulkner's poem "On Seeing the Winged Victory" to describe Cecily Saunders: "'Atthis,'" he said. "'For a moment, an aeon, I pause plunging above the narrow precipice of thy breast'" (SP 227; AGB, Poem XVII 39); the lovelorn George Farr marries Cecily, whom Faulkner modeled partly on Estelle and describes in the novel, in a phrase from one of his New Haven letters about another girl, as a figure by Tanagra (SP 218; TofH 60). In this tangle of associations, there are other literary antecedents, as well. The World War I novelist Thomas Boyd served with the 5th and 6th Marine Regiments in France from 1917 to the end of the war, and Jack Falkner joined the marines as a replacement in August 1918, serving until he was wounded November 1. Both described the theater of war in detail, Jack in his 1967 memoir and Boyd in his widely reviewed novel *Through the Wheat* (1923). Later on Boyd reviewed *Soldiers' Pay* in the *Saturday Review of Literature*.[26] Faulkner certainly would have known Jack's history and his war stories; and in 1925 he was reading W. H. Mottram's *The Spanish Farm*[27] as well as Sassoon and Barbusse, of whom he wrote in "Literature and War." If he also read Boyd's book then he might well have borrowed Boyd's Captain Powers for the Lieutenant Powers in his own novel. Boyd describes Captain Powers's death at the Front in the immediacy of the moment: "On the space where the captain had been lying there was a blood-soaked shoe and a helmet, turned bottom up, and neatly holding a mess of brains."[28] In the postwar setting of *Soldiers' Pay*, Faulkner distances his Lieutenant Powers by portraying him through his wife's tortured reveries and casting his death in the memory of a comrade: "Powers ... a man jumping along a trench of demoralized troops caught in a pointless hysteria. Powers. A face briefly spitted on the flame of a rifle: a white moth beneath a reluctant and sorrowful dawn" (SP 211).[29] Already, such borrowings reveal, Faulkner was sublimating the actual in its various manifestations into the thick fictional realities of the written. Two stories that followed the novel, both set in Europe during the war, illustrate how strongly he brought theater to bear on the gathering pool of his war material.

The first, "Victory," is the story of a Scottish shipbuilder named Alec Gray who enlists in the British Army, rises to the rank of Captain, and is cast aside in November 1918, by the Army and the Empire. In his various avatars Gray is a boy too young to shave, playing at war, an enlisted man who kills his own sergeant-major, and a commoner acting the part of an aristocratic "milord military."[30] Costumed during the war in the uniforms and medals of his steadily changing rank, he still is costumed at the end of the tale, selling matches in Picadilly Circus in his waxed military mustaches and threadbare gentleman's suit. Theatrical artifice here emphasizes the artificiality of wartime identity and the fragility of the military self. Gray's imposture as an officer is one Faulkner knew well, for he had practiced it himself in Oxford and New Orleans. In the story "Ad Astra," he extended the chaos that the Armistice visited on its soldier-actors to the collapse of the theater of war itself. When the war comes to an end on the night of November 11, 1918, and the morning of November 12, the hierarchic order that has scripted the lives of the soldiers in "Ad Astra" dissolves and with it the sustaining structures of artifice. The nameless narrator begins, "I dont know what we were. With the exception of Comyn, we had started out Americans, but after three years, in our British tunics and British wings and here and there a ribbon, I don't suppose we had even bothered in three years to wonder what we were, to think or to remember" (CSWF 407). Faulkner imagines them on a darkened stage, drunkenly abandoning identity with their military ranks and conventions. Monaghan enters, out of costume, wearing "an R.F.C. cap and an American tunic with both shoulder straps flapping loose" (CSWF 410); Comyn declares allegiance to the Irish king Ur Neill (CSWF 420). The captured German pilot, still "Anthony-like . . . rigid, soldierly, with every button in place" (CSWF 412), is treated as a relic rather than as a prisoner of war. "'I once thought of taking one home to my wife,' Bland said. 'So I could prove to her that I have only been to a war. But I never could find a good one. A whole one, I mean'" (CSWF 412). At this desperate extremity, even language fails: "we shouted at one another," the narrator says, "speaking in foreign tongues out of our inescapable isolations, reiterant, unlistened to by one another" (CSWF 413). As Monaghan says of his lost stage identity, "I'm not a soldier. . . . I'm not a gentleman. I'm not anything" (CSWF 414–15). The subadar concludes, "All this generation which fought in the war are dead tonight. But we do not yet know it" (CSWF 421).

Written a decade after the Great War, stories such as "Victory" and "Ad Astra" illustrate not only the place that the war maintained in modern memory, as Paul Fussell has it, but that the theatrical modes of expression it generated continued to serve the modernist literary economy. A decade later, at the outset of the Second World War, Wallace Stevens defined the dilemma of the modern poet as "the act of finding / What will suffice." He wrote in "Of Modern Poetry,"

> It has not always had
> To find: the scene was set; it repeated what
> Was in the script.
>   Then the theatre was changed
> To something else. Its past was a souvenir.

In the soon-to-be-disrupted world of 1940, Stevens asserted, the modern poem once again "has to think about war/And it has to find what will suffice."[31] Faulkner would have agreed. In the interim between the two world wars, he had developed his own modernist version of an earlier Stevens dictate, in "The Idea of Order at Key West," that for the poet-singer of that poem, "there never was a world... / Except the one she sang and, singing, made."[32] For Faulkner the years between *Sartoris* (1927) and *Go Down, Moses* (1942) mark the era of the great Yoknapatawpha County novels in which he sang and made his own fictional world. *Sartoris* is both the first novel set in that emerging cosmos and the last in which the Great War significantly figures until *A Fable* (1954).

In the 1920s and well into the 1930s, Faulkner continued to write short stories about the Great War and characters deeply affected by it, in part because war stories remained popular. And they paid. Five of his war stories were published in magazines in 1930–1932 and republished with five others in the short story collections *These 13* (1931) and *Doctor Martino and Other Stories* (1934). The poems of *A Green Bough* (1933) include six that are war-related, all dating from the years 1919–1920.[33] In Hollywood with Howard Hawks in 1932–1935, he wrote *Today We Live*, a film adaptation of his World War I story "Turn About," worked at MGM to adapt a wartime diary the studio called *War Birds*, and collaborated with Joel Sayre on *The Road to Glory*, which with *Today We Live* significantly influenced the collaborative telling in *Absalom, Absalom!*[34] But the First World War virtually disappeared from the novels. Captain John McLendon, who acts out his postwar frustration in the civil violence of "Dry September," "had commanded troops at the front in France and had been decorated for valor" (CSWF 171), but there are few such veterans in the major fiction after 1927. Darl Bundren has a nominal war record in *As I Lay Dying*, and Ruby Lamar explains in *Sanctuary* that Lee Goodwin is a veteran of the war in the Philippines and served in France between terms in the military prison at Leavenworth. Horace Benbow's Y.M.C.A. service in France in *Sartoris* carried into the original *Sanctuary* (1929), but Faulkner excised direct mention of that when he revised the novel in 1931; Gavin Stevens does not inherit it until after World War II in *The Town* (1957).[35] Percy Grimm's relationship to the war in *Light in August*, like Faulkner's own, lies in his *not* having served; although World War I pilots race planes in *Pylon*, Roger Shumann, the one flier the reporter idolizes, is not one of them.[36]

Still, the heroes of the Great War and military figures from his own past remained for Faulkner larger than life, "in this shadowy attenuation of time," as Mr. Compson says in *Absalom, Absalom!*, "possessing now heroic proportions, performing their acts of simple passion and simple violence, impervious to time and inexplicable."[37] In Phil Stone's rooms at Yale in 1918, Faulkner met a shell-shocked English captain named Bland

and the (to him) equally romantic New Haven poet Arthur Head, both of whose surnames he used for ladies' men in *The Sound and the Fury*, where his Yale became Quentin's Harvard. He met a law student named Nicholas Llewellyn there, who had served in both the German and the American armies in France, and heard Llewellyn argue tactics of the battle of Rheims with a Canadian airman named Jackson Todd (TofH 48). He met hero after war hero, inspiring him to lament in his enlistment letter to his mother and father, "At the rate I am living now, I'll never be able to make anything of myself, but with this business I will be fixed up after the war is over" (TofH 63–64). In *Absalom, Absalom!* two decades later, he would attribute the same despair to Henry Sutpen who lives with the urbane Charles Bon in rooms at the University of Mississippi—"that sharp shocking terrible hopeless despair of the young," Mr. Compson calls it, "which sometimes takes the form of insult toward and even physical assault upon the human subject of it" (AA! 76). Quentin Compson reacts in just this way to Dalton Ames and to his avatars, Gerald Bland and Herbert Head, each of whom in the mythic structure of *The Sound and the Fury* plays a Pluto to Caddy's Persephone. At the penultimate moment of Quentin's day, he says of Dalton, *"with one hand he could lift her to his shoulder and run with her running Running."*[38] A still more personal source of Quentin's anguish, for William Faulkner, is the fact that Dalton *"had been in the army had killed men"* (TSATF 148).

But in what war did Dalton Ames serve? Had he killed men during the Spanish American War in 1898, a year after Faulkner's birth, he would be over thirty in 1909–1910, very long in the tooth to have appealed to the sixteen-year-old Caddy. Yet Dalton's war service clearly was important to Faulkner, for personal as well as aesthetic reasons. When he wrote the novel in 1928, the men of Faulkner's generation who had been in the army and killed men were those larger-than-life heroes from New Haven and Toronto, whose names he used in his novel with other of his New Haven experiences.[39] It seems likely, given such borrowings, that Dalton also is drawn from and shares the experience of soldiers of the Great War like Llewellyn, Todd, Bland, and the veteran British Tommies who inspired the young Faulkner's envy and despair in 1918. Looking back from the moment of composition in 1928–1929 to the fictional moment of 1910, Faulkner borrowed from and, where necessary to the fiction, recast his intense experience at Yale and in the R.A.F. when the Great War had been a constant point of reference and gauge of his morale. In *The Sound and the Fury*, Dalton Ames's anachronistic war service serves the same function for Quentin, whose melodramatic confrontations with Ames and with Head and Bland are cast as duels, likewise rooted in the history of war. Specifically theatrical written performances were on Faulkner's mind at this period. Sometime in 1930–1931, shortly after the publication of *Sartoris* and *The Sound and the Fury*, he drafted a preface for *Sartoris*, where he wrote that he had created the characters of that book "partly from what they were in actual life and partly from what they should have been and were not. Thus I improved on God, who, dramatic though He may be, has no sense, no feeling for theatre."[40] Years later, he would explain to Jean Stein the imaginative process by which a fictional Dalton Ames could be a veteran of an actual war that had not yet been declared or fought. "I can move these people around like God," he famously said, "not only in space but in time too" (Lion 255).

Time had long seemed a fluid condition to the boy who mapped the battle of Verdun in his bedroom with his brothers in 1916,[41] fighting that battle in imagination as, nearly twenty years later, he would have Bayard Sartoris and Ringo fight the battle of Vicksburg on their living map in *The Unvanquished* (1934). Later still, in the essay "Mississippi" (1954), he would reprise their performance in his own name, describing himself, as a child, "with empty spools and chips and sticks and a scraped trench filled with well-water for the River, playing over again in miniature the War, the old irremediable battles—Shiloh and Vicksburg, and Brice's Crossroads."[42] In just this way, his reading of Siegfried Sassoon and Henri Barbuisse and Rupert Brooke stimulated the self-presenting soldier-essayist of the mid-1920s to include himself with them as

> one who has himself slogged up to Arras or its corresponding objective, who has trod the duck boards and felt and heard them sqush [sic] and suck in the mud, who has seen the casual dead rotting beneath dissolving Flemish skies, who has smelt that dreadful smell of war—a combination of uneaten and evacuated food and slept-in mud and soiled and sweatty [sic] clothing—, who has spent four whiskey-less days cursing the General Staff. (One does not curse God in war: certainly anyone who can possibly be anywhere else, is there)[43]

What the Great War provided Faulkner, finally, was not so much the subject matter he described here in detail—he was as fully capable of imagining battle fields on which he had not fought as he was of imagining Temple Drake's emerging sexuality, for example, or the trauma of racial identity in Joe Christmas. What the Great War provided, rather, was a metaphor (theater) and a method (self-presentation) congenial to his sense of himself as a *performer* and of writing itself as a physical *act*. Nor was he writing about himself as he dreamed of being so much as he was using himself and his dreams in order to write—playing with possibilities, including military ones, trying them out, dismissing some and affirming others. Possessed by the idea of war in the 1920s, he discovered both the poses and the means of posing sufficient to the spectacle and display of the written world he would create.

The resulting performance, as Richard Poirier has said of the poetry of Andrew Marvell and Robert Frost, proves "not that the world is too tough for the performer but that he is too tough for the world." He adds, in a passage perfectly descriptive of Faulkner's novel, that "The scene of the poem is more expanded and expansive than is the scene which is the world, and the poet's relationship to the scene of the poem is necessarily dynamic, exploratory, coolly executed to a degree that no comparable 'scene' in life could very well bear."[44] The scene of *The Sound and the Fury* on June 2, 1910, is not the Cambridge, Massachusetts, Faulkner imagined, nor yet the New Haven that he knew, but both together—and more. Characterized by ceremony and spectacle, it is the inclusive, expanded, and expansive scene of Quentin's fevered imagination. Dalton Ames enters and reenters that scene in 1910 in the same "series of delayed repercussions like summer thunder" by which Faulkner said he discovered the larger-than-life figures who had haunted him in 1928–1929, "the Flauberts and Dostoievskys and Conrads whose books I had read ten years ago."[45] In its language and form the Dalton Ames sequence is genuinely theatric, and central to its theater is Faulkner's association of Dalton with the First World War. "When the shadow of the sash appeared on the curtains," Quentin begins, "it was between seven and eight o'clock and then I was in time again, hearing the watch" (TSATF 76). "*I have committed incest,*" he says minutes later, claiming Dalton's role as lover. "*I said Father it was I it was not Dalton Ames*" (TSATF 79). "Dalton Ames. Dalton Ames," he thinks still later, watching Gerald Bland rowing on the river. "Dalton shirts. I thought all the time they were khaki, army issue khaki, until I saw they were of heavy Chinese silk or finest flannel because they made his face so brown his eyes so blue. Dalton Ames. It just missed gentility. Theatrical fixture. Just papier-mache, then touch. Oh. Asbestos. Not quite bronze" (TSATF 92). Then again, on the riverside at noon, "*Dalton Ames oh asbestos*" (TSATF 105). In the fluidity of fictional time, 1918 merges with 1910 in the novel, Faulkner's Captain Bland with Quentin's Gerald Bland, and Gerald Bland with Dalton Ames, the soldier-seducer of the Great War, "*they two blurred within the other forever more*": "*he had been in the army,*" Quentin remembers with William Faulkner, "*had killed men*" (TSATF 148).

NOTES

1. Michael Millgate, "Faulkner on the Literature of the First World War," in *A Faulkner Miscellany*, ed. James B. Meriwether (Jackson: University Press of Mississippi, 1974), 102.
2. Joseph Blotner, *Faulkner: A Biography* (New York: Random House, 1974), 102–3.
3. John Faulkner, *My Brother Bill: An Affectionate Reminiscence* (New York: Trident Press, 1963), 54–56. Future references are cited in the text as MBB.

4. *Thinking of Home: William Faulkner's Letters to His Mother and Father, 1918–1926*, ed. James G. Watson (New York: W.W. Norton, 1992), 55. Future references are cited in the text as TofH.

5. "Literature and War," in Millgate, "Faulkner on the Literature of the First World War," 99.

6. *William Faulkner: New Orleans Sketches*, ed. Carvel Collins (New York: Random House, 1968) 28–33.

7. Sherwood Anderson, "A Meeting South," *Dial* (April 1925).

8. Faulkner to Sherwood Anderson. TLS, early February 1925, Carvell Collins Collection, Harry Ransom Humanities Research Center, University of Texas at Austin.

9. Poem XVII, *A Green Bough*, in *The Marble Faun and A Green Bough* (New York: Random House, 1960), 39. Future references are cited in the text as AGB.

10. See *Selected Letters of William Faulkner*, ed. Joseph L. Blotner (New York: Random House, 1977), 31. Future references are cited in the text as SLWF.

11. "Elmer," ed. Diane L. Cox, *Mississippi Quarterly* 36 (Summer 1983): 381–82; Murry C. Falkner, *The Falkners of Mississippi: A Memoir* (Baton Rouge: Louisiana State University Press, 1967), 102–3.

12. *Lion in the Garden: Interviews with William Faulkner, 1926–1962*, ed. James B. Meriwether and Michael Millgate (New York: Random House, 1968), 133. Future references are cited in the text as Lion.

13. Paul Fussell, *The Great War and Modern Memory* (New York: Oxford University Press, 1975), 192. Future references are cited in the text as Great War.

14. In this regard, Anne Goodwyn Jones argues that in Faulkner's war stories, typically, "War produces manhood again and the storyteller passes on the tale." "Male Fantasies? Faulkner's War Stories and the Construction of Gender," in *Faulkner and Psychology*, ed. Donald Kartiganer and Ann J. Abadie (Jackson: University Press of Mississippi, 1991), 49.

15. Tebbetts to Carvel Collins, TLS February 24, 1962, Carvel Collins Collection, Harry Ransom Humanities Research Center, University of Texas at Austin.

16. Tebbetts to Carvel Collins, TLS December 15, 1963, Carvel Collins Collection, Harry Ransom Humanities Research Center, University of Texas at Austin.

17. Tebbetts to Carvel Collins, TLS December 15, 1963. Carvel Collins Collection, Harry Ransom Humanities Research Center, University of Texas at Austin.

18. Tebbetts to Carvel Collins, TLS March 17, 1963. Carvel Collins Collection, Harry Ransom Humanities Research Center, University of Texas at Austin.

19. The photographs and drawings are reprinted and discussed in James G. Watson, *William Faulkner, Self-Presentation and Performance* (Austin: University of Texas Press, 2000), 18–30.

20. Donald Kartiganer explains that "war for Faulkner is an occasion for gesture, a decisive event that—in the fighting of it, in the telling and the fullest understanding of it—demands something other than concrete involvement: a figurative rather than a literal action, dramatic rather than strategic effect, the miming of battle." "'So I who never had a war. . . .': William Faulkner, War, and the Modern Imagination," *Modern Fiction Studies* 44 (Fall 1998): 619–20.

21. "An Introduction to *The Sound and the Fury*," in *A Faulkner Miscellany*, ed. James B. Meriwether (Jackson: University Press of Mississippi, 1974), 157.

22. Watson, *William Faulkner, Self-Presentation and Performance*, 2.

23. "Landing in Luck," in *William Faulkner: Early Prose and Poetry*, ed. Carvel Collins (Boston: Atlantic–Little Brown, 1962), 42–50. John Faulkner remembered that "some of the graduating class had gone up to celebrate getting their wings and he had flown his Camel halfway through the top of the hangar. The tail of his ship was still outside and they got Bill down from inside the hangar with a ladder" (MBB, 138–39). Jack Falkner repeats much the same story in *The Falkners of Mississippi*, 90–91. Faulkner told the *New Yorker* in 1931 that "He crashed behind his own lines. He was hanging upside down in his plane with both legs broken when an ambulance got to him" (Lion, 23). Faulkner did not graduate or earn wings, he did not crash a Camel or any other plane in Canada, and he did not serve in France.

24. Margaret Yonce says that despite the illusion of several speakers, "the 'conversation' which we hear in the poem is not an exchange of war stories between combat veterans but a single 'voice,' that of a wounded aviator whose shattered mind attempts to sort among the detritus of war experiences to form a kind of composite memory." "'Shot Down Last Spring': The Wounded Aviators of Faulkner's Wasteland," *Mississippi Quarterly* 31 (Summer 1978): 366.

25. Blotner, *Faulkner: A Biography*, 239.

26. Boyd, "Honest but Slapdash," *Saturday Review of Literature* (April 24, 1926), 736.

27. Faulkner to Sherwood Anderson, TLS n.d., William Faulkner Collection, Harry Ransom Humanities Research Center, University of Texas at Austin.

28. Boyd, *Through the Wheat* (1923; New York: Popular Library, 1978), 114.

29. Stanley Cooperman treats the two novels as complementary, arguing that Faulkner was "Less interested than Boyd in the actual process of the military machine, less concerned with the impact of technological combat and mass absurdity." *World War I and the American Novel* (Baltimore: Johns Hopkins University Press, 1967), 159. Faulkner also had far less direct experience in these matters than Boyd.

30. *Collected Stories of William Faulkner* (New York: Random House, 1950), 431. Future references are cited in the text as CSWF. As an R.A.F. cadet in 1918, Faulkner himself was disciplined for failing to shave. See TofH, 80.

31. Stevens, *Wallace Stevens: The Collected Poems* (New York: Vintage, 1990), 239–40.

32. Ibid., 130.

33. The magazine stories are "Honor" (*American Mercury*, July 1930), "Dry September" (*Scribner's*, January 1931), "Ad Astra" (*American Caravan*, March 1931), "Death Drag" (*Scribner's*, January 1932), and "Turn About" (*Saturday Evening Post*, March 1932). "Ad Astra" and "Dry September" were republished in *These 13* with "Victory," "All the Dead Pilots," "Crevasse," and "Carcassonne," which I include because the buckskin pony "with eyes like blue electricity and a mane like tangled fire" arguably describes an open-cockpit airplane (CSWF, 895). "The Leg" was published in *Doctor Martino and Other Stories* with "Death Drag," "Turn About," and Honor." All were reprinted in *Collected Stories of William Faulkner*. The war-related poems of *A Green Bough* are poems I, IV, XVII, XVIII, XXX, and XXXI.

34. See Bruce Kawin, "Faulkner's Film Career: The Years with Hawks," in *Faulkner, Modernism, and Film*, ed. Evans Harrington and Ann J. Abadie (Jackson: University Press of Mississippi, 1979), 163–81. For the influence of the films on the form of *Absalom, Absalom!*, see Watson, *William Faulkner, Self-Presentation and Performance*, 132–33.

35. In the original *Sanctuary*, Belle accuses Horace of incestuous love for his sister, Narcissa, and demands, "How did she come to let you go to the war, even in the Y.M.C.A.?" Faulkner cut the short scene, and with it the reference to Horace's war service, when he revised the novel in 1931. *Sanctuary: The Original Text*, ed. Noel Polk (New York: Random House, 1981), 16. Some evidence in the revised *Sanctuary* of Horace's having direct experience of the war is his "thinking of the expression he had once seen in the eyes of a dead child, and of other dead." *Sanctuary* (Corrected Edition) (New York: Vintage, 1981), 221.

36. John Limon offers an explanation for the absence of World War I from the novels when he writes, "Assume it is true that Faulkner's first three novels were apprentice work, succeeded by two masterpieces that make the case for Faulkner's stature as a high-formalist modernist (followed by other novels that may be better or worse than *The Sound and the Fury* and *As I Lay Dying* but which lack those books' virtuoso perfectionism). It follows that what had to be sacrificed in the fulfillment of Faulkner's most purely modernist aspiration is World War I.... by mentioning, too late in *As I Lay Dying* to affect our conception of the book, that Darl was in the war, Faulkner marks the point at which history becomes form, or, more accurately, where time itself gets stylized." *Writing after War: American War Fiction from Realism to Postmodernism* (New York: Oxford University Press, 1994), 115, 116.

37. *Absalom, Absalom!* Corrected Edition (New York: Vintage, 1986), 80. Future references are cited in the text as AA!

38. *The Sound and the Fury* Corrected Edition (New York: Vintage, 1984), 148. Future references are cited in the text as TSATF.

39. For a discussion of the New Haven matter that carried into *The Sound and the Fury*, see Watson, *William Faulkner, Self-Presentation and Performance*, 55–69.

40. "Text of the Yale Preface [of *Sartoris*]," in Max Putzel, *Genius of Place: William Faulkner's Triumphant Beginnings* (Baton Rouge: Louisiana State University Press), 1985, 296.

41. *The Falkners of Mississippi*, 87.

42. "Mississippi," in *William Faulkner: Essays, Speeches, and Public Letters* (New York: Random House, 1965), 17.

43. "Literature and War," in Millgate, "Faulkner on the Literature of the First World War," 99.

44. Poirier, *The Performing Self: Compositions and Decompositions in the Languages of Contemporary Life* (New Brunswick: Rutgers University Press, 1992), 98.

45. "An Introduction for *The Sound and the Fury*," ed. James B. Meriwether, *Southern Review* 111 (Autumn 1972): 708.

Addie in No-Man's-Land

John Liman

I teach *As I Lay Dying* pretty frequently, and for the last two years I've taught it in a seminar on modernism.[1] I pair it in these seminars with a book about modernism and the Great War, Modris Eksteins's *Rites of Spring*, which makes the haunting, invigorating, yet scattershot point that modernism was created in the same spirit in which Germany fought World War I.[2] The seminar meets for two-and-a-half hours each week, and for the first hour of the second week on *As I Lay Dying*, we kick around Eksteins's claim. We have previously screened a recreation of the Nijinksy-Stravinsky ballet that gives Eksteins's book its title, so the class is prepared to see the merits and limitations of his thesis. Then I coyly introduce *As I Lay Dying*. I wonder, in short, whether the novel has any of the attributes that would qualify it for Eksteins's condemnation: is it irrational, violent, mythic, primitive, and so on? The students muse on that for a while. After a pause, I say: "Of course, there is a direct relation between *As I Lay Dying* and the Great War." Then I wait.

What happens, year after year, is nothing. Silence. After a while, students make a few haphazard and forlorn guesses about what I might mean. Finally, one student—it is one student per seminar who notices this—ventures: isn't it true that Darl, the central character of *As I Lay Dying*, actually fought in World War I? I remain poker-faced, and wonder, "What makes you think that?" Other students are staring at the responding student with mystification and awe. The responding student says, "Well, the book says so." Of course that student is right. Six or seven pages before the end of the book, Darl reveals that he has an obscene spy-glass that he brought home from France after the war (AILD 254).

All right. It's time for the students in the seminar to rally; one of them, every year, now remembers that Darl informs us he has spent many nights beneath strange rooftops, thinking of home (AILD 81). We had been given no reason to believe that these rooftops were the French orange kind, but it had seemed odd when Darl mentioned it: how long have any of the Bundren kids spent away from home? Not long, we would have thought. Other students begin to chime in: perhaps this news about his participation in the Great War *accounts* for Darl. He is the most literate of the Bundrens, the most sensitive; also the meanest and most vengeful. We hold him accountable for the cement cast that does much to cripple his older brother, Cash; we know we can blame him because he is the one who ought to have some expertise in tending to injuries, though for the purposes of resentment he does not, in this case. Is his attitude towards the corpse of his mother—i.e., that it would be good to get rid of it, by burning if necessary—a callous soldier's attitude? The class is eager to make up for its shame in not noticing that Darl was in the Great War by explaining, now, *everything* about Darl in terms of the war.

I am not the only one in the class to observe, but am the only one in the class to make anything of the fact, that Darl, at the site of the very barn fire in which he is trying to incinerate his mother's body, has described the coffin on sawhorses as "a cubistic bug" (AILD 219). This prompts me to wonder aloud, for the benefit of my class, where Darl had gone on his leaves. Did he, like many another American soldier, run into Gertrude Stein in Paris? She would have liked him: he would have awakened in her a nostalgia for American craziness. He perhaps would have seemed to her like the sort of budding young American writer, for Darl seems like a budding young writer, who needed to learn at her feet what the twentieth century signified. She might have taken him back to the rue de Fleurus, and he might have seen a wall full of Braques and Picassos. From then on he would have been inclined to see life as violently fragmented, like *As I Lay Dying*. I am enchanted by this vision of the friendship of Darl Bundren and Gertrude Stein, and I am persuaded that the class at least finds the idea mildly amusing.

But here is the punch line of this story, which I say to you but never to my class, because it would have seemed as if I were toying with them. The punch line is that I find a lot of the story that I've just now elaborated silly. Not all of it, but enough. I do not think that the class was entirely wrong not to notice that Darl was a doughboy, and I do not think that the teacher was entirely right in allowing them to proceed as if that fact were the hidden key to the story. You can turn back, if you want, six or seven pages before the end of *As I Lay Dying* and reread the entire story with Darl's French campaign in mind, but I would not recommend it.

In fact, there has already been a moment in the text when it seemed one had to return to the beginning and start over. I have read *As I Lay Dying* probably ten times now, but I remember the first time; I remember figuring out, at some point, that the whole book revolved around Addie, the Bundren family matriarch, but that Addie would die without ever speaking. That seemed a good literary prank; but the joke was on me, because almost immediately after I figured this out, I was humiliated to read the section in which Addie makes her preposterous, posthumous address. Not only does she speak, but she also provides the only way of making psychological sense of the whole involuted Bundren family sickness. And not only does she make sense of the group psychopathology, she also explicitly provides the linguistic theory on which the whole book has been based. Not only that, she also connects the psychology and the linguistic theory. When you read the Addie section, three-fifths of the way through *As I Lay Dying*, you had better start over. You had been reading things that had to have seemed inexplicable.

We seem to be finding ourselves, reading this novel, in the middle of a Borges story. (Borges loved Faulkner, and a Borgesian retrospective misreading of Faulkner is easy to imagine.) We get three-fifths of the way through the novel to the Addie section, then start again; we get almost to the end of the novel, if upon rereading we move straight through the Addie section, find out that Darl had been in France, and start over again, again. Maybe it's possible to imagine an infinity of these recursive points, and thus a never-ending Zeno's paradox reading of Faulkner that never quite reads the last word.

Well, maybe not. Because, as I say, thinking of Darl as a veteran provides, it turns out, not such a perfectly fitting key to Darl's part of the novel. For one thing: should Darl's psychology require a unique explanation? Though Darl is the only Bundren to be sent away to the madhouse, there is plenty of madness loose in the household. Bringing in the war even to explain Darl's particularly insidious method of madness fails the Ockham's Razor test. It's one premise too many. Darl is covertly vengeful because his mother prefers Cash, her first-born, and Jewel, son of her love affair with the minister Whitfield, to himself, and their relationship with their mother is the only thing in the world that matters to a Bundren son, though each son finds his own way to keep it secret. Darl wants to burn his mother's corpse as revenge against her and those who are still loyal to her desires. It seems likely that he went to the war, if it's possible to speculate far beyond the authority of the book, to get away from his mother's relationship with Cash and, especially, Jewel. If this is so, then the war, far from explaining Darl, is reduced in dimension, at least as far as the novel is concerned, to just another gargoyle on the Bundren family structure.

This is very close to my precise view. If it were in fact my precise view, the talk would be over now and we could call it a night. But I think it is more accurate to assert that in *As I Lay Dying* Faulkner has written a book with alternative locks for competitive keys. And I shall argue that in seeing how the competition fares, we can find out something critical about Faulkner, and what is more, about modernism, and what is more, about the history of American literature, and what is more, about the whole war-obsessed history of literature. Also about war, which is normally preeminent in determining, for literary critics as much as for the culture at large, but not I think for writers, where we are in time.

Oddly enough, the hypothesis that the Great War explains Darl is not as convincing as the hypothesis that the Great War explains *As I Lay Dying*, itself—its characteristic images, its form, its style. For example, what is the reason for the sheer muddiness of *As I Lay Dying*, which is perhaps the muddiest book in all literature? Here is Darl's meditation on the mud that he and Jewel are slogging through, far away from Addie's death, which Darl nevertheless manages to envision and narrate:

> Overhead the day drives level and gray, hiding the sun by a flight of gray spears. In the rain the mules smoke a little, splashed yellow with mud, the off one clinging in sliding lunges to the side of the road above the ditch. The tilted lumber gleams dull yellow, water-soaked and heavy as lead, tilted at a steep angle into the ditch above the broken wheel; about the shattered spokes and about Jewel's ankles a runnel of yellow neither water nor earth swirls, curving with the yellow road neither of earth not water, down the hill dissolving into a streaming mass of dark green neither of earth nor sky. (AILD 49)

Every writer on the human experience of World War I stresses its muddiness. The British trenches were muddy all the time; infantry lived in mud. They also died in mud; the apotheosis of muddiness in Paul Fussell's *The Great War and Modern Memory* is the battle of Passchendaele. The four million shells fired by the British over ten days prior to the battle did not weaken the enemy; rather it tore up the ground. Then "the rain fell and turned the dirt to mud. In the mud the British assaulted and the attack finally attenuated three and a half months later.... Thousands literally drowned in the mud."[3] What is the meaning of this muddiness? The only way to see the meaning of it in Fussell is to see an irony: the British with huge determination and firepower produced the horror of their own devastation. The meaning is in the failure of the preparation to mean what it means to mean.

In his short story "Victory," Faulkner was himself preoccupied with the muddiness of the Great War. In the fighting portion of that story, the word "mud" appears at least once on every page: the hero squats "in the mud with newspapers buttoned inside his tunic"; another, anonymous character on the same page, like the donkeys in *As I Lay Dying*, "slips in the greaselike mud, trying to cling to the crest of the kneedeep ditch"; three paragraphs later we are told that "platoon by platoon they slip and plunge into the ditch and drag their heavy feet out of the clinging mud."[4] We have a right to conclude either that Faulkner's preoccupation with mud has its origin in World War I, or else his personal obsession with mud finds in the trenches of World War I a catastrophic objective correlative. Either way, the question to which we must quickly proceed is: what does mud mean to Faulkner? And in "Victory," a very strange story, I am not sure. But what I can report is that the hero of the story is severely punished for a failure of cleanliness; and later, after he rejoins the army and frags the officer who insisted on his punishment, he is obsessed with his own cleanliness and that of his soldiers. Even when he is poor and homeless after the war, he refuses to relent on his own cleanliness.

In *As I Lay Dying*, muddiness is also met by its opposing principle—cleanliness that takes the form of rectilinearity, manifest in Cash's will to keep everything straight and tidy and hard and discrete. Of course, what he mainly attempts to keep ruled and impermeable is Addie's coffin; when the coffin is on the wagon and Jewel rides up to it, we are told that "a gout of mud, backflung, plops onto the box. Cash leans forward and takes a tool from his box and removes it carefully" (AILD 108–9). Thus one of the contradictory principles of *As I Lay Dying* confronts the other. Cash's neatness and straightness seem to prevail in this skirmish, but as the body within his coffin rots, the ultimate victory would seem to belong to whatever deliquesces and leaks and permeates and stinks.

What seems to fascinate Faulkner most concerning mud is its yellow impurity, or better say its nonelementality. About Jewel's ankle swirls "a runnel of yellow neither water nor earth"; it curves with "the yellow road neither of earth nor water"; it dissolves into "a streaming mass of dark green neither of earth nor sky." That is to say, the mud is rather like Thoreau's streaming mass of clay as it melts down the train embankment at Walden, but rather unlike the pond itself, which holds earth, water, and heaven in its reflection of the ideal harmonious inviolate beauty of the world. What mud means to Faulkner is that the world is nauseating (his Great War stories often feature vomit) because it cannot be contained, categorized, and idealized.

And this again is a lesson that can be learned directly from World War I. If you read Eric Leed's remarkable book on the mythic structure of the war, *No Man's Land*, while you are thinking about Faulkner, you cannot avoid the sensation that Leed is writing about *As I Lay Dying*, though Faulkner is not mentioned once in the book. For example, Leed adopts the anthropologist Mary Douglas's notion of "pollution" to understand what the soldier in the trenches was experiencing. Leed quotes Douglas—"In short, pollution behavior is the reaction which condemns any object or idea likely to confuse or contradict our cherished classifications"—and applies it to war:

> The most unsettling feature of the landscape of war, for many combatants, lay in the constant transgression of those distinctions that preserve both order and cleanliness. The men in the trenches lived with the rats that grew fat from eating the corpses of men and animals. The smell of the dead pervaded the front lines,

penetrating even the deepest living quarters. The war literature is full of surprising encounters with corpses, complaints of being unable to prevent dirt, mud, and vermin from invading the most personal spaces.[5]

The sensation, while reading such passages, which link corpses and mud, that I was reading Faulkner criticism was so strong that I began to think that the title of *As I Lay Dying* was *No-Man's-Land* (for Addie dies partly to escape the men of her family), and I began to fantasize a novel in the form of a memoir written by a wounded, unevacuated, and finally dead but unburied soldier in *No Man's Land* entitled *As I Lay Dying*.

It is of course one thing to imagine a world in which, generally, boundaries and classifications do not hold, and another thing to imagine that the boundary between life and death does not hold. But that is what *As I Lay Dying* does imagine: Dr. Peabody says that Addie was dead ten days prior to her medical passing, and in another sense she stays alive for ten more days as she awaits, if that is the right word, her burial. Once again, we may trace Faulkner's interest in this Gothic horror to the Great War: his story "Crevasse" is about the fear of burial alive—which seems to be the complementary phobia to the fear of nonburial dead—in a cave in World War I. Again, this is standard World War I horror: Leed discusses the invariant dream of living burial, "of being held motionless by the weight of the earth while [and now he quotes a memoir] 'a heavy shell, howling and gurgling, with ineluctable slowness then with a mad shriek came down upon me'" (NML 22). The front, Leed summarizes, "is a place that dissolved the clean distinction between life and death" (NML 21).

And not just Faulkner was writing, in the last years of the 1920s, about the experience of seeing one's coffin while one is alive, preposthumously. In Erich Maria Remarque's *All Quiet on the Western Front*, the narrator, on the way to the front, passes a shelled schoolhouse. "Stacked up against its longer side is a high double wall of yellow, unpolished, brand-new coffins. They still smell of resin, and pine, and the forest. There are at least a hundred. . . . The coffins are really for us."[6] In Richard Aldington's *Death of a Hero*, a soldier "peered through and saw that the whole of the inside had been cleared of débris, and was stacked with quantities of wooden objects. He shaded his eyes more carefully, and saw that they were ranks and ranks of wooden crosses. Those he could see had painted on them R.I.P.; then underneath was a blank space for the name."[7]

Muddiness almost signifies death for Faulkner, as it seems to in the conjunction of muddy drawers and Damuddy's passing in *The Sound and the Fury*. More exactly, it seems to signify the incapacity for patrolling the boundary between death and life, or, more exactly yet, it serves as the emblem for Faulkner's capacity for feeling death in every life. Even pregnancy feels to Dewey Dell like the invasion of her body by mud (or, as she says, guts); and after death, humans live in each other's minds like demons and ghosts, which is where and how they had always lived. In short, the way to feel death in life is to feel the incapacity for knowing where one begins or ends. Temporally, this point is made by Faulkner's treatment of the fetus as a half-life, and of the moment of dying as a half-death. Spatially, the point is first made by way of Darl's capacity to narrate a scene of death from which he is miles distant. *As I Lay Dying* is a book not without boundaries, but with always trespassable boundaries, and in fact one of the strands of the plot, Dewey Dell's search for an abortion, has no ending, which means that the death we are inhabited by cannot be killed off.

What is the appropriate linguistic theory for such a conception? Addie's speech provides it. Here is the point at which Faulkner's conception of reality leads him to his modernist project: the linguistic experimentation of *As I Lay Dying* derives from Addie's theories. When Addie thinks of her husband Anse, she thinks of his name:

> Anse. Why Anse. Why are you Anse. I would think about his name until after a while I could see the word as a shape, a vessel, and I would watch him liquify [sic] and flow into it like cold molasses flowing out of the darkness into the vessel, until the jar stood full and motionless: a significant shape profoundly without life like an empty door frame; and then I would find that I had forgotten the name of the jar. (AILD 173)

This suggests that the way to produce an actual death—the once and for all kind—is to produce a name like a coffin. Naming is the only way to effect what Dewey Dell needs: it is the manufacturing of containers to rigor mortise the amorphous, irreducible, death-in-life and life-in-death of the muddy world.

This is the theory we need to understand some of the oddity of the way that *As I Lay Dying* was written. For example, the way that words liquefy and coagulate and liquefy—like Anse in Addie's imagination, but not the labeled jar he flows into. In honor of Dewey Dell's pregnancy, the trees are said to be "swollen, increased as though quick with young" (AILD 76). Within a few pages, this phrase is echoed by the following linguistic flurry:

"Yes, sir. It will rain some more."
"It come up quick." (AILD 87)

"It's been there a long time, that ere bridge," Quick says. (AILD 88)

"A fellow can sho slip quick on wet planks," Quick says. (AILD 90)

This is either bizarrely incompetent writing, or very interesting. I would choose interesting, particularly insofar as the word "quick" is a noun, an adjective, and an adverb, and refers simultaneously to birth, injury, and (because it is anticipated that the quick rain will cause the crop to wash out of the ground) abortion. Or take what happens to the word "bore," within one page of text:

> And the next morning they found [Vardaman] in his shirt tail, laying asleep on the floor like a felled steer, and the top of the box bored clean full of holes.
>
> And when folks talks [Anse] low, I think to myself he aint that less of a man or he couldn't a bore himself this long.
>
> Cora said, "I have bore you what the Lord God sent me." (AILD 173)

The word suggests endurance, maternal nurturing, and violent maternal penetration. Also, tenses are confused, as they always are in Addie's virtuosic use of the word "lie" and cognates—"Then I would lay with Anse again—I did not lie to him" (AILD 175)—which muddles intimacy and isolation, intercourse and nonintercourse, past and future, from the title of the novel onward.

Nouns, particularly, irritate Addie, as well they might, as the existence of nouns keeps the world from liquefying or muddying. "[M]otherhood was invented by someone who had to have a word for it because the ones that had the children didn't care whether there was a word for it or not. I knew that fear was invented by someone that had never had the fear; pride, who never had the pride." And Anse "had a word, too. Love, he called it" (AILD 171–72).

We have forgotten the Great War for a while, but here we are compelled to remember it. For every modernist author worthy of the title had to consider, in the wake of the war, where all the high, abstract locutions, nouns especially, had gone. Hemingway's dictum on the subject in *A Farewell to Arms* is famous: "abstract words such as glory, honor, courage, or hallow were obscene beside the concrete names of villages, the numbers of roads, the names of rivers, the numbers of regiments and the dates."[8] In this remark, we may register the distinction between Hemingway and Faulkner: Hemingway wants the names of rivers, Faulkner wants the river itself. That is, Hemingway wants less abstract, more concrete naming; Faulkner wants less concrete, muddier naming. Another skew is that Hemingway wants to outlaw the word "courage," but does not mention, as Addie does, the word "fear": Hemingway's mode is disillusion, but Faulkner's is disintegration. Still, what the two theories have in common is that words, unreformed, elevate and etherealize the world, and Fussell—who provides a long list of recently outmoded words ("comrade" for friend, "steed" for horse, "peril" for danger, etc.)—assumes that the best place to learn about the treachery of nouns was the western front (MM 21–22).

But here, at long last, the argument has to take a turn; because the looming question about the psychological theory of the book (egos fail to function to divide body from body, subject from subject), the ontological theory of the book (the world is undivided heavy flow), the linguistic theory of the book (words are not units), and the formal theory of the book (reality belongs to characters whose streams of consciousness overflow their banks), is why they are all announced by Addie, rather than Darl.

Granted that Addie is rather violent. In fact, she seems to resemble a type of soldier that Eric Leed gets interested in. Leed's book is about the way World War I invited soldiers into the dynamic of the rite of passage, separating them, defamiliarizing the world for them, acquainting them with death, but failed to give them a world to return to, restored. The war was not a revivifying escape from the ordinary trials of life; it was a nearly infinite magnification of those trials. One way out was hysteria; another was identification with the war machine itself. The latter case is epitomized by the soldier-litterateur, Ernst Jünger. Jünger is the sort of German, familiar to us from Klaus Theveleit's great book on the German Freikorps, *Male Fantasies*, who writes passages like this:

> But now [in a breakthrough] we will rip away this veil [of trenches and firepower] instead of gingerly lifting its corner.... We will force open the closed door and enter by force into the forbidden land. And for us who have, for so long, been forced to accumulate in desolate fields of shell holes, the idea of this thrust into the depths holds a compelling fascination. We will demolish the dikes and break like a stormflood into the broad, untouched region. Every day new villages and cities appear to our gaze and rich booty falls into our fist. (NML 158–59)

Leed has recourse to Wilhelm Reich on sadism and masochism to understand this. "The most consistent fantasy of the masochist is that of being punctured and of obtaining 'liberation from the outside, provided by someone else.' Similarly, the fantasy of the sadist is that of puncturing another, of finding gratification in the assertion of his will upon a passive object" (NML 157). Leed judges that in Jünger the sadistic element is dominant, and he also intuits signs of the incestuous in Jünger's penetration of the forbidden. It is hard not to think of Addie, whose unorthodox pedagogical techniques probably were frowned upon even in her day. She would look forward to her students' mistakes, so she could "whip them. When the switch fell I could feel it upon my flesh; when it welted and ridged it was my blood that ran, and I would think with each blow of the switch: Now you are aware of me! Now I am something in your secret and selfish life, who have marked your blood with my own for ever and ever" (AILD 170).

You need blood, apparently, one way or the other, if you yearn to escape the ordinary bounded weariness of your life. We might be inclined to wish that Addie, rather than Darl, had been allowed to go to war to do so. But the fact is that Addie, unlike Jünger, and unlike all the German Freikorps writers quoted by Theveleit, does not thwart the vulnerability of her passions by an identification with the rigid and unyielding machine; she wants complete mutual penetration of liquescent flesh and liquescent flesh. And she proposed to find satisfaction not in war but in what we would have called, if she had not warned us away from the term, motherhood. Pregnancy is for her a kind of dying, in the Renaissance sense (it is dying for Dewey Dell in the usual sense); it is how Addie performs a ritual sacrifice of her identity to her passions.

I hope two things are clear. The first is that *As I Lay Dying* is very nearly a perfect specimen of the Great War novel, written during the outpouring of Great War writing that commenced a decade after the armistice. The second is that the Great War is very nearly irrelevant to it. It is from Addie's autobiography that we learn almost everything we need to know to understand the Bundrens and the novel and world they are in. From Darl's war experience, we surmise nothing. So why write a war novel in which war is irrelevant?

My guess is that Faulkner began his career as a novelist on the assumption that coming to terms with the Great War was the first obligation of the modernist. If in fact you look at Faulkner's odd-numbered novels at the beginning of his career, you find a series that arrives, if I am reading it correctly, at the peculiar use of the war in *As I Lay Dying*. In *Soldiers' Pay*, Faulkner teaches himself the technique of making his narrative spiral around an almost mute character, Donald Mahon, who is dead while still alive—"The man that was wounded is dead and this is another person, a grown child"[9]—who is permitted a single section in which to recall the circumstances of his wounding (recalling it permits him finally to die as a medical matter), and whose physical death seems a perfection of the immobility of his final days. That Donald was an aviator in the Great War makes his always waning afterlife typical of "all the dead pilots." Yet Faulkner will determine, for reasons we need to understand, to transfer all his attributes to a woman whose adult experience consists of being a schoolteacher and mother.

In the short story I just alluded to, "All the Dead Pilots," we are told that all the pilots are dead in the Donald Mahon-Addie Bundren sense, with one exception, John Sartoris, who was shot down.[10] And Faulkner's third novel, *Flags in the Dust*, is of course largely about Bayard Sartoris, who probably most resembles Jewel in *As I Lay Dying*, as he careers around town on horseback or in cars trying to replicate his brother John's death.[11] Yet there is a peculiar turn in the novel, by the end of which the subject is not so much Bayard's suffering as it is his great-aunt Miss Jenny's and his wife Narcissa's. There is a moment in every Great War memoir when the returning soldier is informed—much to his disgust—that sacrifices on the home front have been heroic. Miss Jenny makes a similar speech, but as the victim of Grant's total warfare, she has a right.

> "Men cant seem to stand anything," she [Miss Jenny] repeated. "Cant even stand helling around with no worry and no responsibility and no limit to all the meanness they can think about wanting to do. Do you think a man could sit day after day and month after month in a house miles from anywhere and spend the time between casualty lists tearing up bedclothes and window curtains and table linen to make lint and watching sugar and flour and meat dwindling away and using pine knots for light because there aren't any candles and no candlesticks to put them in, if there were, and hiding in nigger cabins while drunken Yankee generals set fire to the house your great-great-grandfather built and you and all your folks were born in? Dont talk to me about men suffering in war." (FD 45–46)

Meanwhile, Narcissa, to whom this diatribe has been spoken, gives birth on the day her husband crashes and dies; this means, in Faulkner's view, that she has fought her war more successfully. She surrounds her infant with "wave after wave of that strength which welled so abundantly within her as the days accumulated, manning the walls with invincible garrisons" (FD 349). With Faulkner's approval, apparently, Narcissa "thought how much finer that gallantry which never lowered lance to foes no sword could ever find, that uncomplaining steadfastness of those unsung (ay, unwept, too) women than the fustian and useless glamor of the men that theirs was hidden from" (FD 350). So Faulkner, in moving from *Soldiers' Pay* to *Flags in the Dust*, moves from the fading of Donald Mahon, who is indeed a man, but whose blinding in the war is always, very nearly explicitly, treated as castration, to the endurance of a woman, Narcissa, in the quotidian battles of prenatal and parental life. We are ready to think of Addie as a warrior, birthing and dying, though the point that must be made about her is that she did not need to have anything to do with the Great War to earn her wings.

It is not merely that women are warriors, too. It is that they are warriors who do not fight literal wars. And this is not merely to congratulate them on a stalwart endurance that does not require murder and destruction for its occasion. It is to say that they live in a different historical time from men. Male temporality can only seek climaxes. This means either that men achieve their climax in war, like Donald Mahon, who symbolically loses his virginity and his potency in a single act of air combat, and are condemned thereafter to a life of ebbing anti-climax, or they fail to achieve their climax in war, like Bayard Sartoris, and are condemned thereafter to seek it in a furious peacetime. Here is how aviator sex is described in *Soldiers' Pay* by Januarius Jones: "Do you know how falcons make love? They embrace at an enormous height and fall locked, beak to beak, plunging: an unbearable ecstasy. While we have got to assume all sorts of ludicrous postures, knowing our own sweat." His lack of sweat makes the falcon's fall peculiarly unfallen; it seems to be marked by a fearlessness of post-Edenic anti-climax: "The falcon breaks his clasp and swoops away swift and proud and lonely, while a man must rise and take his hat and walk out" (SP 227). Faulkner, like the virginal cadet Lowe, never got this high; but as a "falconer," perhaps he has an instinct for this kind of proud and lonely falcon intercourse. Mahon experienced it; but he is a man after all, and his detumescence is always gravewards.

If you have that sort of climax, you have that sort of anti-climax. On the other hand, if you are a man, and you don't, you can only perpetually seek it. *Flags in the Dust* seems to be based on the endless repetition of traumatic memory, from the Civil War to the Great War and thereafter, which amounts to an endlessly glimpsed and sought confrontation with death. Old Bayard Sartoris, grandfather of the protagonist, fleeing Yankees as a youth, sees in his reflection in the spring "the cavernous sockets of his eyes ... and from the still water there stared back at him for a sudden moment, a skull" (FD 82). This connects two generations later to the "rusting skeleton of a Ford car," whose "two lamps gave it an expression of beetling patient astonishment, like a skull" (FD 123). When young Bayard gallops past Narcissa Benbow, whom he will marry, on his way to a painful accident, he "remark[s] for a flashing second a woman's face, and a mouth partly open and two eyes round with serene astonishment," later recalled as "two eyes round with grave astonishment" (FD 120,126). At the *next* memory of the woman, Bayard recalls her "two eyes round with grave astonishment, winged serenely by two dark wings of hair" (FD 134). Then we hear of the "fallen dark wings of her hair" moved upon by air "with grave coolness" (FD 138). The skull is the car is the woman; the woman—to whom the word "grave" is, like Bayard, always attracted—has wings and falls like an angel. Young Bayard's car accelerates "on a roar of sound like blurred thunderous wings" (FD 105). Pedantic Dr. Alford's hair, something like Narcissa's, is parted into "two careful reddish-brown wings" (the point is to reveal the skull); the horse on which young Bayard is injured "burst [out] like unfolding wings"; the literary Horace Benbow "is borne aloft on his flaming verbal wings" (FD 111, 119, 154).

There are wings everywhere, associated with skulls, speed, falling, and burning, because Bayard, flying with John, knew John was in trouble when he saw "the flame streaming out along his wing" (FD 239). This is why Bayard seeks death; but it is also why the book always seeks the same imagery. This is the thematics and stylistics of traumatized memory, when the memory is your own but not quite the trauma; it is, in other words, how you write and act when you are stuck on the near side of your climax.

It makes sense for Faulkner to write that way, on behalf of the Sartorises and the South, which has been stuck in a style and theme since the trauma of the Civil War. It is not merely that Bayard seeks John's death. It is also that John seeks to die on behalf of a missed encounter with death; what John wants to do is die in his grandfather Bayard's Civil War. If Faulkner starts his career on the assumption that he must be a novelist of the Great War, the Great War he is drawn to is not the one that defined modernity—the Great War fought in the wet, noisy, noisome, pointless, immobile trenches—but the one fought swiftly and purely in the sky. The air war was of course in a sense the most modern aspect of Great War combat; but its appeal to Faulkner was that it was, in one way, so out of date as to be virtually prehistoric.

I once posited, grandiosely, that one of the reasons for the invention of literature was the failure of war to be beautiful; I hypothesized that one of the most urgent meta-themes of *The Iliad* was the decline of warfare, from the time of the Trojan War to the time of its epic, from war-as-duel (symmetrical, bounded, complete) to asymmetrical, squalid strategic warfare.[12] It always seems to observers that the next-to-last war was beautiful and the last one was the first not to be; but there is some validity to the view that the Great War was the last moment for duel war on a grand scale in the West. In fact, the end of the possibility, in Western warfare, for duel war on the grand scale can be dated with some precision. Liddell Hart tell us that

> The year 1917 was marked . . . by an increasing development of the method of fighting and flying in formation, which tended to replace the Homeric combats of individual champions. . . . Henceforth, knight-errantry yielded to tactics and air-fighting gradually assumed the more developed forms of warfare, although carried out on a different plane. By the end of the war an attack was often delivered by formations of fifty or sixty machines which manoeuvred—the actual squadrons compact—with the aim of breaking up the enemy's formation.[13]

What Faulkner was after, in other words, was warfare that allowed him to fulfill the Southern dream of knightly, personal, duel-like, beautiful combat, which the Civil War certainly was not but should have been. He looked to the most technologically advanced aspect of the most brutal and technologically revolutionary war to fulfill his dream of a type of gallantry already antique in the time of Homer, in order to fulfill his dream of a better, or a redeemed, Civil War. But he could not have it. He could not have it, of course, because it did not exist. But I am more interested in the aesthetic impossibility of this dream of aviator combat. In Januarius Jones's conception, the appeal of air combat is that it is climax without detumescence. In fact, however, missions end and wars end, and if you want to use air combat as your model for literature, what you get is a book like *Soldiers' Pay*, all anti-climax, or *Flags in the Dust*, which seems to be driven towards a climax always personally too late and aesthetically too soon.

What Faulkner sees, when he comes to write *As I Lay Dying*, is that to join the twentieth century, he will have to come to terms with the trenches. This confrontation alone will allow him to put to rest his dream of a redeemed Civil War. He understands three things more. The first is that in order to realize the meaning of the trenches he needs an entirely new idea about time, a conception of a time that does something other than approach celestial climaxes or fall earthwards away from them. The horizontal trenches almost never move, and between them people are neither alive nor dead. The second is that he needs some conception of woman's time—time that does not move swiftly and surely from beginning to end, like a Hemingway sentence, but time that swirls and slows and backloops. Dewey Dell sees a sign that says "New Hope three miles." To which she appends this apparent non sequitur: *"That's what they mean by the womb of time: the agony and the despair of spreading bones, the hard girdle in which lie the outraged entrails of events"* (AILD 121). She translates from hope (New Hope) to despair as she translates from space (three miles) to the womb of time. This is time that takes the form of a womb: neither eschatological nor fallen, history merely grows in place.

Third, Faulkner realizes, since he had not fought in the trenches nor pretended he had, that it was his obligation to prove the possibility of mastering all the lessons of the twentieth century—the undoing of traditional hierarchies, the devaluing of rituals, the absurdity of faith—from a Yoknapatawpha family that seems, at first glance, to be as primitive as cave dwellers. That is why Darl and Addie compete for the key to the novel; that is why Darl's revelation is in the climactic position of the novel but weaker; that is why Addie's revelation is in the interior of the novel but is stronger, darkness radiating into the novel.

Perhaps I have made it seem that Faulkner was peculiar in his relation to the Great War. But Hemingway's draft of *The Sun Also Rises* had more of Jake and Brett's meeting during the war than was permitted to remain in the novel, and Fitzgerald's draft of *The Great Gatsby* had more of Gatsby's war heroism. Apparently the highest works of high American modernist fiction had of necessity to begin with the war but could not continue or end with it. Imagine, for example, Fitzgerald's problem: how to get us interested in a character known as the "great" Gatsby so soon after the Great War had inflated and devalued the idea of greatness; how to get us interested in a few lives and deaths so soon after, if you don't count civilians, eight-and-a-half million deaths; how to make it seem remotely plausible that you might take the Great War merely as a complication in a relationship, so that the relationship cannot continue only because another one has intervened, not because everything in the world has changed. You need to invent a new way of thinking of time outside history; and though Fitzgerald invents a catastrophe for his conclusion—described both as a holocaust and an accident, which sounds like a Great War oxymoron—the novel cannot breathe at all unless you allow momentarily for the fantasy of time that alters nothing.

It had been assumed that the modernist response to the Great War was primarily outrage or despair, until Modris Eksteins argued that World War I was a modernist war. I do not want to minimize the difference between these views, but I do not subscribe to either of them because I do not think history is so lockstep as both theories imply. In America we feel a special seductiveness in the idea that history is ruled, in two senses, by war, since we had an originary war. Feminist war theorists have occasionally speculated that war is the preferred form of male birth envy—it is the male form of suffering to bring forth new life, the way that the Civil War, in memory of forefathers who brought forth on this continent a new nation, conceived in liberty, would issue in a new birth of freedom, according to one famous formulation.[14] If your nation was born in war, you will look to each war to be born again.

But I believe that Washington Irving, named after one of those forefathers, gave us the characteristic tone for much postwar—post-any-war—writing in "Rip Van Winkle," whose hero seems to go to sleep for twenty years to give his wife time to die before returning to the village, but who in fact manages to miss the Revolutionary War in the process, and the possibility of his own premature death. When he arrives back in the village, everything has of course changed—America is more bustling, disputatious, and venal after every single war, according to the mythology—but Rip has not himself changed. Gatsby is his descendant, but does Rip one better by actually fighting in the war that changes everything without noticing that everything has changed. Malamud's Roy Hobbs, in *The Natural*, who reawakens after World War II into a corrupt world, is in the same tradition, though of course, given the novel's belatedness, it is also *about* that tradition.

Now I will once again recall the grandiose claim that literature began in Homer's disappointment in contemporary warfare, and add as corollary that this American tradition of missing or minimizing war is not so much a counter-Homeric tradition as the authentic Homeric tradition itself. Harold Bloom, bemused by feminism, pronounced his judgment that if there is in fact a women's literary pedigree, it amounts to a revolution in literary history, since the great tradition would not be exclusively descended from *The Iliad*.[15] I disagree. I don't think of *The Iliad* as being war literature, an insane statement except in one specialized sense: I don't think that it is formally beholden to war. I think that it is about war but not of it. I think that the Homeric tradition is the history of the literary determination to keep style free of the ugliness of the latest war. John Keegan and Richard Holmes tell us that

> the onset of mass-produced weapons, something approaching which was made possible by the introduction of iron about 1200 B.C., confronted the champion of single combat with a threat he had not previously had to face. It was that of a body of enemies who, because they could match him both in quantity and quality of weapons, did not need to equal him in skill in order to beat him. Not, at least, if they were prepared to undergo collective training and to conform vigorously to drill and to orders during the course of action.[16]

Organized armies began to appear around 1000 B.C., which is to say abut half way from the Trojan War to *The Iliad*, so that a warrior began to be transformed into a soldier. Previously, Keegan and Holmes write, "Hector and Achilles [had fought] as individuals, indeed, as the poet tells us, almost as performers under the eye of their assembled supporters" (Keegan and Holmes 25). But in fact what seems to me to preoccupy Homer in *The Iliad* is the failure of the Trojan War to take the form of duels: the Akhaian side cannot cohere; attempts at duels to epitomize and end the fighting are foiled by goddesses; when individual combat momentarily occurs, very frequently other soldiers rush to the defense of the weaker warrior, ruining the duel; and occasionally the war descends into pure melee. That is, the war fails to be beautiful, and Homer can only maintain the war as his aesthetic object by continually bowing to the ideal of combat beauty that has been lost.

This ideal never stops being lost. The history of warfare is a continuous falling away of war from the symmetrical, closed, and complete form of the duel. Consider the place of the Civil War in this decline. Keegan and Holmes write that

> in the middle of the nineteenth century, the technological equilibrium which had endowed the European infantryman with his battle-winning capacity was suddenly upset. New firearms, rifled to enhance accuracy at unprecedented ranges and then furnished with a magazine to decuple firepower, rendered close-order infantry tactics not merely ineffective but dangerous and self-defeating. The character of the battles of the American Civil War ... had issued that warning in stark terms.... By the end of the first decade of the twentieth century it was clear to any dispassionate observer that the era of the primacy of man in warfare was drawing to a close and that the era of the primacy of the machine was at hand. (14)

Was the primacy of the man in warfare absolutely at an end in the first decade of the twentieth century? Not quite, because, ironically, the airplane revived, for a few years, the beauty of the duel as the last, best hope of aesthetic warfare. That returns us to Faulkner, who hoped to find, in his fantasies about flying in the war, a way to maintain his nostalgia for knighthood, gallantry, and the duel without sacrificing his determination to find his way to the heart of modernity. If this is your project, paradox will have to be your mode, and here is the central paradox of this aspect of Faulkner's war writing: that disillusion exists to maintain illusion. That is, aviators will have to be disillusioned after the war as tribute to the illusion that properly aesthetic climaxes can still be found in duels.

As I Lay Dying, however, is a melee; it is uncertain where the alliances are; it is certain that death is not climactic; it is certain that nothing, by the action of the book, has been settled. Does war, on the other hand, ever settle anything? The question is critical for literature because, if it does, then fiction is aesthetically inferior to history. The traditional American view is that war's capacity to settle things is its very essence. William James considered the Civil War to be the perfect example of this: interrupting what would have been a protracted history of compromises on slavery, the Civil War simply abolished it. And in his book, *The Moral Equivalent of War*, which might as well have been titled *The Aesthetic Equivalent of War*, James, trying to imagine how war might be transcended, felt forced to grant "the unwillingness of the imagination" to "envisage a future in which . . . the destinies of people shall nevermore be decided quickly, thrillingly, and tragically."[18] But Faulkner, in the midst of what Winston Churchill (as Warwick Wadlington reminded a previous convoking of this society) called "another Thirty Years War,"[19] and at the end furthermore of a great decade of lynching as resistance to the proper outcome of the Civil War, would come in *As I Lay Dying* to believe that the only way to defend his own right to speak after the Great War was to develop a form of the novel that had its own reasons for inconclusiveness. Thus, in one gesture, he would absorb the lesson of the Great War and depreciate his obligation to consider war as the beautiful-in-history, as the only closure history makes available.

Elaine Scarry's work succeeds in making the standard view—that wars are conclusive—seem very odd.[20] Why, once wars are over, do they not start up again at the next available opportunity? Scarry's view, to reduce hundreds of closely reasoned pages to a sentence, is that the violated flesh of soldiers on both sides is thought to bear ritual testimony to the righteousness of the victorious side. Though I do not know if I would have been able to think clearly about the conclusiveness of wars without her work, nevertheless I want to register here my sense that she perhaps overestimates the extent to which they do conclude. We live in an era in which the best available object for considering this proposition is war in the

Balkans. It seems to me that the only generalization that can be made is that whether wars conclude or not is a historical contingency. In any case, Addie herself is proof that the joy of violated flesh may be transitive rather than conclusive.

Perhaps *A Fable* provides the best evidence that Faulkner conceived of the Great War as inconclusive. The book as you know concerns a French army mutiny in May of 1918. Faulkner seems to consider it a tragic irony that

> by mutinying, the regiment had stopped the war; it had saved France (France? England too; the whole West, since nothing else apparently had been able to stop the Germans since the March breakthrough in front of Amiens) and this [mass execution] was to be its reward; the three thousand men who had saved France and the world, would lose their lives. . . .[21]

Ah yes, we are eager to say, how ironic that those who saved the world from war are killed for their trouble! But then something occurs to us: the war, without the mutiny, would be over in six months, anyway. England, France, the West and the world were not, as it turns out, in mortal jeopardy. The only thing that Faulkner might have meant, as far as I can see, by this apparent amnesia is that what the mutiny was saving Europe and the West and the world from was the *second* World War (recall that Faulkner began *A Fable* in 1943). Germany, not seeing, in all the dead soldiers, ritual testimony to the unjustness of its cause, had reopened the war at the next opportunity—and had not yet been stopped. The reason, furthermore, that not just England and France but also the West and the world were in jeopardy was the Bomb (remember that Faulkner completed the novel in 1954). The world was Bayard Sartoris of *Flags in the Dust*, seeking climaxes in mimetic pursuit of earlier, unsatisfied passions. The point of the strike in May 1918 was to prevent the final masculinization of history; but in Addie Bundren's dying—as opposed to her death—Faulkner had already offered a ritual sacrifice to the same end. The Great War was inconclusive, but it created a nostalgia or longing for beautiful climaxes. One of the achievements of *As I Lay Dying* is that it found a way to incorporate muddy inconclusiveness into its form without fostering, at the same time, by the same act, a pre-nostalgia for the apocalypse that would bring the world, in the year of Faulkner's death and the Cuban missile crisis, to the brink of clean closure.

NOTES

1. William Faulkner, *As I Lay Dying* (New York: Vintage International, 1990). All further references to this edition, abbreviated AILD, will be inserted in the text.

2. Modris Eksteins, *Rites of Springs: The Great War and the Birth of the Modern Age* (New York: Anchor/Doubleday, 1989).

3. Paul Fussell, *The Great War and Modern Memory* (New York: Oxford University Press, 1975), 16. All further references to this edition, abbreviated MM, will be inserted in the text.

4. William Faulkner, *Collected Stories of William Faulkner* (New York: Vintage/Random, 1995), 444–45.

5. Eric J. Leed, *No Man's Land: Combat and Identity in World War I* (New York: Cambridge University Press, 1979), 18. All further references to this edition, abbreviated NML, will be inserted in the text.

6. Erich Maria Remarque, *All Quiet on the Western Front*, trans. A.W. Wheen (New York: Fawcett, 1929), 99–100.

7. Richard Aldington, *Death of a Hero* (Garden City, N.Y.: Garden City Publishing, 1929), 325.

8. Ernest Hemingway, *A Farewell to Arms* (New York: Scribner's, 1929), 185.

9. William Faulkner, *Soldiers' Pay* (New York: Liveright, 1926), 118. All further references to this edition, abbreviated SP, will be inserted in the text.

10. William Faulkner, "All the Dead Pilots," in *Collected Stories*, 511–31.

11. William Faulkner, *Flags in the Dust* (New York: Random House, 1973). All further references to this edition, abbreviated FD, will be inserted in the text.

12. John Limon, *Writing after War: American War Fiction from Realism to Postmodernism* (New York: Oxford University Press, 1994).

13. B. H. Liddell Hart, *The Real War: 1914–1918* (Boston: Little, Brown, 1930), 316.

14. See Nancy Huston, "The Matrix of War: Mothers and Heroes," in Susan Rubin Suleiman, ed., *The Female Body in Western Culture: Contemporary Perspectives* (Cambridge: Harvard University Press, 1986), 133.

15. Harold Bloom, *A Map of Misreading* (New York: Oxford University Press, 1975), 33.

16. John Keegan and Richard Holmes, *Soldiers: A History of Men in Battle* (New York: Viking, 1986), 23. Hereafter cited as Keegan and Holmes.

18. Bruce W. Wilshire, *William James: The Essential Writings* (Albany, N.Y.: State University of Albany Press, 1984), 355.

19. Warwick Wadlington, "The Guns of *Light in August*: War and Peace in the Second Thirty Years War," in Donald M. Kartiganer and Ann J. Abadie, ed., *Faulkner in Cultural Context* (Jackson: University Press of Mississippi, 1997), 125–47.

20. Elaine Scarry, *The Body in Pain: The Making and Unmaking of the World* (New York: Oxford University Press, 1985).

21. William Faulkner, *A Fable*, in *William Faulkner Novels, 1942–1954*, Joseph Blotner and Noel Polk, eds. (New York: Library of America, 1994), 782.

Daughters of Necessity, Mothers of Resource: White Women and the War in *Absalom, Absalom!*

PAULA ELYSEU MESQUITA

> *The world is in a crisis and always has been in a crisis, and the only time it was worse off than when it was in a crisis was when it wasn't in a crisis, because it was when it wasn't in a crisis that we tried to accommodate ourselves to slavery. We tried to accommodate ourselves to the superiority of the male. We tried to accommodate ourselves to some other fool inconclusive or incomplete idea. So crisis—there is strength in it.*
> —ARTHUR F. RAPER[1]

After the end of the Civil War a South Carolina woman sighed in her writings, "Oh! To see and be in it all. I hate weary days of inaction. Yet what can we women do but wait and suffer?"[2] Kate Stone's lament for the womanly condition that had relegated her to the impotent anxiety and monotony of the "safe places" during wartime conveys a sense of unwilling endurance of socially appointed gender roles. It also clearly resonates with Mr. Compson's condescending remark to Quentin: "So what can we do, as gentlemen, but listen to them [Southern women] being ghosts?"[3] At issue in both Stone's and Mr. Compson's comments is the assertion that women's participation in the war and in postbellum life was insubstantial and stood no real comparison with the *effectual*, valid action of men in warfare.

By 1936, Faulkner seemed to be shifting away from former portrayals of romantic Southern femininity, of subversively seductive young girls and charismatic matriarchs. *Absalom, Absalom!*'s setting during the Civil War allowed him to explore further the mysteries of domestic inertia, which in the belligerent South of his fiction seemed to enclose the female principle like a deadly cocoon. The female profiles he created for the Sutpen saga served as functions of stasis in a narrative obsessed with the dying spirituality of the South. While in novels like *The Sound and the Fury* the emotional crisis that triggers the Compson tragedy originates in Caddy's dynamic, destabilizing actions, *Absalom* is peopled by women who seem to experience only existential paralysis. Their lives are utterly determined by men's external feuding, both at familial and military levels. On the surface the one truly remarkable feature shared by characters like Rosa, Judith, and Clytie is a somewhat inexplicable tolerance of all instances of emotional and material loss, while the social world around them gradually disintegrates through the destructive action of males within and without the limits of Sutpen's Hundred.

In this sense, Faulkner's fascination with the image of femininity as an irreducible force of nature appears to have changed direction slightly: pulling woman away from the center of chaos, as we had seen her in *The Sound and the Fury* or *As I Lay Dying*, he here studies her powerful spirit of endurance in adversity. His representation of feminine impassivity went so far as to suggest not only that these women withstood the inhospitable reality of wartime hardship, but that they actually seemed to exist outside reality. Their only refuge seemed to be the fictional modes of existence they carved for themselves.

Several questions emerge. In what category does this form of action fall? Was the stasis real? What role did these women carry out, as individuals and as citizens in the military engagement of the Confederacy? What was the significance and range of their intervention and what sociopolitical meanings lie therein? And, perhaps most significantly, did their reactions to the changes brought on by the war represent the unified response of a self-aware gender collective? The Civil War battling, as Faulkner well knew, worked as a perfect metaphor for parallel contests of gender and race unfolding simultaneously within the white household. Moreover it illustrated, more than half a century on, that the South would still benefit from present thought-provoking social crises. His view and that of many other Southern intellectuals was that if the benighted South was ever to awaken from its long sleep and fulfill its rich economic, cultural, and human potential it could not escape painful but necessary spiritual purging.

The entire spectrum of Southern society was hard hit by the violence, the shortages, the loss of human and material resources, not to mention the ideological crises—all of which became more and more unbearable as the conflict progressed. However, it must be recognized that, at some levels at least, one particular section of society obliquely benefited from the social and economic rearrangements imposed by the war, and all the more as the South became more and more engulfed in warfare. I am of course referring to white Southern women, notably the wives, sisters, and daughters of the men who in their hundreds of thousands abandoned the rule of household and property to join the Confederate army. Women in turn found themselves with no alternative but to step in for their absent male relatives. They took over the duties of property management and social organization formerly retained by their men, most frequently unsupervised by other males. At a time when the ideology of domesticity was deeply ingrained in middle- and upper-class mentality, not all women necessarily saw this uncalled for increase in responsibilities—not to mention "unbefitting" *masculine* responsibilities—in a positive light. Yet many eventually began to realize that in the midst of catastrophe and misfortune a blessing in disguise had been lurking. A new source of political power was made available to them as they inadvertently became the champions of Southern liberties on the home front. Still, what did it mean, this new power? For men in such troubled times, marching off to war was sufficient definition of their maleness. But what were women to think of the new position in which political developments they were never consulted about had landed them? One thing they could probably guess—no "beautiful lives"[4] lay immediately ahead. As Miss Jenny remarks in *Flags in the Dust*, the popular and literary construction of the war was deceptively one-sided:

> Do you think a man could sit day after day and month after month in a house miles from anywhere and spend the time between casualty lists tearing up bedclothes and window curtains and table linen to make lint and watching sugar and flour and meat dwindling away . . . and hiding in nigger cabins while drunken Yankee generals set fire to the house your great-great-grandfather built and you and all your folks were born in? Dont talk to me about men suffering in the war.[5]

1. ". . . *since waking I shall never sleep again*"

Significantly, *Absalom* opens with the ritualistic encounter between a young man born in the postbellum South and an older woman who has had first-hand experience of the war: the reluctant Quentin and the ghostly Miss Coldfield, the latter consistently described (especially by Quentin and his father) in terms that suggest immateriality and detachment.[6] Rosa's life-span determines a precocious need for fictionalizing life in her surroundings and sharpens our perception of her existence as ulterior to palpable reality. Still in her mid-teens when the Civil War broke out, Rosa had grown up in a relatively quiet antebellum South. She suffered the abrupt upheaval and unprecedented deprivations of the wartime period and went on to live yet another forty-five years of emptiness and angry frustration, apparently the only legacy left to her by the war experience. The emotional barrenness of her childhood years was manifest in an inclination to observe reality through romantic abstractions in her teenage years. The hiatus that separated her eventless life from the exclusive, almost exotic world of Sutpen women allowed her to transform them (as well as Thomas and Bon) into mythical creations. Through their actions she attempted to compensate for the vacuum in her own life (not that Rosa actually wished to be Ellen or Judith, for whom she occasionally expressed if not pure contempt at least total incomprehension; but clearly she was interested in playing out in an imaginary dimension the more fulfilling female roles—mother, lover—which were theirs in the real world).

That vacuum was suddenly inundated with the very tangible chaos unleashed by the war. The trail of social and economic disarray of the 1860s and the Reconstruction era only added to the environmental complexities that had already jammed her early development. The evident psychological impact of the political crisis stemmed greatly from the aggravating effect it had on existing familial, gender, and racial tensions. Also quite determining for Rosa and young women in the South—and most irrevocable of all—mass recruitment and the high number of casualties in the battlefield resulted in the virtual effacement of young males from southern towns and cities. This crisis naturally led to serious gender imbalance in the region and for the next two decades spinsterhood would remain the likeliest fate for young females. Yet undoubtedly the war also brought forward a promise of meaningful venture for lonely, action-starved women like Rosa. At least temporarily they could channel their energies to a visible form of communal enterprise and simultaneously project their own unsolved inner tensions onto the national conflict.

Contemporary Civil War rhetoric on both sides frequently turned to the metaphor of the family quarrel.[7] As the daughter of an unrelenting antisecessionist, the metaphor held quite literally true for Rosa, a fervent Rebel supporter in the Coldfield household. Her status as a young single—that is, economically dependent—daughter both prevented her from leaving her father for the Southern cause and to a great extent silenced her in her political stance. Or did it?

Unlike Judith and Clytie and the majority of women in the seceding states, Rosa did not see the head of her family or her master march off towards enemy lines. Given her political loyalties this put her in an even more challenging position: she must not only live under the same roof as, but also be supported by, an ideological opponent. Bound by the tight limits of filial and gender obedience, Rosa was forbidden not only to take any part in ceremonial gatherings supporting the departing regiments but also even to peek at passing soldiers or in any way to manifest her views on the current state of affairs. To be in any way associated with Confederate activity had become the most serious transgression of domestic rules dictated by her father. It would appear, then, that more than ever Rosa's scope for speech or action as a woman was tightening because of the war. Nonetheless, what we witness right from the declaration of war is an interesting gender role reversion between father and daughter.

When the inevitability of war became evident towards 1861 the ideological beliefs of many antisecessionists in the South subsided and regional identity proved the stronger sentiment. The North was generally perceived as an adversarial culture and specific political disagreements amongst Southerners were neutralized by this view at crucial moments. Consequently, as the region prepared for the hostilities, many antisecessionists joined the Confederate regiments, a gesture that attested to their regional loyalty as well as their manhood. But in Mr. Coldfield's case, religious convictions and disillusionment over the outcome of the national debate had just the opposite effect; they caused him to relinquish rights and duties socially assigned to males—namely his freedom of speech and his duty of action. Before the war Mr. Coldfield freely exercised his authority and discursive powers both in private and in public life.[8] But at the time of the conflict we see him receding gradually into invisibility and silence, nailing the entrance to the small attic where he hid permanently after his store was broken into by Union soldiers. Three years later he would literally abandon all forms of action by dying, a denouement symbolically anticipated by the disposal of the hammer used for self-incarceration.

Conversely, as her father's presence gradually faded into nonexistence after 1861, Rosa was gradually forced to confront the social convulsion that the war represented. At many levels this meant that like most other young women in the Confederacy she had to step out of her own political nonexistence into a new mode of active social participation. A complete redefinition of Southern womanhood was evidently in order. Up until the actual declaration of war, the average woman's access to all matters political was fiercely limited by patriarchal restrictions. Women's involvement in politics was widely opposed. Their reluctance to allow them to participate in such "manly" affairs revealed the fear that it might generate "unsexed" women. As far as citizenship was concerned, in the words of a Rebel, "woman . . . has but one right and that is the right to protection."[9] Such "protection" led to widespread female unawareness that the conflict was turning into one of unprecedented dimension. Moreover, it explained their underestimation not only of the issues at stake but also of the extent to which their lives would be affected. The prevailing view of womanhood as synonymous with domesticity is still evident in Rosa's main (pre-)occupation when the first rumors of war came to Jefferson: ". . . whipping lace [for her niece's trousseau] out of ravelled and hoarded string and thread and sewing it into garments while news came of Lincoln's election and of the fall of Sumpter, and she scarce listening, hearing and losing the knell and doom of her native land between two tedious and clumsy stitches" (AA 61). "She was still doing it when Mississippi seceded and when the first Confederate uniforms began to appear in Jefferson . . . beneath the regimental colors which [Sutpen] and Sartoris had designed and which Sartoris' womenfolks had sewed together out of silk dresses" (AA 63).

While Faulkner seemed to be having a little fun at Rosa's expense with this parody of the crucial female war effort,[10] there is nonetheless a real sense here of how distanced from war issues many women seemed to be until stern impoverishment and the mounting death toll became unmistakably palpable to them. However, abrupt changes in the public sphere were followed not long after by structural transformations in the private world of home. As Mr. Coldfield retreated to the "safe," womblike attic, Rosa had to take on new responsibilities not only of supervision but of actual production. In other words, the same war that condemned her father to immobility and silence endowed her with agency and a voice. Whether Rosa's conventionality allowed her to fully realize this or not, her new dynamic mode was in its very essence defiant of the antebellum gender-oriented work distribution. And if the matter of changing race relations was pivotal in Rosa's experience of the war and its aftermath, as I will suggest shortly, witnessing the breakdown of gender delimitation was no less an issue:

> "and soon she, who had never been taught to do anything practical because the aunt had raised her to believe that she was not only delicate but actually precious, was cooking the food which as time passed became harder and harder to come by and poorer and poorer in quality, and hauling it up to her father at night.... She did this for three years, feeding in secret at night and with food which in quantity was scarcely sufficient for one, the man whom she hated." (65)

It is revealing that Rosa's stated hatred for her father only surfaces during wartime. Mr. Coldfield's radical stand against both slavery and secession only worsened her identity crisis. It threatened to rob her simultaneously of two cardinal tenets shaping identities in Victorian Southern culture: the supremacy of maleness and whiteness. There is a strong sense of dislocation when Rosa is initially forced to take on the lead of the household. She performs what she perceives as exhausting and demeaning chores which by the standards of the genteel tradition were below her white womanhood. She was doing the jobs of the absent white male and of the freed slaves her father had refused to buy or keep—and too aware of it. Providing for the family was also indisputably equated with masculinity, yet it is Rosa now who must feed her father. Her bitter resentment indicates that she sees him as having failed at manhood; she sees his refusal to join the Rebels and fight for the perpetuation of slavery as a form of self-effacement. Ultimately it constitutes neglect of that all-important Southern cultural backbone: the protection of the white woman, that is, the preservation not only of her sexual purity but of her spiritual superiority as well. At the turning point of 1861 neither quality seemed compatible with the prosaic worldliness of cooking, cleaning, and manufacturing. The very physical displacement of the upper- and middle-class white woman from the social environment of the parlor to the less-inspiring spaces of menial labor in the home was in itself regarded as symptomatic of social downgrading.[11]

Yet the prolonged battling, which had always been constructed as a male domain, put such assumptions into perspective. When it became inevitable for women to join the war effort and they were forced to participate as actively as the men—albeit in different areas—clear-cut gender distinctions became more problematic than ever. The war did indeed make it very difficult for white women to overlook the fact that while the old social order might have privileged them in terms of race, it notably ranked them as subordinate—as slaves too were subordinate—on grounds of gender. The war did not turn ladies into slaves, but it made it inescapably evident that both groups shared a common experience of subservience to white masters. At the same time that the white women's crucial contribution to the cause in industry, enterprise, and agriculture leveled them with white men in terms of productivity and ideological commitment, these women began to claim other male-identified activities as also rightly theirs. They were beginning to recognize that their traditional role in society was actually expanding because of the war. In fact, stepping into men's shoes became a fantasy which was ever easier to fulfill—literally. Historical records tell us of women occasionally experimenting with transvestitism, trying on their absent husbands' and brothers' clothes. These women were certainly aware of the audacity of their transgression and its latent political significance;[12] yet the men's military defeats were alarming, and the women were certainly justified in their growing uneasiness about a situation of utter dependence which they had never had reason to question before. At any rate they appeased women's confused guilt for getting involved in what they had always been taught to see as men's affairs. The same desire for surpassing gender barriers and craving for action of real consequence is recurrently expressed by Rosa in terms that question biological destiny: *"That was the miscast summer of my barren youth which . . . I lived out not as a woman, a girl, but rather as the man which I perhaps should have been"* (116). Her growing interest in the figure of Thomas Sutpen, who though a notorious "demon" joins the Confederate army and even becomes a senior official, reveals Rosa's correlation of effectual praxis with masculinity.

Writing had likewise remained ostensibly a man's business so far, but it was now being undertaken by thousands of anxious, pensive women. They turned to producing diaries, poetry, and prose in their search for a space where political views and personal feelings could be vented spontaneously. Writing became an important instrument for women's political growth, as it allowed them to express themselves without fear of social censorship at a time when for women to discuss public affairs was still frowned upon.

Initial motivation for women's Civil War writing was undoubtedly of a confessional nature. However there is no denying that their documental legacy became of utmost historical importance, as it offers a vivid insight into the changing moods of the wartime Southern communities both at private and public levels. It is telling, then, that Rosa Coldfield finds her voice at the very moment when her father loses his.[13] How seriously Faulkner himself takes her writing is perhaps predictable; no doubt Quentin and his misogynous father see her as a true "scribbling woman," as having "established . . . herself as the town's and the county's poetess laureate by issuing to the stern and meagre subscription list of the county newspaper poems, ode, eulogy and epitaph, out of some bitter and implacable reserve of undefeat" (6). But I am more interested in the exuberant, fountainlike prolificacy of her composition rather than its actual literary quality, which we can't even describe, since Faulkner gives us no samples. Considering that Rosa's existence until the start of the war has been one of virtual muteness, her warborn inclination towards writing suggests that she has discovered a meaningful form of expression whereby inner conflicts can be creatively played out. Rosa's poetic object-choice may be the gallant Confederate army, but a clear sense of obsession and the fact that she writes late at night indicate that she is rather addressing her own "dark," unspoken tensions.

In a curious *mis-en-âbyme* of sorts with her creator's appropriation of the war setting for aesthetic purposes in *Absalom, Absalom!*, Rosa too has found in the war motif a perfect artistic frame for conflicting personal and political loyalties. Her praise of the Rebels allows her to conceptualize the antagonism she feels towards both her abolitionist father and the omnipresent yet elusive African Americans, both of whom she perceives as threatening to the integrity of her white womanhood. The theme and the language of rebellion in her poetry are also in agreement with her insurgence against her father's prohibitions. She uses writing as a subversive form of agency, a means for breaking the silence imposed on her with regard to Confederate matters. It is also through her wartime writing that Rosa seems to rediscover speech. She becomes more verbal in her interaction with others after the war, and at the opening of the narrative, when she is sixty-five years old, Quentin actually complains of her incessant talking. Indeed one of her very few gains from the war was a new awareness of language and its powers of representation and transformation. A great part of what happens in *Absalom* is either told first-hand by Rosa or modified by Rosa's telling, and that in itself illustrates how vital to the Sutpen story her voice really is. That is why she must *tell* Quentin about the war, to enable him to *tell* or even to *write* about the South.[14] For Rosa language has become the only way the South could try to make sense of history and eventually come to terms with what had happened. And whether she recognizes the importance of it or not, it has also become a vital means to correct the strange absence of the female element in popular constructions of the Civil War and to perpetuate the memory of women's manifold participation in the mind of the following generations.

2. "Not the boy"

But for all of Rosa's repressed admiration for masculine notions of honor, valor, and outdoor physical activity embodied by Sutpen and Charles Bon, the war years consign her to the feminine solitude of the house. Deserted by father and aunt, it is only after Bon is killed that she moves in with Judith and Clytie to await the return of Sutpen. As a result of the sapping demands of the Rebel army her social interaction is still confined to an exclusively female cosmos. Women moving in with other kin or friend females was a common arrangement amongst Southern communities during the war. Yet since there was rarely any real spontaneity in such decisions, it is not clear-cut that all women should find it easy relating to one another on the sole grounds of gender identification. Rosa indeed describes how it would have been unnatural for her to seek emotional support in Judith or Clytie:

> *I had for company one woman whom, for all she was blood kin to me, I did not understand . . . and another who was so foreign to me and to all that I was that we might have been not only of different races . . . not only of different sexes . . . but of different species.* (AA 123).

In reality, Rosa's difficulty in bonding with either of the two women lies not so much in a lack of same-sex empathy, but rather in a clash of social philosophies. Judith and Clytie's living arrangement presents a real challenge to the inflexible gender and racial categorizations that still shape her view of human reality. In fact, their very kinship and harmonious coexistence are in themselves the material negation of the logic behind the Civil War.

To begin with, Judith's behavior has always been problematic from a perspective of gender alignment, notably in her contiguity with brother and soul mate Henry. Faulkner elaborates their close-knit relationship before the war ("that single personality with two bodies" AA 73) through one of his favorite themes, the inherent sexual ambiguity of gender. While Henry is consistently depicted in feminizing terms, Judith has inherited her father's tenacity and resolve and certainly has the more "masculine" profile of the two children.[15] The paradoxical nature of their tight bond functions as a synecdoche of the ideological chasm dividing the nation. Faulkner makes this evident by investing their storyline with recurrent military overtones, following traditional representations of the Civil War as a family feud. As the historical background for the complex liaisons within the Judith-Henry-Bon triangle, the war becomes a determining factor for the development of the lovers' plot as it places the private implications of fraternal and amorous affairs against the wider picture of nationwide political commotion. It also puts Judith's nonconforming female identity in a more revealing sociological perspective. Instead of breaking her defiant spirit, the war actually stresses the contrast in the conceptualization of womanhood that she embodies. At a time when dependence and helplessness were no longer affordable attributes of femininity, the conflict emphasized the incipient breakdown of purely biological assumptions about womanhood. What it had taken a war for Rosa to realize Judith seems to have known and acted upon all along:

> *"It did not even require the first day . . . to show us that we did not need . . . any man . . .—I who had kept my father's house and he alive for almost four years, Judith who had done the same out here, and Clytie who could cut a cord of wood or run a furrow better . . . than Jones himself."* (124)

In fact, for Judith, taking the place of men has been a permanent mode of existence rather than a wartime necessity. In one of the first instances of her willing surrogacy she is merely six years old. When Sutpen gives up his wild Sunday morning horseracing excursions, Judith takes it upon herself to command one of his wild slaves to make the team of horses run away, much to the bewilderment of her entire family. Such boldness and initiative in a young girl, let alone a child, is radical for the 1860s and accordingly she is punished for her *action*. Her early interest in male-identified activities involving danger, physical action, and violence reveals her awareness of her father's dynastic design and a powerful will to overcome the paralyzing constraints of gender.

Judith's relationship with Henry is consistently described in terms of psychological twinning. One metaphor, with its imagery of military homogeneity, blurs all those social distinctions that make up civilian life: theirs is "a curious relationship: something of that fierce impersonal rivalry between two cadets in a crack regiment who . . . chance the same destruction and who would risk death for one another not for the other's sake but for the sake of the unbroken front of the regiment itself" (AA 62–63). Yet their identities are quite contrasting, and never more clearly than in the episode of the stable fight described at the end of the first chapter. While Henry runs away, traumatized by the crude display of violence among his father and the wild slaves, Judith remains calm and collected, secretly watching the fights from the entrance to the loft. There is a strong element of subversion in Judith and Clytie's inconspicuous infringement of the father's prohibition. It is upon Henry that Sutpen means to inculcate some sense of primal virility and certainly not on either of his female descendents. Judith perceives the spectacle of the combat as yet another field of action off-limits to her on account of her sex. Energy, regardless of its manifestation, is equated only with masculinity. Thus in her identification with Sutpen's forceful temperament she strives to accomplish her own design: to prove herself as worthy a successor as any male descendent. Ironically (or not) she does indeed end up ruling Sutpen's property with the help of the inseparable Clytie. However, this opportunity only becomes available to her through the demographic and societal readjustments imposed by the war.

As previously with Rosa, the war initially appears to perpetuate the fundamental paradox in her family: "unmanly" men can take their rights of agency for granted and go to war, while women, no matter how "masculine" their demeanor, must remain passive in their inconsequential housekeeping. The irony seems even greater when one remembers the young Henry screaming and vomiting just from watching the slaves fight. Henry is never more out of place than on the battlefront, but even if Judith is psychologically better equipped than he to face the carnage of war, she is the one who must stay behind. As Alice Ready from Tennessee wrote in her diary in 1862, "I never before wished I was a man—now I feel so keenly my weakness and dependence."[16] More than ever women felt that gender distinctions went much beyond mere sexual differentiation. Particularly at times like these, for them it also meant social exclusion and political encumbrance. Having to stay at home gave many women a sense of unimportance; but, as we have seen in Rosa's case, others seized it as an opportunity for meaningful, unhindered activity. The importance of this is that more often than not such freedom led them to question established political assumptions of gender and racial discrimination, down to the very core of social organization. Judith's nonconforming character allowed Faulkner to take this view further than he possibly could with the more Victorian Miss Coldfield.

Underneath the apparent quietude of the *"busy, eventless lives"* (AA 124) that the three women live in that period between the end of the war and the return of Sutpen, the political storm that has long been brewing at home can no longer go unnoticed. Henry and Sutpen and Bon and hundreds of thousands of other men went to war to fight for the submission of African Americans—on which the submission of white women greatly relied. Yet back home everything about the way the women live undermines the very ideology that the men have set off to defend and even die for. Like many white women in the South, Judith steps down from the pedestal of morality and fragility that was reserved for the upper- and middle-class white woman and into a more pragmatic field of sociological reorganization, starting with the reassessment of social relations between white women and slaves.

3. Sleeping with the Enemy

Whiteness and maleness were the most determinant referents for self-definition in the nineteenth-century South; one's social existence was rigidly determined by sectional perceptions of race and gender. But the initial glorification of the Civil War quickly subsided and gave way to an upheaval that shook even the most basic social values. In *Absalom* this contrast can be seen in the steep descending curve of popular mood, from Rosa's initial oblivion of the implications of the conflict to women's endurance of dreary wartime routine over the next few years: *"We were afraid. We fed them [the returning soldiers]; . . . But we were afraid of them.), we waked and fulfilled the endless tedious obligations which the sheer holding to life and breath entailed"* (AA 126–27). White Southern women appeared to be the social group who had the most to lose with the war. On the one hand, they depended greatly on the white men for protection and livelihood. On the other, they needed slaves to free them of domestic work and to allow them the less mundane existence that was constructed as ideal femininity. Now the war had shattered their reliance on male provision and *black* no longer meant *bound*. When these fundamental accessories of white womanhood could no longer be taken for granted, how was their perception of African Americans affected? After all, they were the ones who had to live under the same roof as them without the protection of male whites, at a time when fears of slave insurrection were greatly widespread.

It was indeed a delicate and complex situation and one which fascinated Faulkner. For many women, bitterness over the loss of status resulted in great resentment towards the black servants. They often pretended not to acknowledge the change in labor relations and expected blacks to behave in a servile manner even after emancipation. This is clearly the case with Rosa and her neurotic construction of Clytie as an indifferent arch-rival. Blacks had always been perceived as an inscrutable race, but when the war threatened the institution of slavery, the cornerstone of Southern civilization, slaveowners and whites in general had good reason to be apprehensive about the reaction of slaves. Mary Chestnut, a plantation mistress from South Carolina, wrote in 1861: "Their faces are as unreadable as the sphinx. Certainly they are unchanged in their good conduct."[17] Although Chestnut like many white women initially tried to believe that slave loyalty was unshakable, the silence in which the latter had always been kept now posed a real problem, as whites had no access to slave thoughts. As the war unfolds, Rosa's paranoiac hostility against the "sphynx-faced" Clytie (109) mounts perceptibly. This is no doubt a consequence of what she sees as a blurring of the color line that unequivocally separated their worlds before. As we have previously seen, in the initial period after Rosa moves in with the two sisters, she still perceives Clytie and her blackness as completely alien to everything that constitutes her world: *"not only of different races . . . , not only of different sexes . . . , but of different species . . ."* (AA 123). But the experience of contiguity gradually erodes this stubborn sense of difference: *"It was as though we were one being, interchangeable and indiscriminate . . ."* (AA 125). The necessity for white women to work side by side with black servants precipitated a new and uncomfortable sense of sameness amongst mistresses and white women in general, which was most often translated into a fear of assimilation or racial merging. This fear may explain Rosa's hysteria at the moment when Clytie not only speaks her name to her face but also touches her hand to prevent her invasion. The actual physical contact between the two races surpasses any metaphorical interpretation that Rosa might infer: *"Because there is something in the touch of flesh with flesh which abrogates, cuts sharp and straight across the devious intricate channels of decorous ordering . . ."* (AA 111–12). Rosa was only now beginning to acknowledge the radical and very material implications that the distant war would actually have for the coexistence of the two races in the household.

In addition, creating the special relationship between Clytie and Judith, Faulkner addressed an aspect of this sociological turning point which was for a long time greatly underestimated. His focus was on the disruption of race relations as a two-way process. As white women were gradually (if temporarily) forced to accept a condition of commonality with blacks, so were the blacks presented with an opportunity to prove their human worth to others and themselves in a social setting that challenged segregation. Clytie had always enjoyed the companionship of Judith since their childhood, but only extraordinary conditions like the Civil War could explain the gradual leveling of their leadership in the house, to the point that Rosa sees them as indiscriminate. Unlike Rosa, Judith actively encouraged this sense of equity, allowing Clytie to take charge of specific responsibilities at home. Yet this in itself would not have been enough for Clytie's psychological emancipation. Many white women who had lived experiences of greater proximity and understanding with their black servants during the conflict took back the trust and friendship they had shared with them when the war came to an end. This was not, of course, the case with Judith. But the symbolic importance of Clytie's character lies in her capacity to free herself spiritually and to confront the groundless white arrogance of those that Rosa stands for, without even needing the support or validation of Judith. Clytie may not have abandoned Sutpen's Hundred during or after the war, but she was genuinely emancipated by then. Because of her special position in the household she stays to take care of her family, even die for her family, but not to serve former masters.

NOTES

1. In Arthur F. Raper Oral History Memoir (January 18, 1971), in Columbia Oral History Collection, 162, Columbia University Library, New York.

2. Katharine M. Jones, ed., *Heroines of Dixie: Confederate Women Tell Their Story of the War* (Indianapolis: Bobbs-Merrill, 1955), 70.

3. William Faulkner, *Absalom, Absalom! The Corrected Text* (New York: Random House, 1986), 12. Cited as AA in the text.

4. "*Beautiful lives—women do. In very breathing they draw drink and meat from some beautiful attenuation of unreality in which the shades and shapes of facts—of birth and bereavement, of suffering and bewilderment and despair—move with the substanceless decorum of lawn party charades* [. . .]" (AA 171).

5. William Faulkner, *Flags in the Dust* (New York: Random House, 1973), 53.

6. In fact, physical descriptions of female characters in *Absalom, Absalom!* often recreate psychological remoteness from reality: "the small slight child whose feet, even when she would be grown, would never quite reach the floor even from her own chairs" (AA 51); "Judith gone . . . into that transition stage . . . where she was even more inaccessible . . . — that state where, though still visible, young girls appear as though seen through glass and where even the voice cannot reach them" (AA 52).

7. "It is desirable that brothers & sisters in a family should live in peace & harmony & do kindnesses for each other, but if strife commences and all efforts at reconciliation fail, rather than that they should continue under one roof to be *always* wrangling and quarreling it is better that one party go off & set up for themselves. As with a family so with our Union." Henry Watson, Jr., letter fragment, January 27, 1861, in Henry Watson, Jr., Papers, Duke University Library, Manuscript Department, Durham, North Carolina.

8. ". . . before war was actually declared and Mississippi seceded, his acts and speeches of protest had been not only calm but rational and quite sensible." (AA 64).

9. George Fitzhugh, *Sociology of the South: Or the Failure of Free Society* (Richmond: Morris, 1854), 214.

10. "Silk dresses were displaced by cotton ones, the parlor was deserted for the kitchen, the piano for the sewing machine. The grind was upon us. We were too pressed in finances to hire anything done but laundry work and wood cutting." Belle Kearney, *A Slaveholder's Daughter* (New York: Negro University Press, 1966), 23.

11. "I never expected that my wife would come to have to come to the wash tub, but so it is." Samuel Agnew, *Samuel Andrew Agnew Diary*, January 1, 1866, Southern Historical Collection, University of North Carolina, Chapel Hill.

12. A young Louisiana girl wrote in her diary in 1862 that she had considered putting on her brother's suit: "I advanced so far as to lay it on the bed. . . . I was ashamed to let even my canary see me." Halfway through she abandoned the idea, explaining: "my courage had deserted me, and there ended my first and last attempt at disguise. I have heard so many girls boast of having worn men's clothes; I wonder where they get the courage." Sarah Morgan, *The Civil War Diary of Sarah Morgan*, ed. Charles East (Athens: U of P, Georgia 1991), 167.

13. As Mr. Compson tells Quentin, "the first of the odes to Southern soldiers in that portfolio which when your grandfather saw it in 1885 contained a thousand or more, was dated in the first year of her father's voluntary incarceration and dated at two o clock in the morning." (AA 65).

14. "So maybe you will enter the literary profession as so many Southern gentlemen and gentlewomen too are doing now and maybe some day you will remember this and write about it." (AA 5).

15. "No: anything but a fatalist, who was the Sutpen with the ruthless Sutpen code of taking what it wanted . . . of the two children Henry was the Coldfield with the Coldfield cluttering of morality and rules of right and wrong" (AA 95).

16. Alice Ready Diary, April 13, 1862, Southern Historical Collection, University of North Carolina, Chapel Hill.

17. Mary Chestnut, *Mary Chestnut's Civil War*, ed. C. Vann Woodward (New Haven: Yale University Press, 1981), 233.

Fraternal Fury:
Faulkner, World War I, and Myths of Masculinity

JOHN LOWE

Beware a brother,
For every brother plays the role of Jacob,
And every friend spreads scandal.
One deceives the other . . .
Fraud upon fraud, deceit upon deceit.

—Jeremiah 9:3–5

That was something that probably every soldier in war has
felt . . . that my brother is the man I am trying to kill.[1]
—WILLIAM FAULKNER

Last summer I was in Atlanta with a German graduate student and decided to take him to see the Cyclorama in Grant Park, the world's largest painting, and a circular one at that, which depicts the Battle of Atlanta. The gray-haired Daughters of the Confederacy who used to supervise the viewing have now been replaced by a sound and light show, one seen from a state-of-the-art revolving set of seats. But one thing hasn't changed: the robot voice movingly intones the story of two young men, who now get picked out by the automated spotlight. A Yankee finds a wounded Rebel on the field, gives him water, and discovers the man is his brother. I had always thrilled to this story, for the soldiers are my great-great-grandfather and his brother. Later, I told my mother about the changes at the Cyclorama and the way the story still gets told. She snorted contemptuously: "they're still getting it wrong!" I was surprised to learn that my ancestors were in fact both Rebels from Georgia, but that one had to go to Tennessee to enlist because he was too young in Georgia. The people at the Cyclorama had been told this, because my progenitor was at one time one of the oldest living Confederates, and was alive when the Cyclorama was installed, after its completion in *Milwaukee* by German artists. So why does the story still get told? Because, of course, it's a great myth we like to believe. One of the unstated meanings of the portrait is that the Union brother very easily could have fired the shot that killed his sibling. This family scene encapsulates the romance of reunion, but against the backdrop of fraternal struggle.

Faulkner's Fraternal Fury

I would like to interrogate this myth of fraternity, to suggest that it lies deep in the heart of our culture, and that it permeates the work of our greatest writer, William Faulkner, especially the magnificent stream of writing he produced from 1926 through 1936, from *Soldiers' Pay* to his masterwork, *Absalom, Absalom!* A review of Faulkner's troubled relations with two of his brothers has led me to believe that many of the narratives he created during these turbulent years had much to do with what I call his "fraternal fury." I will argue that this obsession led Faulkner into much more than biographical fiction, for in his quarrel with Jack and John Falkner he found a metaphor for war, regional animosities, finance capitalism, the split consciousness of literary modernism, and, finally, the tragic racial history of the region and nation.

In what follows I trace the arc of fraternal fury in the early World War I fiction, culminating in the first Yoknapatawpha novel, *Flags in the Dust* (1973; first published as *Sartoris* in 1929), which interbraids the World War I combatants, John and Bayard Sartoris, with the mythical story of their Civil War ancestors who bore the same names. However, the other book Faulkner published in 1929, *The Sound and the Fury*, also details a story about brothers; they have virtually no contact with each other during the course of the novel, and in the "Appendix" Faulkner added later, one of them, the retarded Benjy, is eventually castrated and then incarcerated in an insane asylum on the orders of his brother Jason. In Faulkner's next published novel, *As I Lay Dying*, the entire narrative centers on the desperate struggle between two brothers to control the disposition of their mother's body; although their journey to her burial site in Jefferson is ostensibly led by their father, in fact the sons must decide the issue. Eventually, the son who *has had military service in Europe in World War I*, Darl, is deemed mad, is physically attacked by one of his brothers and a sister, who scream "kill him!," and is, like Benjy, sent to the asylum in Jackson.

While Faulkner was writing yet another book about fraternal rivalry, *Absalom*, he did something new: instead of just having one brother die, he finally took the step of creating a character who kills his brother.[2] As this was set against a larger narrative of Civil War, always a conflict characterized as "brother against brother," but also against a complex narrative of racial love and hate, epitomized by the white and black brothers, Faulkner was perhaps seeking to force the issue that had haunted his personal life into a new dimension, finally to exorcize it by making it into the stuff of overwhelming fiction, a novel that would in many ways encapsulate the most troubling and enduring issues in American democracy.

It was therefore devastating when Faulkner's beloved brother Dean died in a fiery plane crash, in the very plane William had given him and taught him how to fly; the disaster occurred right in the middle of the writing of *Absalom!* I once asked a friend, a fellow Faulkner aficionado, which of his novels she thought the greatest. She said she didn't know if *Absalom* was the greatest, but it had impressed her the most, because she said, "it's the most anguished." And indeed it is a skein of narratives of fraternal rivalry moving toward a fictional actual act of fratricide, which was written before and after the most despairing moment in Faulkner's life, when he had to face that fact that he in some ways had been responsible for the death of the one brother he loved without reservation. In *Absalom*, Charles Bon and Henry Sutpen, like my Martin ancestors, are not on opposite sides of the Civil War either; in fact, they are best friends who roomed together in college, and only during the war does the long-hidden fact that they are indeed brothers come out. Despite their deep love for one another, a love that has a biblical resonance, Henry feels forced to murder Charles when the latter, who has been revealed to have African ancestry, persists in his plan to marry their sister.

Why was Faulkner so drawn to the story of brothers who love and yet hate each other? It is my contention that this is precisely the way he felt about his brothers Jack and John, that he saw this was a problem, and that he tried to work through it in his art. Eventually, Faulkner came to believe this conundrum was a metaphor for America itself; fraternity, in its larger sense, was an integral component in the construction of the default mode of the nation, white manhood. Fraternity was also a natural equivalent term for democracy and social organization, and for what Whitman called the "love of comrades." On other levels, it became the ground for cutthroat competition that led to outrages against women, minorities, and nature itself. On a still different level, Faulkner surely saw the story of children who come to be enemies as a metaphor for the strange realities of Southern culture, where the most intimate forms of communal life were permitted between black and white on many levels, but never formally sanctioned matrimony and legal transmission of family name and property. In several narratives, Faulkner tells the story of two boys, inseparable as children, who must sleep in separate beds once they approach manhood, beds on two distinct levels that signify social position and racial hierarchy. Faulkner used this story twice in Civil War narrative, in *Absalom* and *The Unvanquished*, whose sometimes comic story of white Bayard and black Ringo has strong parallels with Faulkner's other tales of cross-race "brothers."

The story in some ways was modeled on Thomas Nelson Page's classic *Two Little Confederates*, which tells the tale of Southern brothers during the Civil War. Faulkner would later expand this to biracial sets of brothers, as in the tale of Tomey's Turl in *Go Down, Moses*, which utilizes the biblical myth of Joseph to underscore the horror of two men enslaving their own brother. We now know that Faulkner was aware of black descendants of his great-grandfather Falkner,[3] so the issue cuts close to the bone. When lines of racial descent become hidden, one cannot only possibly murder one's brother without knowing it, but also rape one's sister (the subject of the Absalom, Amnon, and Tamar story in the Bible).

The Falkner Brothers and World War I

War became for Faulkner a central pole of masculine identity, partly through the legacy of his ancestor, the Old Colonel, but more significantly from the circumambient legend of the Lost Cause. Throughout the period of Reconstruction and continuing into our own time, the fascination with the Civil War has been largely a masculine preoccupation. It used to be, in fact, that a white Southern man was expected to talk knowledgeably about its battles and events, somewhat like today when any man not able to talk in a detailed way about SEC football is looked at askance in male circles.

Faulkner seems always to have viewed war as a magnification of fraternal struggle, which he knew firsthand in his family. How did this fraternal enmity begin? Identity of any sort begins with the mother. As Maud Falkner's firstborn, Faulkner always had a special relation to her. When he was a child, his position as eldest son and for a time, the largest child, presented him with privilege and power (figure 1). Faulkner's reign as the only child ended in 1899 when his brother Murry Charles Jr. ("Jack") was born. Two years later a second rival, John Wesley Thompson III ("Johncy"), joined the family. Ominously, Johncy was born on September 24, a day before William's fourth birthday. This meant that for the rest of their lives, his birthday would be celebrated the day before William's, even though William was born first. As the brothers aged, Jack and John came to exceed William in size and in athletic ability and success with women.

Eventually both Jack and John would publish memoirs that told their own versions of the Falkner family history and their relations with their famous brother. John, whose rivalry with William would keep fraternal thematics alive in Faulkner's work for some time, did not use the logical "four sons" picture for his frontispiece to *My Brother Bill*, but rather chose a picture featuring only the three oldest; Johncy, not Bill, is at the center, towering over the others, an effect enhanced by a large circular hat that rather has the effect of a halo.

Figure 1

Further, when the book was reissued as a paperback, the editors wanted an adult picture of the two brothers. However, there was only one photo of them together, which was snapped late in their lives during a minor quarrel, when William had come to John's house to demand he return a lawn mower and gas funnel he had borrowed (figure 2). Both

Figure 2

men stare at the camera stonily. When the picture appeared on the cover, it was cropped, so as to remove the funnel.

This small detail speaks volumes about the problem both Jack and John faced in writing their memoirs after William's death. They knew readers wanted to hear about William more than about themselves. Accordingly, they subtracted the volatile material from the narrative. As in any autobiography, there was a need to look positive, and in these, pressure to seem loving, loyal brothers. However, their texts do reveal the many tensions between the brothers, sometimes between the lines, often more overtly. In a longer study, I am providing ample evidence of the ways in which both brothers slip in numerous indications of the conflict under the surface. Faulkner never wrote an autobiography, although he thought of doing so at one time;[4] nevertheless, the many treatments in his fiction of fraternal relations, his constant reinscription of Falkner family history through various avatars, and his many comments in letters and interviews about this subject may be placed alongside the "testimonies" of his brothers to provide a kind of meditation on fraternal fury in a small Mississippi town in the first half of the twentieth century.

There was, of course, the fourth son, Dean; however, as the beloved baby brother, he was, as so often is the case with lastborns, a pampered favorite and no threat to the William's firstborn position of power in the family. Psychologists have demonstrated that in multiple-sibling families, the process of *deidentification,* whereby siblings define themselves as different from each other in a buffering tactic that sometimes reduces competition and comparison, occurs most often between first and second born dyads, and rarely between the first and last-born dyad.[5] Further, the three younger Falkner brothers, rather ordinary mortals in comparison to their gifted sibling, had identities of their own quite apart from William; increasingly, photos of the Faulkner children were of these three, without William, as he drifted apart from them as a teenager; eventually, Phil Stone, an older intellectual, and rather aristocratic Oxford resident, would function as a kind of older brother/teacher/mentor for Faulkner, in many ways displacing the blood brothers.

The masculine ancestors had their say too. Many critics have noted the profound influence on all the Falkner boys of their great-grandfather, "Old Colonel Falkner," but Kevin Railey has recently asserted that the flesh and blood figure of the young Colonel, Faulkner's grandfather, had far more of an effect on William. J. W. T. Falkner was raised by the Thompson family rather than by his father, the Old Colonel, and was prepared by them to lead an extremely successful life as an entrepreneur. He held political office and had much to do with the modernization of Oxford. As patriarch of the extended family, he, more than Murry, provided Faulkner with a model of male authority. It was his grandfather Falkner who told William tales about the first William's fabled Civil War exploits, which he also heard from veterans who frequented J. W. T. Falkner's home. From his grandfather Faulkner inherited a love of elegant clothing, courtly behavior toward women, and a fascination with the military; despite the fact that the Young Colonel had never served in a war, he was a Mason, loved his martial uniform, and was buried in it. We might note here that there was thus a family tradition of supporting a military tradition where there was none. The Falkner family memorabilia contains uniforms, braid, swords, and many military portraits. Faulkner relished these objects and no doubt would have liked more of them, especially the ones that had passed to brother John; they confirmed his fantasies. As Frederic Jameson has observed, "Unbeknownst to us, the objects around us lead lives of their own in our unconscious fantasies, where, vibrant with manna or taboo, with symbolic fascination or repulsion, they stand as the words or hieroglyphs of the immense rebus of desire."[6]

Faulkner's maternal great-grandfather, Dr. John Y. Murry, was quite religious, and insisted his family come to the table with a verse of scripture memorized. Also a respected member of the local community, he too provided his family with a model of what has been termed the "Christian gentleman." Susan Curtis stresses the conforming pressure of this model in nineteenth-century American society, through "social gospelers" and masculine clubs such as the Masons, the Red Men, and the Odd Fellows, a process of role identification that began early in Faulkner's life with his subscription to magazines such as *The Youth's Home Companion* and *The American Boy*.[7] William Faulkner came to dislike group organizations later in life, but in his youth they were vital to his masculine identity; like his grandfather and men all over America at this time, fraternal organizations were a mode of establishing cultural capital and a default mode for the model citizen as white male. The Young Colonel was a force in local business groups. Although we usually think of Faulkner as a loner who went his own idiosyncratic way, he too sought masculine company, and in fact was a popular little boy who usually thought up the best games. As a teenager, despite his diminutive size, he desperately fought to succeed in team sports, but it was his brothers who excelled on the playing field. Even when they were small boys, there were signals of the rivalry that would come later: one of the most interesting involves airplanes, which would function in the lives of all the Faulkner boys and in William's fiction in particular. Little Bill had talked Jack and John into building an airplane, which he "casually announced" that Jack would fly. Significantly, Bill had found the plans for the airplane in the pages of *American Boy*, a kind of early century scriptbook for early masculine development. When their grandiose plans for a biwing got scaled down to a one-wing, Jack became "apprehensive"; later in life, he wrote, "Bill had a ready reply, but somehow it seemed to lack conviction; after all, it was my neck that was to be laid on the chopping block of progress and invention."[8] Little brother Dean was brought in by Mammy Callie to watch. The launch over the edge of a deep ditch wasn't accomplished easily, and eventually Bill took Jack's place in the cockpit, getting only barely scratched as the plane slid down to the bottom of the ditch.[9] In this vignette, Faulkner acts out a fantasy against the intimate world of "boy culture," possibly involving a subsumed fratricidal urge which he subsequently inverted onto himself. The fact that he ponders two "scripts" here, first thinking of sending the brother over the cliff to possible flight or death, and then, taking his place, is proleptive of the way Faulkner would split these two aspects of himself and his brother in his fiction; in *Soldiers' Pay*, for instance, Cadet Lowe is obviously a parody of Faulkner's own noncombatant stance; Donald Mahon, however, represents not only Jack Faulkner, the real wounded hero, but also the doomed and romantic figure Faulkner yearned to be. This would be a constant pattern in his fiction, leading up to *Absalom*, in 1936.

As a young man, rejected by his sweetheart Estelle, and with no prospects in Oxford, William left for Connecticut to join Stone, who was now a law student at Yale. Brother Jack once had the temerity to date Estelle, although nothing came of it; she soon married Cornell Franklin. Faulkner was working in a Northern weaponry plant when they wed, but Johncy served as the driver who brought Estelle to her wedding and then to the station where she and Cornell left for a honeymoon. Both of William's brothers played a part in Estelle's "betrayal," and, in fact, Jack recounts how even though he was away working in Memphis in 1929, he made a point to tell Bill not to marry Estelle, that he couldn't afford it.[10]

The outbreak of World War I created a new aspect to William's rivalry with Jack. Thirsting for the validation of combat experience, but rejected by U.S. recruiters, Faulkner joined the R.A.F. in Canada and trained to become a pilot. It seems certain, however, despite his claims to have crashed into a hanger upside down, that he never actually flew a plane, for the war ended before he could earn his wings. Undaunted, Faulkner procured an officer's uniform decked with these wings, which he used in his homecoming pose as a decorated war hero (figure 3). Blotner, telling of Faulkner's sashaying around the Oxford Square in this unauthorized uniform, replete with gloves and a cane, spinning spurious tales of combat and a wound in Europe, asks, "How could he wear the wings he had not earned, the pips that had not been awarded, the uniform of a rank he had not attained?"[11] More seriously, he did this when the family feared brother Jack was dead. In May 1918, Jack Falkner began Marine training at Parris Island. By August he was in France and was soon sent to the front. In September he was gassed, but kept fighting, and on November 1, in a trench near Argonne Wood, he was severely wounded; the family didn't hear from him for weeks. When William returned to Oxford in December, Jack was still incommunicado. It was only the week before Christmas that the family received a letter Jack wrote from a French hospital telling of his wounds and assuring them he was alive. When the veteran returned to a hero's welcome in Oxford, his brother William must have writhed inwardly with shame, but simultaneously burned with jealousy. We should remember, however, that Faulkner's initial lies upon his return to Oxford (and well before news of Jack's injuries) were in part necessary because of the many false flying stories his letters to his mother from Toronto contained. These tales are still disturbing, and only seem to be amusing today because of his subsequent career and the distance of time.[12] Why did Faulkner repeat these tales throughout his life? Perhaps he considered his fictions a form of life story. Timothy Dow Adams flatly asserts, "All autobiographers are unreliable narrators, all humans are liars, and yet . . . to be a successful liar in one's own life story is especially difficult." For Adams, what writers decide to misrepresent is as revealing as what really happened. He usefully reminds us that the mere facts of our

Figure 3

life often seem to us to "distort" who we think we are, and points to the difficulty of consistent misrepresentation.[13]

Now let me relate this to the continued telling of the false story about my own relatives in the Cyclorama. A myth is a story that people believe is true, but it can also be a story that they wish to believe is true. Faulkner wanted to believe his story, and in some ways he did, for his fictionalizing of the experience no doubt meant almost as much to him as if he had really lived it. His various love affairs at this time kept the stories bubbling. When he was wooing Helen Baird, she reports, he charmed her with "fairy stories," but he told her and several other women about his "wound," which sometimes included a metal plate in his head.[14] We remember that Othello won Desdemona with his moving stories of combat. Faulkner, a failure in just about everything before the war, desperately needed some stable catchhold as he struggled to reenter the society he had failed to satisfy already. The fiction he created was used to win over women, fellow writers like Sherwood Anderson, male communities, and most importantly, perhaps, his family, and especially his mother, whose attention was also sought by his brothers. It was unfortunate that he had no other "niche" available to him, since this military pose overlapped with Jack's, but it was all he had at the moment. Fortunately, his gift for personal "fiction" intertwined with the enduring niche he carved out for himself as an artist, something he had explored through painting and poetry earlier.

Earlier, however, the rivalry with Jack continued on another front after the war; both Jack and Bill entered the University of Mississippi in 1919, Jack to study law. Both joined SAE. Faulkner tried to reintegrate himself into the community and the university through fraternal organizations. He had been a boy scout, so he signed up as a scout master, and was severely humiliated when he was dismissed from that post for drinking. At Ole Miss, in addition to his initiation in SAE, William also joined the American Legion Club; however, he often found ways of being unusual in groups; in one club photo, he is looking away from the camera belligerently, and smoking a cigarette. In light of Faulkner's reputation as an artsy weirdo on campus, one wonders how he got into SAE; however, since all the Falkners had been members, the SAEs no doubt felt they had to accept a legacy. Faulkner eventually irritated many men on campus, through his affected dress, frequent stony silences, and especially through his newspaper pieces, many of them translations or poems, that other Ole Miss boys found pretentious. Nonetheless, Faulkner somehow managed to overcome the suspicions of many other male groups, perhaps because he could easily code-switch between masculine forms of dress, activity, and vocabulary, but also because his false military record made him secure in his identity as a "real man." He regularly went hunting with rather ordinary folk, but also liked to go to the refined Stone family's camp in the Delta.[15]

Jack got his degree, but Bill dropped out, and they seem to have spent little time together at the university. Jack had little interest in the poetry his brother was writing then: "I had no ideas about the nature of his writing and, since he apparently felt no inclination to talk to me about it, I had even less to inquire about it.... Even in later years... we never sat down and talked about his work."[16] In 1924, however, Jack moved to Washington, eventually became an FBI agent, and still later worked for the Veterans Administration. He never returned to live in Oxford, never had children, and thus was no longer a rival. John, the younger brother, became a competitor in several realms, but most menacingly, as a fellow writer.

Faulkner eventually left Oxford to travel in Europe and to hang out in New Orleans with fellow Bohemians; there he began to spin his fantasies out in short stories, sketches, and magazine and journalism work. Sherwood Anderson helped him to get *Soldiers' Pay* published, and his commitment to writing deepened.

Estelle, with her two children in tow, returned from China where she had been living, divorced, and, in 1929, married Faulkner, who by this time felt mainly a sense of duty toward Estelle rather than love. However, he had generated fiction out of his romantic "wound," as he suggested in his second novel, *Mosquitoes* (1927). "'Lucky he who believes that his heart is broken: he can immediately write a book and so take revenge (what is more terrible than the knowledge that the man you just knocked down discovered a coin in the gutter while getting up?) on him or her who damaged his or her ventricles. Besides cleaning up in the movies and magazines. No, no,' he repeated, 'you don't commit suicide when you are disappointed in love. You write a book.'"[17] We might add as a corollary to this: if your brother comes home a wounded war hero and makes a mockery out of your pretended combat experience, don't get sad: write a book and kill him off. This is exactly what Faulkner did, not only in *Soldiers' Pay*, but in several stories and subsequent novels as well.

Many of these literary/personal fantasies were caught up with aerial exploits. Faulkner was excited by the airplane, for he immediately saw it as an extension of his family's long-standing pride as expert horsemen, and a way to overcome his small stature. After all, once on a horse or at the controls of an airplane, physical diminutiveness ceases to be a problem. Faulkner and his brothers had ponies at an early age; ultimately, a fall from a horse precipitated Faulkner's death. He saw to it that daughter Jill was trained as a horsewoman, and Jimmy Faulkner recently described his daughter Meg DuChaine's success as a horse trainer as part of the family's heritage: "We all like horses. I guess it's the sense of animal power, just as the airplane gives you a sense of mechanical power. The faster you can go, the better."[18] Later in life, Faulkner, never a particularly good pilot, lost interest in flying; as he told a Japanese audience, "it has become so mechanical that the pleasure I had once is gone. One has to be a mechanical or technical expert to fly any more. The days when anyone with an airplane and a tank of fuel could fly where he wanted is past."[19]

Faulkner told his stories of aerial combat so often that he perhaps came to believe them himself. In the year before his death, he told his doctor that the pain in his back originated in a World War I injury. Faulkner had a way, however, of making some of his lies into truths. Eventually, he surreptitiously took flying lessons, bought his own plane and dashing sartorial accouterments. In light of Faulkner's expected role as leader in the family, it should have been no surprise to him that all three of his brothers took to flying. It must have been galling to him, however, that the adulation of his young nephews had to be shared with their father John, who once again became his competitor in a new arena by proving to be a better pilot, and by setting up a flying service, factors that may explain William's *real* loss of interest in flying. "The Flying Faulkners" staged an air show in 1935. Faulkner had written a novel about stuntpilots, *Pylon*, published in March of 1935, which concludes with a fatal crash.

There was a third level to this world of planes and horses, eventually, in the elegant milieu of the fox hunt; Faulkner loved to pose in his pink coat, and delighted in taking group portraits in front of his columned mansion, mingling the hierarchical trappings of Old South and merry Old England, with him installed as the patriarch. Significantly, his brothers are not among the group. When he died he was eagerly anticipating moving into a classic English style mansion in Charlottesville, where he could ride to the hounds with true FFVs (First Families of Virginia).

John too sought the Southern mode of this pose, as a picture of his extended "plantation mode" family, replete with servants who were no doubt considered "one of the family," demonstrates. Houses, furniture, heirlooms are shifting signifiers of patriarchal identity and power as well. After the war and his initial successes as a writer, William sought to go beyond contemporary standards of masculinity and to replicate the refined, aristocratic, and chivalric world of his ancestors. Certainly his purchase of the run-down Rowan Oak was an attempt to assert the revival of the ancient patrimony, with him in its castle. Uncle John Faulkner inherited many of the cherished family antiques such as the Old Colonel's dining table and other artifacts, many of them military in origin; they subsequently, however, passed into the hands of Jimmy Faulkner, Johncy's son, who had already inherited Falkner heirlooms from his father; all these objects are now in Jimmy's antebellum home, which closely resembles Rowan Oak, and in fact both houses were designed by the same architect. Jimmy's home is somewhat of a shrine to the memory of both his father and his uncle, replete with a sideboard set out like the one in *The Sound and the Fury* and a line of family portraits going up the stairs.

This is fitting; Faulkner's relation with his two nephews, Johncy's boys Jimmy and Chooky, was warm, and in some ways they came to be the sons he so badly wanted. Revealingly, he insisted in his own family compound that Jill and others call him "Pappy," the appellation that had been used for the ancestors, but not for his father Murry. But he got his nephews to call him "Brother Will," which suggests another angle of approach, a recreation of a fraternal relation that this time was untroubled by competition. When Miss Maud died, William went to select a coffin with Jimmy and Chooky, not with his brothers.

Thus by having these sons, John ultimately won the family feud, for it is through him the family name has lived on; William clearly saw these nephews as surrogate sons, or alternately, as invented brothers.

"Brother Will": Born to Rebel?

At this point we need to ask about the underlying forces in the relations between the brothers. This discussion represents a sampling from a book-length study I am developing, *Faulkner's Fraternal Fury*, which attempts a new angle of approach to some familiar texts, utilizing some recent work on the construction of gender, a reassessment of the meaning of Faulkner's biblical typology, developments in narrative theory, and most significantly, family systems theory, and studies of birth order, especially Frank J. Sulloway's *Born to Rebel: Birth Order, Family Dynamics, and Creative Lives*.[20] Sulloway's work in turn should connect (as he often does not) with the new discourse on masculinity, which has taught us that manliness is a human invention, one that has been shaped and reshaped by different cultures in different ways.

Faulkner told Malcolm Cowley "I am telling the same story over and over, which is myself and the world."[21] His brother John said "I have never know anyone who identified himself with his writings more than Bill did. . . . Sometimes it was hard to tell which was which."[22] Faulkner admitted too that Quentin Compson was a self-portrait.[23] He had little to say, however, about the other Compson brothers' models. Still, his major works from *Flags in the Dust* through *Absalom* would seem to validate Sulloway, who asserts that "siblings raised together are almost as different in their personalities as people from different families."[24] They are also locked, in most cases, in a battle for family resources, key among them, of course, parental affection.

In nature in general, as Darwin demonstrated, recurring conflicts stimulate adaptations that increase the odds of survival. Particularly in his study of the birds of the Galapagos, Darwin found evidence of how species would over time differentiate, as they responded to varying access to specific foods and territories, such as the different heights of rocky seaside promontories. Bills, talons, flight methods, all represent adaptations, successful achievement of "niches." Humans also develop different qualities in order to compete for scarce commodities, and this is exactly the pattern the Falkner brothers followed.

One of the reasons we have not had a study of Faulkner and fraternity until now is that Faulkner scholarship, like virtually all American literary criticism of identity formation, still relies on Freud, whose obsession with the Oedipal syndrome hardly needs detailing here. It has been forgotten that one of Freud's associates, Alfred Adler, studied birth order, a subject Freud ignored. Adler theorized that if firstborns are unable to regain parental favor, they sometimes rebel. The secondborn, Adler felt, "behaves as if he were in a race, is under full steam all the time, and trains continually to surpass his older brother and conquer him."[25] Youngest children never occupy the "throne" of the eldest, and are thus not subject to dethronement and, especially if they are the baby of the family, are prone to become pampered and lazy. Often, however, they are the most likely to rebel against familiar patterns, and also to be creative. Faulkner fits the pattern of one of the exceptions to these patterns. When the firstborn for some reason is bypassed in the family pecking order, he or she often becomes a functional laterborn, and rebels, seeking a new way to gain resources. This does not mean, however, that second or later-borns are more aggressive than the first-borns; on the contrary, Carlfred B. Broderick asserts that "at every age, first-born siblings exhibit more aggressive feelings and behaviors than their younger competitors" partly because they understand that their "throne" position is constantly under attack.[26] Thus Faulkner's rage, so to speak, burned at both ends of the birth-order spectrum and was therefore unusually intense.

Again, Faulkner's critics have occasionally been drawn to the fraternal nexus I have been describing, but usually wind up viewing such struggle as a variation of the Oedipal, with the brother standing in for the real enemy, the father. Richard Gray's impressive biography of Faulkner takes this tack. Certainly recent and convincing psychoanalytical studies of Faulkner's works by Doreen Fowler and Noel Polk have been worthwhile;[27] I am not here to discount Freudians; Faulkner was profoundly Freudian in much of his writing. I am arguing, however, that the Freudian tends to push out other approaches; if we are always looking at the relation between the child and the parents, then we tend to ignore, as Freud himself did, the relation between siblings; by the way, Freud, not surprisingly, was a firstborn.

Anthropology, gender studies, and the new masculinity studies are astonishingly silent on sibling relations; even Levi-Strauss's seminal *The Elementary Structures of Kinship* skirts the subject, all proof of the way the Oedipal trumps other possibilities, even in an age when Freud's theories have supposedly been discounted.[28] Under the guise of recuperation through Lacan, Freud is still providing us with the dominant way of reading the family.

In nature, firstborns are more assertive, "socially dominant, ambitious, jealous of their status, and defensive."[29] The family environment determines how these competitive tendencies are expressed. In terms of personality, firstborns who get displaced can become, functionally, like laterborns, and the reverse is also true. As siblings interact, and as parents seem to favor one over another, secret hurts develop that may last for decades. These wounds can lead to loss of respect for parental authority, which then sets the stage for rebellion, and the creation of sibling strategies. Sulloway explains: "As children become older and their unique interests and talents begin to emerge, siblings become increasingly diversified in their niches. One sibling may become recognized for athletic prowess, whereas another may manifest artistic talents. Yet another sibling may be good at mediating arguments and become the family diplomat. Because siblings ... occupy different niches, they experience the family in diverse ways."[30]

Early childhood sets the paradigm; the firstborns are bigger, stronger, often smarter, and they dominate siblings. Laterborns have to work around size and power difference, so they use acquiescence, cooperation, pleading, and whining to appeal to parents for protection; later they become altruistic and peer-oriented. Firstborns are more conscientious; they become used to being the model and to taking care of siblings. Firstborns are more emotionally intense than laterborns, who are more risk accepting: "laterborns are more likely to engage in dangerous physical activities, such as contact sports," while firstborns "specialize in strategies designed to subordinate rivals. By pursuing disparate interests and abilities, siblings minimize direct competition."[31] Thus laterborns are more open to experience, because it helps them find new and thus empty "niches" within the family.

According to psychoanalytic theory, siblings are unconsciously preoccupied with the wish to kill other family members. When the intended victim is not a parent, it is a surrogate sibling. This diversification of talents is good for society: "When older siblings already excelled at hunting, it was time to develop an aptitude for fishing."[32] A constant across classes: firstborns choose the most direct path, while laterborns' more unconventional paths make them more inclined to dangerous sports and physical risks. (Baby brother Dean was a far better athlete than William, even though both were small.) Also, younger sons travel further away from home. Firstborns time and again pass up opportunities to travel, but secondborns are especially likely to do so; this proved true of secondborn Jack.

The separation of the Falkner brothers after puberty and, more dramatically, after the war, offers an illustration of how these disparate interests worked, but also an example, in the case of William and John, how similar interests caused clashes. Nor were presumably finished conflicts always over; as a kind of coda to Faulkner's tales of World War I; his military rivalry with his brothers continued during World War II, when Jack served as a major in intelligence in North Africa, John joined the Navy, and his son Jimmy was a Marine pilot. Jack was involved in the invasion of Elba; Jimmy was shot down but survived and won service medals. John was involved in a jeep wreck, and thus received a medical discharge. In a disgraceful letter to Jimmy, Faulkner enclosed a pip from his lieutenant's RAF uniform, advising his nephew to weld it onto his dog tags for good luck. "I would have liked for you to have had my dog-tag, R.A.F., but I lost it in Europe, in Germany." This is followed by sage advice about how to act in combat.[33] Although Faulkner melded his feelings for his brothers into his fiction throughout his career, Jack and Johncy only appear a total of nine times in Faulkner's voluminous correspondence, and none of his letters are directed to them.

By contrast, the doomed Dean continued to be present in Faulkner's life and literary imagination through the presence of Dean's daughter, also named Dean (eerily echoing the Quentin/Miss Quentin pattern Faulkner had used in *The Sound and the Fury*); Faulkner helped Dean's widow raise the young girl. Although brother Dean never served in the military, Faulkner always associated him with martial valor; stricken to the core by Dean's accidental death, he sat up all night with the undertaker trying to help reconstruct the shattered body so that their mother could bear to see it. The funeral was on November 11, Armistice Day, which paid tribute to "All the Dead Pilots," as Faulkner had called them in a story. Against Miss Maud's wishes, Faulkner used the same tombstone inscription for Dean's grave that he had created years earlier for John Sartoris, who also fell like Icarus from the sky: "I bare him on eagles wings and brought him unto me."

Soldiers' Pay

These theories find their first fictional illustration in Faulkner's work in *Soldiers' Pay*, where he transformed searing personal pain into a first novel. The wounded veteran Donald Mahon, horribly scarred, a stand-in for Faulkner's brother Jack, returns to his native Georgia virtually a vegetable, blind and unable to communicate. Private Julian Lowe, who accompanies Mahon on the train, seethes with envy, much as Faulkner must have over Jack. By novel's end, Faulkner the artist "kills" Mahon, while Lowe, long-vanished from the narrative, seems to have found success out in California.

In the novel's rather silly opening scenes on the train, the rough-acting conductor nevertheless wants the drunken veterans he's chastising to know he appreciates soldiers: "Listen, soldiers, I got a son in France. Sixth Marines he is. His mother ain't heard from him since October. I'll do anything for you boys, see, but for God's sake act decent" (11).[34] Although the amateurish comedy of the first few pages focuses on the drunken clowning of the returning soldiers, it is punctuated by Gilligan's quotation, "Hark! The sound of battle and the laughing horses draws near. But shall they dull this poor unworthy head?" This passage from the profound last section of the Book of Job (chapter 39) hints at the despair Faulkner felt personally at this juncture, an emotion that lies just beneath the surface of the banter, especially Lowe's. When Jack returned from France, it must have been galling to Faulkner to see the welcome his father gave him, and to watch his efforts to get Jack an immediate discharge from the Marines, and then to secure him a job at the university, where Jack had been accepted for the fall term. As an added bit of revenge, Faulkner named the femme fatale who dumps Mahon in horrified reaction to his wounds, Cecily, after the woman who became Jack's first wife.

The book gets its true momentum only when Margaret Powers and Joe Gilligan arrive with Donald in the latter's home town. The outsider status of Gilligan (a returning soldier, but a non-Southerner) and Powers (the "new," Northern woman) make them ideal "eyes" for the reader as the inner workings of the sleepy hamlet unfold. Above all, however, their sympathy for Donald stands in marked contrast to the stunning indifference, even horror, of the townsfolk, who are represented most forcefully, if oddly, in the person of Cecily, Donald's epicene fiancée. Her revulsion at his scar seems to overrule even the sense of his impending death. Even the rector Mahon, Donald's father, seems disturbed that his romantic mourning over his presumed dead son has to be interrupted. Better, all of them seem to feel, that he had stayed dead rather than returning in this state to die again.

The homecoming anticipated for Donald depends on his returning "whole," as Cecily says before she knows of his condition, "to be engaged to a man who will be famous when he gets here" (61). This was no doubt precisely the way Faulkner felt about the imminent return to Oxford of his wounded brother just before Christmas.

It takes little imagination to see that Julian Lowe, a minor character who nevertheless opens *Soldiers' Pay*, is a mirror image, in his disappointment over not seeing duty overseas, of William Faulkner. Known sarcastically as "one wing," "He suffered the same jaundice that many a more booted one than he did . . . they had stopped the war on him" (7). This line casts further light on the fact that when Faulkner appeared in Oxford after the war wearing unearned military accouterments, they included a *pair* of aviators' wings.

These thematics echo those in Hemingway's 1925 story "Soldier's Home," in which the veteran Krebs finds his own hometown more alien that wartime Europe. Krebs, who, like John Falkner, had been a marine and fought in some of the fiercest battles, does not want to talk about the war; eventually he does, but no one wants to hear about it. "Krebs found that to be listened to at all he had to lie"; he acquires "the nausea in regard to experience that is the result of untruth or exaggeration, and when he occasionally met another man who had really been a soldier and they talked a few minutes . . . he fell into the easy pose of the old soldier among other soldiers: that he had been badly, sickeningly frightened all the time. In this way he lost everything" (69).

Similarly, Gilligan tells Lowe on the train, "Us soldiers got to stick together in a foreign country like this" (9). This seems especially urgent later when Mrs. Saunders, no doubt speaking for the town, predicts that Donald won't want to work, and will make a bad husband: as she tells her husband, "You know yourself how these ex-soldiers are" (70).

Donald Mahon's return takes place in early April. This date allows Faulkner to interbraid two of his literary passions; first, the brutal sweetness of T. S. Eliot's "April is the cruellest month/Breeding lilies out of the dead land," and the drowning, overdone nature poetry of Swinburne and the fin-de-siècle decadents, with Faulkner using overripe phrases such as "a delirium of swallows." Yet Faulkner seems to want to have his cake and eat it too. Januarius Jones, a sarcastic, narcissistic, goatlike pedant, and not a veteran, stands in for the "sophisticated" reader that Faulkner was, quoting any number of au courant decadent and modernist writers, but also commenting ironically and bitingly on the romantic traceries, precisely the ones that Faulkner is on the other side of the ledger embroidering. As Jones asks Emmy, "how is the dying hero today?" (94).

A key passage relating to Jack Falkner's return occurs when Margaret Powers mocks "their funny little paper" (104), which, like the *Oxford Eagle*, has a story along the lines of "War Hero Returns." The tone of her remark suggests Faulkner's own attempt to belittle the newspaper tribute to his brother.

Michel Gresset has pointed to the book's chief defect; it is Faulkner's only novel that really aims at a kind of verisimilitude.[35] Its many assets, however, include a telling portrait of the new woman, Cecily (named after Jack's wife, but obviously modeled on Estelle); a presentation of the myriad changes initiated by the war and consumer society; and a telling analysis of the quick evaporation of interest Americans had in returning soldiers.

Flags in the Dust

Flags in the Dust is another matter; it is a much more successful book, and a bolder presentation of fraternal rivalry. It is not too much to say that Faulkner's Yoknapatawpha fable really begins with a version of the Icarus myth: two men, flying near the sun, though in fighter planes, involved in a World War I dogfight with a German pilot. Johnny Sartoris is hit; his stricken counterpart, not a Daedelus/father but in fact a twin/Icarus brother, Bayard Sartoris, watches horrified as John falls from the smoking sky. These fated avatars of a glorious heritage, which their heroics over France are meant to mimic and transcend, are the first in a long line of brothers in Faulkner's fiction. In their planes, they replicate their Civil War ancestors and namesakes, the brothers Bayard and John Sartoris on horseback. The modern pair exemplify in part their creator's lifelong fascination with biblical motifs, whereby one brother sees his birthright threatened by the other, but also with seeing in the events of his own life biblical typology, sacral significance, and the basic raw material of fiction.

Bayard Sartoris and his twin John represent many things; on the one hand, their failures and tragedy speak for the writer, and for the larger modernist disillusionment with supposed "progress" and the trumpeted value of the "war to end all wars," the "war for democracy." In Bayard's alienation and despair we see a martial, far more masculine version of the aimless Prufrock; Faulkner had of course modeled his earlier character, Mr. Talliaferro of *Mosquitoes*, more closely on Eliot's figure, replete with dandyish dress and effete mannerisms. Yet Bayard has his brutal, repellant side too, and we see it both directly and indirectly through contrast with his dead twin. To comprehend this fully, we need to return to the original Bayard and John, Aunt Jenny's brothers who grew up with her in the plantation country of Virginia, in a family equipped with all the mythological trappings of such a heritage. The original Bayard, we learn from Jenny, set a pattern of foolish and flamboyant daring that animates the entire male declension of the family. Faulkner created a biblically repetitive pattern of ritual death with the first Bayard, who dies in Virginia in a foolish raid on a Yankee camp in search of anchovies. Aunt Jenny lovingly tells the tale, once again, to an astonished visitor from Scotland. The story has the effect of underlining the modernist, existentialist alienation of young Bayard. The original Bayard was, in romantic parlance, a "wild man," a type that frequently goes to an early but heroic death. As such, he is a rebuke to the comparative timidity of any sane, rational man.

However, Miss Jenny is quite hypocritical in her stance toward the Sartorises. Her supposed critique of their foolhardiness is reversed in her teasing yet taunting of young Bayard: "Do you think nobody else ever went to a war? Do you reckon that when my Bayard came back from The War, he made a nuisance of himself . . . he was a gentleman: he raised the devil like a gentleman, not like you Mississippi country people. Clodhoppers. Look what he did with just a horse. . . . At least he got himself decently killed. . . . He did more with a horse than you could do with that aeroplane" (259).

When Dean Faulkner's plane crashed, William, as patriarch of the family, inscribed the death date in the pages of the family Bible, which he inherited when Murry died the preceding year. In *Flags in the Dust*, in a scene whose importance is signified by the fact that it originally began the novel,[36] Old Bayard climbs the stairs to a storeroom to open a cedar chest untouched since 1901. We learn that he only goes here to record deaths in the family Bible, which he did when young Bayard's father, John, died of yellow fever and an old Spanish bullet wound. Old Bayard could have made entries earlier *this* year when young Bayard's wife and son died, and then again when Bayard's twin died; however, believing in the "curse," Old Bayard had waited, expecting his other grandson to join John in death, "expecting to kill two birds with one stone, as it were. Thus each opening was in a way ceremonial, commemorating the violent finis to some phase of his family's history . . . it seemed . . . that a legion of ghosts breathed quietly at his shoulder" (93–94).[37] Old Bayard fingers some old brocade, then a Toledo rapier: "its stained fine blade and shabby elegant sheath the symbol of his race . . . the instrument had become a little tarnished in its very aptitude for shaping circumstance to its arrogant ends" (95). Other martial items include twin dueling pistols in a rosewood box, possessing the "lean, deceptive delicacy of race horses," accompanied by what Old Man Falls calls "that 'ere dang der'nger," lying "between the other two weapons . . . like a cold and deadly insect between two flowers" (95). Old Bayard muses that "the man who professes to care nothing about his forbears is only a little less vain than he who bases all his actions on blood precedent. And a Sartoris is entitled to a little vanity and poppycock, if he wants it," a memory that flushes another, Old Bayard's flight as a young boy from a Yankee patrol, during which he comes upon a skull looking up at him from the stream from which he drinks. Here too, he confronts skulls, as he adds the names of the dead: young Bayard's wife and child, and John Sartoris, "July 5, 1918." Faulkner aficionados have previously remarked on the coincidence that Faulkner died on the Old Colonel's birthday, July 6th; here Faulkner has John die one day short of that magic date, surely no accident.

As eldest male Sartoris, Old Bayard has the solemn responsibility of entering births, deaths, and marriages in the Bible, the mythic paradigm for Southern life that itself is rife with genealogical declensions. Record keeping of this nature is a sacred duty, one that brings home the repetitive nature of time and human life, and the ways in which every family inevitably creates a narrative. As historian, scribe, creator, and destroyer of fictional generations, Faulkner multiplied this priestly role exponentially. Here it is crucial to note that toward the end of his life, Faulkner cared very much about who inherited this function. Shortly before he died, Faulkner gave Jimmy, as the oldest Faulkner male *in the next generation*, the family Bible.[38] Accordingly, it would be Jimmy, not John, who would enter the information about William's death. One wonders what Jill Faulkner Summers thought about this patriarchal act of primogeniture.

Old Bayard's scene in the attic has a pendant; after one of his car wrecks, Bayard goes into the room he shared with John and opens a chest that contains the withered paw of John's first bear and the shell that killed it; John's New Testament inscribed by their mother on their seventh birthday, March 16, 1909, a day away from the fate-ridden Ides of March (fittingly, the Rubicon is mentioned on the next page), which establishes the Twins as Pisces, one of the several signs of the Zodiac involving paired figures. Bayard picks up the bloodstained hunting coat: "'Johnny,' he whispered. Suddenly he raised the garment toward his face but halted . . . he looked swiftly over his shoulder [then] lifted the garment and laid his face against it, defiantly and deliberately and knelt so for a time" (240). Bayard then gathers the book, the trophy, and the coat, along with a picture of John's Princeton eating club, and ritually burns all of it in Elnora's washing pot fire. Unlike the scene in the attic, this appears to be a ritual exorcism, one rendered blasphemous by his burning of the Bible.

This complex scene richly suggests both profound love and burning jealousy. However, the case that Bayard would resent John is somewhat difficult to make since Faulkner provides quite variant views of John in different texts. In *Flags*, John is clearly favored over Bayard by almost everyone in Jefferson because of his sunnier personality, his generosity, and his verbal abilities, all of which Bayard, a melancholy and somewhat solitary figure, lacks. Faulkner also states that John attended Princeton without indicating that Bayard did, thus providing a kind of intellectual disparity between the twins. This detail is somewhat puzzling in that in the short story "All the Dead Pilots," John Sartoris is pictured as a boor, whose letters home are said to be like those "a third-form lad in Harrow could have written, perhaps bettered."[39] Narcissa's memories of John provide further evidence of his elevation over Bayard, and her marriage to the latter almost seems a case of seizing the second best as what's left.

John seems to have been a favorite with the backwoods MacCallums too, who ask after him when Bayard visits.

However, in general, the novel's portrait of John does indeed suggest covert resentment on Bayard's part, as does the ritual exorcism we have examined. Still, we might feel that Faulkner has not really developed this enough to justify the anguished admission from Bayard late in the novel: "Then again something bitter and deep and sleepless in him blazed out in vindication and justification and accusation; what, he knew not, blazing out at what. Whom, he did not know: You did it! You caused it all: you killed Johnny" (359). This quite confused and confusing statement nevertheless suggests the love-hate he feels for his dead twin. In an intriguing essay, Dexter Westrum claims that Bayard is, in fact, part of a balancing equation that twins always form, and that with his beloved brother John dead, Bayard can only look on life as impossible, as he is now incomplete. Westrum bolsters this argument by examining those other notorious twins in Faulkner's canon, Uncle Buck and Uncle Buddy, of *Go Down, Moses*.[40] However, I would take exception to two points of Westrum's argument; first, his idea that one either loves or hates, but not both, is surely wrong; second, the differences between Uncle Buck and Uncle Buddy, both elderly and seemingly confirmed bachelors, are quite distinct from those that separate Bayard and John Sartoris. Finally, Westrum's reliance on sociological and psychological studies of twins assumes that this is the norm Faulkner acknowledges and seeks to reflect. I would add that *Flags*, coming as close as it does to Faulkner's desperate attempt to prove his manhood through war, necessarily takes a quite different view of the fraternal relation between these twins than the much later *Go Down, Moses*, which, I would argue, was composed after Faulkner had had a shattering but ultimately therapeutic resolution to his fraternal anxieties through the death of Dean.

John S. Williams has provided a quite persuasive reading of the Sartoris twins' complex relationship. He too cites John's beloved status in Jefferson, and also views the two scenes I have just examined as complementary. He even posits a homosexual, incestuous attraction for John on Bayard's part (which I find somewhat extreme).[41] Yet he never locates the source of Faulkner's obsession, and that is perhaps the reason why Bayard's declaration of fraticidal guilt, to use Mr. Compson's words in another context, just does "not explain," in his own troubled family history.

The construct of fraternity led Faulkner to many corollary considerations. To his credit, he provides us with yet another story of homecoming in *Flags*, that of Caspey, Elnora's brother, the first example of a militant African American in Faulkner's work. Caspey alarms his family, just as Bayard has alarmed the Sartorises, for similar yet ultimately very different reasons. Both men represent the "polluted" element of the returning warrior, whose hands, figuratively or literally, have been immersed in blood, whose focus has been murder. The reintegration of unleashed barbarism is properly the concern of every postwar society. Bayard's guilt over Johnny's death blocks any possibility of curbing his furious, pointless motion which eventuates in his death. Caspey's family rightly fears, conversely, that his pointed views and motives will endanger not only him, but the entire family. As he proudly asserts that American blacks have "saved France and America bofe" he proclaims "I dont take nothin' f'um no white folks no mo'. . . . War done changed all dat. If us colored folks is good enough to save France f'um de Germans, den us is good enough to have de same rights de Germans has. French folks thinks so anyhow, and if America don't, dey's ways of learnin' um" (53). Significantly, Old Bayard physically forces Caspey into his prewar submission. However, it is important to note that in another Sartoris story, Caspey's sister Elnora is revealed to be John Sartoris's child borne by her mother, Old Simon's wife, Euphony.[42] Thus this errant "brother" is in *fact* like "one of the family." Here we remember too that Euphony's supposed child by Simon is Ringo; it appears likely that Faulkner at least toyed with the notion of making Ringo Old Bayard's blood brother in *The Unvanquished*, which would have constituted a parallel and contrast to the relation he was writing at the same time between Bon and Henry. Perhaps he drew back because of this; but the comparison would have been interesting as Bayard admits that Ringo is smarter than he is. In any case, Faulkner returned to this black-white configuration powerfully in *Go Down, Moses*, where Tomey's Turl is blood brother to Uncle Buck and Uncle Buddy.

The World War I Short Stories

I have remarked on the rather striking lack of geopolitical observation on Faulkner's part in these two early treatments of World War I. It is only in the short stories that he began to write in the thirties that one finds a broader, more historical and philosophical view. We might also suspect that it was only then that the writer had had time to research matters that he pretended to have knowledge of in the earlier texts. But here too, war and fraternity are commingled.

Faulkner is always better when he is making things up after mastering the basic material; accordingly, his World War I stories, written after these two earlier novels, when he had established a full arsenal of literary skills, are much more persuasive in terms of their presentation of the war itself, especially the gripping battle stories "Victory" and "Crevasse," and the tour de force "Turn About," which is set amid aerial and then sea combat.

Although John Faulkner claimed that William never researched his books, the latter spent hours in the University library where many books documenting the war were on the shelves.[43] One book I have found there is a first-edition account of the sinking of the *Zeebrugge*, which may well have provided a pattern for the attack on the German ship in the latter part of "Turnabout." Aerial combat over France, the topography of the country, and the various technical and specialized slang terms of these glamourous warriors had become common currency. There were many songs, for instance, about the war, that incorporated the lingo such as Irving Berlin's "Yap, Yap, Yaphank," which obviously contributed to Gilligan's portrayal in the opening pages of *Soldiers' Pay*. Faulkner had certainly acquired technical terms as a cadet in Toronto, and likely much of the slang too, since the Canadians at that point were far more British than they are today. Many first-hand accounts of the aerial war appeared; *Above the French Lines: Letters of Stuart Walcott, American Aviator: July 4, 1917, to December 8, 1917* (1918) is still in the open stacks in the university library in Oxford, and has likely been there since its publication by Princeton University Press, which rushed it out soon after Walcott's death through heroic aerial combat on December 12, 1917—he was a Princeton man. We remember here that John Sartoris went to Princeton as well, at least in *Flags in the Dust*. Walcott enlisted first in the French air corps, and was in the process of transferring to the American forces when he was killed; in *Soldiers' Pay*, Lowe states to Gilligan: "You don't have to be a foreigner to be with the British or French. Look at Lufberry. He was with the French until we come in" (25). Lufberry appears in person in Walcott's account, as both were in the legendary Lafayette Escadrille.[44]

Faulkner's stories about World War I were mostly published in 1931, after the great innovations of *The Sound and the Fury* and *As I Lay Dying*. They were clearly informed by the reading I have just suggested, but probably too by the stories about the war that Faulkner's literary "brothers" such as Hemingway, Dos Passos, and Fitzgerald had published. These writers were thus sibling rivals too, especially Hemingway, whose heroic wound authenticated him and contrasted powerfully to Faulkner's lack of combat experience; indeed, this likely played a large part in Faulkner's repetition of his war tales late in his career. Here we might consider that the townspeople of Oxford were not the only ones who had scorn for noncombatants. Hemingway, proud of his combat record, wrote caustically to Edmund Wilson about Willa Cather's Pulitzer Prize novel about the war, *One of Ours*: "Prize, big sale, people taking it seriously. You were in the war weren't you? Wasn't that last scene in the lines wonderful? Do you know where it came from? The battle scene in *Birth of a Nation*. I identified episode after episode, Catherized. Poor woman she had to get her war experience somewhere."[45] Because many had sentiments like this, Faulkner did his homework before depicting scenes of actual combat, which he does superlatively.

I cannot provide here an exhaustive analysis of any of these tales, but I would like to point to a few details in "Victory" and "Ad Astra." In the latter, American soldiers in a French dining hall have a German prisoner in tow. The German's story proves absorbing; the eldest of four brothers, he has rejected the baronry that is his by primogeniture. His next brother went into the army, the third led a wastrel life in Berlin, the baby became a dragoon. The German rejects his title because at the university he has learned to value brotherhood, not the fatherland. We then learn that his first brother was killed by a jealous husband, the second was shot by one of his own troops, and the youngest was killed by the American aviator Bishop. The German's conversation is mostly with the Indian subadar, who echoes him in urging brotherhood. The story ends ironically, however, as the French attack their allies for daring to bring a Boche into the hall.

"Victory" is the story of the Scot Alec Gray, a shipbuilder who is sent to the brig for not shaving, something that actually happened to Faulkner in Toronto. Alec takes revenge later, during battle, by killing the man who reported him. Eventually, his bravery, which results as a circumstance of the murder (he's an unwilling hero) makes him an officer, creates innate pride in him and a compelling desire to rise in class after the war. He takes to formal suits and a twisted moustache that complements his now silver hair. Think of the similarly posed picture of Faulkner featured at this conference! People seeing Alec and his distinguished air feel he is "a milord military."[46] His civilian job evaporates, however, and his new friends desert him. Unable to join his family or to take up shipbuilding again, and without other skills, he chooses to beg in London. Significantly, he has three brothers at home, and one is married and doing well. In both stories Faulkner is retreating a bit from the siren call of war; although the glamour of the military is still there, Faulkner seemingly draws a line through it. It is tempting to read the story as Faulkner's bravely honest appraisal of where he might have ended up after the war, *even if he had come home a hero*, without his writing. You will note too Faulkner's penchant for getting even with people who offend him in his writing; observe what happens to the critic of his moustache!

In both stories, however, he is still thinking in terms of brothers. Gray foolishly sacrifices everything, including his family, to maintain a slim hope of rising above them. The German's story seemingly creates a shadow family for the doomed Sartorises, and perhaps the curse that Faulkner feels still lies over the Falkners. Significantly, Bayard Sartoris plays a minor role in "Ad Astra"; it is reported that his twin was shot down earlier, and the German's two middle brothers are twins. These parallels were perhaps intended to complement the German/Subaltern alliance, and to extend Faulkner's overall attempt to create the idea of global fraternity; tellingly, however, all of it is mocked by the French-inspired melee. Further, the ideal of transnational brotherhood can hardly take place when the tensions within families themselves can't be resolved, as the background of both stories suggests.

War as Prelude to Greatness

Faulkner ruthlessly appraised his own failures over the years and was acutely conscious of the guilt he felt at hating his kindred. Whitman transformed his homosexuality from a "problem" into a generative impetus for his art and a creative metaphor for America, the love of comrades. Similarly, Faulkner wrote out much of his resentment of his brothers into novels, from his first one, *Soldier's Pay*, up until *Absalom*. In many of the novels he destroys models of his brothers but ultimately uses fraternal struggle as a metaphor for democracy, gender formation, and, most significantly, racial struggle. Thus, Faulkner's own mother, the initial source of identity, ultimately, through art, becomes America herself. But, in personal terms, even late in his life, Faulkner's mother was the battleground on which this struggle was played out. Dozens of studies of sibling rivalries have shown that the degree of competition depends on the way the mother handles the rivals (Broderick, 118). Both William and John were obsessively dependent on their mother, and John Faulkner often said that the binge drinking of his brother was done to prompt attention from their mother. As Doreen Fowler has discussed, Faulkner would go to bed partly clothed or nude, drink himself into oblivion, awake, and repeat the drinking. His stupor could go on for days or a week and necessitated the most basic kind of cleaning and tending, which his mother sometimes provided even after her son's marriage. Fowler does not pursue her implication, however, for Faulkner's securing of a "return" to the mother, which Fowler interprets as a death wish, is also a way of triumphing over the brother.[47] In any case, Miss Maud, who died at the age of eighty-eight, exerted a powerful hold on William and John until the end. In the years before her death, she posed proudly for pictures with John when one of his novels was published, joined him in condemning William for "stealing" the plotline of one of John's tales, and shared John's and Jack's contempt for William's belief in rights for African Americans.

In writing these early novels and stories, Faulkner attempted to show his mother that he too, like her, could be an "artist"; he also wanted to redeem his failed experience to participate in the Great War; this gained urgency from his smoldering sense that his younger brother had once again eclipsed him. he also saw, however, that these emotions, which could not be expressed verbally, could find expression in writing, and further, that the personal could be transcended through the transformation of experience and fraternal fury into art; more importantly, art was now the way out of his aimless wandering, a foothold in life, and the way to its summit. Eventually, the family as metaphor became Faulkner's constant impetus, certainly in all of his historical fiction, which builds in so many cases on Falkner family history, but also in the novels set in the contemporary moment, for he was keenly aware that the novelist can and should reinscribe his own times as well. This has been described as the mode of the scriptures by Northrup Frye, who asserts that the reinscription of history can lead to a higher form, what Frye calls redeeming history, following the German terms of *Weltgeschichte* and *Heilsgeeschichte*.[48]

Faulkner's translation of his family's own history into fiction grew out of those pages appended to the family Bible that charted the births, deaths, and marriages that were shorthand for the magical tales his aunts told him, the counterpart of Aunt Jenny's rapt musings on the Sartoris clan in *Flags*. These ritualistic modes of dealing with death found dramatic expression in his early novels and stories, which seem half in love with death. In the wake of Faulkner's failed attempt at military heroism, he succumbed to romantic notions of the hero while at the same time killing off the figures that represented his brothers. In *Flags* this may be seen in the tombstone Faulkner creates for John Sartoris, which later is echoed in the actual tombstone Faulkner had made for his brother Dean's tomb. Both John and Bayard Sartoris, and then later Dean, seem to have been avatars of tragic heroes for Faulkner. In ancient Greece, heroes were intimately associated with death, and often died young. Cults developed that gathered at these figures' tombs, where they were not worshiped as gods but rather transfigured through reverential memorial. Faulkner was keenly aware of the aura exuded by the Old Colonel's commanding marble statue in the Ripley graveyard; he recreated it in the final pages of *Flags in the Dust* as the tomb of patriarch John, and would no doubt have been pleased by the monument erected over his own body, and by the ritual offerings of whiskey poured over him by tipsy admirers in the dead of night. But he also intended Dean and his black nurse, Caroline Barr, to be read, after death, as heroic scripts. Faulkner created a special tombstone for "Mammy Callie" that seems quite problematic today, as it reads: "Mammy/ her white children bless her";[49] one wonders just what her black children thought about such a memorial. But like "all the dead pilots," she was the raw material for the myths that sustained him and fueled his art. Barthes has stated that myth is a script that history dictates, and oftentimes that history can be quite personal.

The aforementioned letters of the American airman Stuart Walcott contain a biographical note by his father that states: "When the *Lusitania* was sunk he felt strongly that the United States should take a positive stand in favor of the freedom of the seas, that the rights of America should be protected even if it meant war, and he was ready to fight for it."[50] There is no such rationale for the Sartoris men, for fighting either in World War I or in the Civil War. Indeed, Old Bayard asks Old Man Falls, "what the devil were you folks fighting about, anyhow?" to which Falls replies "damned if I ever did know" (252). If there is a major problem in the books I have described, it is that Faulkner never really considers the political aspects of the war in any detail, preferring a highly personal, suggestive story and style that forces the reader to supply the context and interpretation, a mode not unlike Hemingway's. His more meditative pronouncements on this war would have to wait for *A Fable*.

The title of this conference is Faulkner and War, and I would like to read one final passage from Jack Faulkner, who really did go to war:

> Fragments of the shell thumped into the ground and walls of the trench. Then our platoon sergeant called out from his position a few paces down the trench, "Down, damn it, down in the trench." At that instant I felt as though someone had slipped up beside me and blasted my head with a steel rail. My rifle was knocked out of my hands, and I dug handfuls of mud out of the side of the trench trying to keep from toppling . . . the next thing I knew I was flat on my back in the three years' accumulation of dank oozy slime. . . . I could barely hear someone calling, "Medic! Medic! This way! . . . my right trouser leg was ripped open. . . . I found blood there. By the time they lifted me out of the trench, several other wounded were on stretchers . . . artillery shells were exploding all around. . . . Did I pray? I don't remember. I was too occupied in wondering what the doctors could do to help me before I got around to asking the Good Lord to lend a hand. The medics attached to the Marines in France . . . the danger in which they lived was no less than that of the Marines they served with so much courage. I never saw one I would not have been proud to call brother."[51]

Jack's fictional avatars did not fare so well in the war narratives of brother William, and none of his returning soldiers express sentiments such as these. What these early tales do ponder, however, is the power of fraternal repetition within the family's generations, and the creation of tradition through naming, ritual, and forms of activity. These aspects of the family have continued to the present moment. Two days ago I was fascinated to hear that Jimmy Faulkner's four grandchildren are named Sally, John, Jack, and William after the constant foursome of the older generation's childhood. Jimmy Faulkner tells me these newcomers were born in the order I listed them, so William is the youngest. Apparently he already has a reputation for rebellion, just like his namesake, and if the theory of birth order is correct, he is indeed "born to rebel" and will have the ideal background for the creative life, perhaps one in literature. That might be the perfect coda for a troubling, but energizing, family feud, one that has contributed forcefully to the great literature of the larger world.

NOTES

1. *Faulkner at West Point*, ed. Joseph L. Fant III and Robert Ashley (New York: Random House, 1964), 102.

2. Noel Polk has demonstrated that there is no firm evidence in the text that Bon is indeed Sutpen's son, or that Bon had African ancestry (*Children of the Dark House: Text and Context in Faulkner* [Jackson: University Press of Mississippi, 1996], 139 ff.). However, most critics have accepted Quentin and Shreve's speculations on both these issues as (fictional) fact, and Faulkner himself referred several times in interviews to Bon as Sutpen's son; see, for instance, *Faulkner in the University: Class Conferences at the University of Virginia, 1957–1958*, ed. Frederick L. Gwynn and Joseph L. Blotner (New York: Vintage, 1965), 35; 79; 93; 272.

3. See Joel Williamson, *William Faulkner and Southern History* (New York: Oxford University Press, 1993), 64–71.

4. There is, however, the partly autobiographical sketch "Mississippi," which was published in abbreviated form in *Holiday* in 1956; the full text, taken from the manuscript, appears in *Essays, Speeches, and Public Letters by William Faulkner*, ed. James B. Meriweather (New York: Random House, 1966), 11–43. It barely mentions the three Falkner brothers, and not by name.

5. See F. F. Schachter et al., "Sibling De-Identification," *Developmental Psychology* 12 (1976): 418–27.

6. Fredric Jameson, *Marxism and Form* (Princeton: Princeton University Press, 1972), 99.

7. Susan Curtis, "The Son of Man and God the Father: The Social Gospel and Victorian Masculinity," in *Meanings for Manhood: Constructions of Masculinity in Victorian America*, ed. Mark C. Carnes and Clyde Griffen (Chicago: University of Chicago Press, 1990), 67–78. Faulkner's boyhood magazine reading is discussed in Joseph Blotner, *Faulkner: A Biography*, 2 vols. (New York: Random House, 1974), 1:101.

8. Murry C. Falkner, *The Falkners of Mississippi: A Memoir* (Baton Rouge: Louisiana State University Press, 1967), 57.

9. Blotner (1974), 1:135–36.

10. Falkner, 125.

11. Joseph Blotner, *Faulkner: A Biography*, 1-volume edition (New York: Random House, 1984), 66.

12. Let me rephrase the situation in a new way: an acclaimed writer who has won the Pulitzer Prize is found to be lying about having combat experience. This describes not only the William Faulkner we know, but also the recent and notorious case of Joseph Ellis, a professor of history at Mount Holyoke who came under fire for having told his classes over a ten-year period that he saw combat in Vietnam. Significantly, his Pulitzer Prize winning book is entitled *Founding Brothers*, and in it he adheres strongly to the centrality of fraternity in American culture. In the recent debate over Ellis (Anna Marie Cox, "In Wake of the Scandal Over Joseph Ellis, Scholars Ask 'Why?' and 'What Now?,'" *Chronicle of Higher Education* 47, 44 ([July 13, 2001]: 10–12), Robin D.G. Kelley, a professor of history at New York University

feels that professors are more and more likely today to draw on personal experience to illustrate history or fiction because students believe their source of knowledge is themselves. "Professors have to trump that. Scholars feel pressure to be authentic—more than authentic" (11). The *Chronicle* article presents other scholars' angry reactions, and at least some of it is attributed to professional jealousy of Ellis, who committed the grievous sin not only of winning a Pulitzer for what some feel is psychobabble history, but of reaping a financial bonanza and public glory when the book became a best-seller. But the *Chronicle* also reveals that many other men have made up fictional stories about combat duty in Vietnam. Indeed, sociological studies have indicated that telling lies is an indispensable component of the development of the man of words; most men at one time lie—particularly to other men—about their sexual exploits, fish they've caught, or achievements on athletic fields. Certainly Southern oral traditions and the more formal written mode of Old Southwest humor are two obvious examples of this syndrome.

13. Timothy Dow Adams, *Telling Lies in Modern Autobiography* (Chapel Hill: University of North Carolina Press, 1990), ix.
14. Ben Wasson, *Count No Count: Flashbacks to Faulkner* (Jackson: University Press of Mississippi, 1983), 14.
15. Blotner (1974), 1:163.
16. Falkner, 118.
17. William Faulkner, *Mosquitoes* (New York: Boni and Liveright, 1927), 228. The passage is spoken by the Semitic man.
18. Sally Wolff with Floyd C. Watkins, *Talking about William Faulkner: Interviews with Jimmy Faulkner and Others* (Baton Rouge: Louisiana State University Press, 1996), 30.
19. *Faulkner at Nagano*, ed. Robert Jellife (Tokyo: Kenkyusha, 1962), 90–91.
20. Frank Sulloway, *Born to Rebel: Birth Order, Family Dynamics, and Creative Lives* (New York: Pantheon, 1996).
21. *Selected Letters of William Faulkner*, ed. Joseph Blotner (New York: Random House, 1977), 185.
22. John Faulkner, *My Brother Bill* (New York: Trident Press, 1963), 225.
23. Blotner (1984), 213.
24. Sulloway, xiii.
25. Alfred Adler, *The Individual Psychology of Alfred Adler: A Systematic Presentation in Selections from His Writings*, ed. and annotated by Heinz L. Ansbacher and Rowena R. Ansbacher (New York: Basic Books, 1956), 379.
26. Carlfred B. Broderick, *Understanding Family Process: Basics of Family Systems Theory* (Newbury Park, Calif.: Sage, 1993), 117.
27. Polk, *Children of the Dark House*; Doreen Fowler, *Faulkner: The Return of the Repressed* (Charlottesville: University Press of Virginia, 1997).
28. Claude Levi-Strauss, *The Elementary Structures of Kinship*, rev. ed., trans. James Harle Bell, John Richard von Sturmer, and Rodney Needham (Boston: Beacon Press, 1969).
29. Sulloway, xiv.
30. Ibid., 21.
31. Ibid., 79–86.
32. Ibid., 98.
33. Blotner, *Letters*, 171.
34. William Faulkner, *Soldiers' Pay* (New York: New American Library, 1968). All further citations are from this edition.
35. Michel Gresset, *Fascination: Faulkner's Fiction, 1919–1936*, trans. Thomas West (Durham: Duke University Press, 1989), 71–83.
36. Blotner (1984), 194, reports the original manuscript of *Flags*, which Faulkner preserved, began with this scene.
37. William Faulkner, *Flags in the Dust* (New York: Vintage, 1974). All further citations are from this edition.
38. Personal communication from Jimmy Faulkner, July 2001.
39. William Faulkner, *Collected Stories of William Faulkner* (New York: Vintage, 1977), 517.

40. Dexter Westrum, "Faulkner's Sense of Twins and the Code: Why Young Bayard Died," *Arizona Quarterly* 40, 4 (1984): 365–76.

41. John S. Williams, "Ambivalence, Rivalry, and Loss: Bayard Sartoris and the Ghosts of the Past," *Arizona Quarterly* 43, 2 (1987): 178–92.

42. In "There Was a Queen" (originally published in 1932 but written in 1930), Faulkner states Elnora and Old Bayard are half brother and sister, "though possibly but not probably neither of them knew it, including Bayard's father"; (*Collected Stories*, 727). Interestingly, in this story Caspey is not Elnora's brother, as in *Flags*, but her husband, and he has been incarcerated for stealing.

43. Personal communication from Jimmy Faulkner, July 2001.

44. Stuart Walcott, *Above the French Lines: Letters of Stuart Walcott, American Aviator: July 4, 1917, to December 8, 1917* (Princeton: Princeton University Press, 1918).

45. Edmund Wilson, *The Shores of Light: A Literary Chronicle of the Twenties and Thirties*. (New York: Random House, 1951), 118.

46. *Collected Stories*, 431.

47. Fowler, 29. See also Blotner (1974), 1: 19–20 and John Faulkner, 116–17.

48. Northrup Frye, *The Great Code: The Bible and Literature* (New York: Harcourt Brace Jovanovich, 1982), 47.

49. Blotner (1984), 413.

50. Walcot, 91.

51. Falkner, 99–101.

Quentin, Listen!

David Madden

Ernest Hemingway once declared that "All modern American literature comes from Huckleberry Finn," and there is some truth in that pompous pronouncement.[1]

Risking pomposity, I wish to make not one but several declarations: that all Southern literature *comes out* of the Civil War and Reconstruction, that all Southern novels are *about* the Civil War and Reconstruction, that *Absalom, Absalom!* is the best example of that phenomenon, not only in the Faulkner canon, but in all Southern literature, that *Absalom, Absalom!* is my choice as the greatest Civil War novel, that Colonel Thomas Sutpen, man of action in the Antebellum, Civil War, and Reconstruction eras, is *not*, as he is often held up to be, the protagonist of *Absalom, Absalom!*, that Quentin Compson, the most passive of Sutpen's vicarious witnesses, *is* the protagonist, that the most pertinent way to show that Quentin is the protagonist is to examine the techniques of the art of fiction that Faulkner employs in this novel, that Quentin Compson's consciousness is the most trenchant expression of the legacy of the Civil War at the deepest existential level.

How is it that all Southern literature *comes out* of the Civil War and Reconstruction, and that all Southern novels are *about* the Civil War and Reconstruction? The effect of the war and Reconstruction has so permeated Southern history and consciousness that anything a Southerner writes derives from that prolonged effect process, and that process itself is delineated in *Absalom, Absalom!* more deliberately and clearly than in any other Southern novel. By contrast, there is no such thing as a Northern novel, nor a true Civil War novel by a Northerner—*The Red Badge of Courage*, for instance, is about war per se—because there is no such thing as a Northerner, except in the minds of Southerners, who are, however, both very real and very surreal to Northerners.

A catalytic experience for civilizations throughout history, *war*, especially the Civil War, is a catalyst for Faulkner personally and for his characters, especially Quentin Compson, whose consciousness is at the center of Faulkner's creative consciousness. Every force seeks a form. I use "Civil

War" as an all-embracive term for Antebellum, Civil War, Reconstruction force and legacy eras because the Civil War is a catalyst for all lines of trajectory. The lines of trajectory of Antebellum forces converge and explode in the Civil War, the lines of trajectory in the Civil War are tangled, the lines of trajectory in Reconstruction spread out and hang like a web until Quentin's last year, 1910, four years before World War I; the web was reshaped by Jim Crow, World War I, the Depression, and the civil rights movement, and it hangs still over us all. Obsessive talk of the myriad trajectories of those external forces ignites forces of emotion, imagination, and intellect in Quentin's consciousness and unconsciousness.

Absalom, Absalom! is my choice as the greatest Civil War novel, *not even though* it does not directly depict war, but *because* of the ways in which the war is more alluded to and its effects implied than dramatized. Faulkner implies ways in which life in the South led up to the war, was profoundly traumatized by it, and, more emphatically, by Reconstruction; and we may infer that it permeated, in myriad ways, Faulkner's own life. In *not* dealing directly with battles, Faulkner evokes, in his pervasive use of the technique of context and implication, what is more important—the war's effect on Americans, especially Southerners, right on up to you and me today.

In the works in which he figures, Quentin so seldom acts upon or interacts with other characters that readers are enabled to respond only to his consciousness as he passively reacts to and reluctantly but in anguish meditates upon the actions of others. Quentin is Faulkner's expressionistic embodiment of the process that makes all Southern literature about the Civil War. There is no character quite like Quentin in Southern fiction, not in Carson McCullers's *The Heart Is a Lonely Hunter*, all of whose four major characters are locked in the isolation of their own psyches, but do, at least, tell their personal stories, even if only to a mute, who is himself somewhat like Quentin; not in William Styron's *Lie Down in Darkness*, although that novel resembles *The Sound and the Fury*; not in Thomas Wolfe's four epic novels, even though they feature the same hero; not in any Civil War novels by Southerners, although the hero of *The History of Rome Hanks and Kindred Matters*, by Northerner Joseph Pennell, faintly resembles Quentin-as-listener. Having found nothing in all fiction as fascinatingly complex as Quentin's shifting role in the works of Faulkner, I would claim for Quentin a significant uniqueness in all world literature, while lamenting that he is one of its most neglected characters, even though several critics, especially John Irwin in *Doubling and Incest, Repetition and Revenge* (1975), Estella Schoenberg in *Old Tales and Talking* (1977), and Noel Polk in *Children of the Dark House* (1996), have made us more aware of him.

That, compared with his other characters, Quentin was always a vital, sharply focused presence in Faulkner's consciousness is demonstrated by the fact that when he discussed his characters in public he referred to the males as "the boy" and often had lapses of memory about them, but he almost always called Quentin by name, and about *him*, his memory was always clear. Several major and numerous minor characters reappear in Faulkner's work but Quentin has the distinction of being a major character in two of Faulkner's major works and in four short stories, "That Evening Sun," "A Justice," "A Bear Hunt," and "Lion." That Horace Benbow resembles Quentin, especially in the early versions of *Sartoris* and *Sanctuary*, that Faulkner "rehearsed" Quentin and Sutpen in the short story "Evangeline," and that one *might* imagine Quentin as the anonymous "we" narrator of "A Rose for Emily" emphasize Quentin's centrality in the Faulkner canon.

The other three narrators of *The Sound and the Fury*, Benjy, Jason, and Faulkner himself, seldom refer to Quentin. Benjy's stream of consciousness expresses pure being in timelessness. Had Faulkner allowed Caddy (his "heart's darling"), to whom all the narrators relentlessly refer, to speak, would she have spoken of Quentin? I think not. Caddy's naming her daughter Quentin seems an ironic dismissal of Quentin and his incestuous longing for her.[2] Quentin's obsession with Caddy is so strong that his confession is that of a man whose life flashes before him as he drowns. Jason's tough guy narration is realistic self-justification. But to whom do these brothers speak? Isolated within their very different egos, none of the three brothers have listeners. Faulkner presents their narrations as pure literary artifice. But Faulkner narrates the fourth section of *The Sound and the Fury* in full awareness that *he* has what his characters, especially Quentin, his alter-ego, *lack*, but do not crave, a community of readers, of listeners.

I am now proposing to publishers that the two novels and four short stories in which Quentin is either the protagonist or a major character be brought together in a single volume of about 600 pages. My study of those works and their effect on me personally and as a fiction writer has led me to the conviction that if they are gathered into a single volume, with an introduction explaining why, the average Faulkner reader may grasp the essence of this elusive character.

Colonel Thomas Sutpen, man of action in the Antebellum, Civil War, and Reconstruction eras, is not the protagonist of *Absalom, Absalom!*[3] I am convinced that the repeated focus on Sutpen by many readers and critics distorts the novel, and turns Quentin into a mere narrative device at best and makes him gratuitous at worst.[4]

On the surface, *Absalom, Absalom!* is a dramatic rendering of the ways in which Thomas Sutpen the legend becomes the creation of the Southern oral storytelling tradition, a tradition nurtured in Antebellum wilderness, magnified in Civil War defeat, and transmuted in humiliation, resentment, and self-loathing through Reconstruction on into 1910, Quentin's twentieth year.

As a little boy, Sutpen, who sprang from poor white trash, was commanded by a black servant to enter a mansion by the back door. This wound to Thomas Sutpen's very identity inspired his dream of becoming the owner of a mansion and slaves. He obsessively and savagely pursued a grand design to force that dream into reality, a dream that became a nightmare for everyone around him, especially his wives, white and black, and his sons and daughters, white and black, his sister-in-law, Miss Rosa, the children of his black son, the poor white trash man who worshipfully served him, and that man's granddaughter and great-granddaughter. Sutpen himself was satisfied only with the image of himself that the design was created to produce, the image of a man above all other men, who were to be merely witnesses to his rise and to the perpetuation of his blood, while he seemed to take little pleasure in the land, the mansion, the women, the children, or in the many other men and women who figured in his operatic design.

From the moment the townspeople set eyes upon the wild stranger who would become known as Thomas Sutpen, the demon, the ogre, leading his gang of wild slaves through the town, the exaggerated and conflicting stories began, stories that told how he bought a hundred square miles of wilderness, tamed the wilderness, built a mansion, amassed a fortune, married the daughter of a prominent citizen, on whom he begat a son and daughter, Henry and Judith, how he went off to war to protect those products of that design, how during Reconstruction, his fortunes so declined that he became the keeper of a store and how Wash Jones, his poor white trash Sancho Panza in this Quixotic epic slew Sutpen with the scythe he had borrowed from Sutpen.

That is far more than enough for storytellers—that is, *everybody*—in any impoverished Deep South small town to thrive on. Faulkner thrived on such stories until he could become a writer and reimagine and expand upon them, until he could imagine what is missing, the answers to the many mysteries and secrets that always germinate behind the façade of such legends. So Faulkner creates the keepers of the secret answers to the mysteries that seem to constitute the very identifies of the later storytellers and their children. They are motivated, in that later era, a time of no grand actions such as the Civil War, in that long, trancelike era of "old tales and talking" (243), to bring the dark mysteries out into the daylight. They discover finally: that Charles Bon, Henry Sutpen's roommate, at the University of Mississippi, who followed a design of his own, schemed to go with Henry to Sutpen's Hundred to confront Sutpen for abandoning his mother and to reveal that he is Sutpen's son, but that he meets Judith, who falls in love with him; that the confrontation with Sutpen was delayed by the war; that when his father revealed to him that Bon was his half-brother and part Negro, Henry shot Bon to defend his sister's honor, then fled; that when Sutpen's wife Ellen died, he proposed that her sister, Rosa, become a mere body out of which he could produce a male heir, and that he was refused; that the Negro house servant Clytie was also Sutpen's daughter, and that Sutpen had not only begotten children of his slaves but had turned at last to a poor white trash girl and begot a child by her, all three of whom the grandfather, Wash Jones, slaughtered; that Charles Bon's child, too, came to Sutpen's mansion and was taken in by Judith and Clytie; and finally that Henry returned from exile almost forty years later and hid in the now-derelict "dark house," until discovered by his Aunt Rosa and Quentin, and that it was Clytie the slave daughter who applied a scorched earth climax to the Sutpen epic by setting the mansion on fire, perishing with her white brother Henry.

Although the long postwar era of the Lost Cause produced few men of action like Colonel Sutpen, it produced a legion of storytellers and multitudes of listeners, and this backward marching, backward looking parade of storytellers and listeners comes finally to a dead end in Quentin Compson.

Given the obvious fact that lives like Colonel Thomas Sutpen's have been the stuff of fiction, both very good and very bad, from Homer and Sophocles to the present, why do I feel compelled, almost messianically, to urge, along with several scholars, that greater attention must be paid to Quentin, whose affinities are all with the palest of postmodern anti-heroes?

Sutpen's story expresses the desire of Southerners to be both civilized, as in Jefferson, and wild, as in the Civil War. Quentin can be neither nor does he even aspire to be either. Both the South and Quentin are transfixed between the nightmare of the past and its legacy in the present. Jason gives his son the same name Sir Walter Scott gave his man of action, *Quentin Durward*, the young Scot who fought for a foreign king in 1468, an ironic contrast to Quentin Compson. Quentin's grandfather's storytelling does not inspire Quentin's father, Jason, to a life of action, and Jason's storytelling fails to inspire Quentin to a life of action; Jason's only act is to pass on the story, imbued with his own character and personality. Quentin's only acts are the passive ones of reluctant listening, anguished retelling, of going along with his father to the Sutpen cemetery and going along with Miss Rosa into Sutpen's house, of staring at his father's letter in his room at Harvard.

Unlike his father, Jason, Quentin does not want to know, understand, become involved in the story of Sutpen and others, and tell it to future kin, to a community of listeners. Part of Quentin's problem is that he knows that, like people, like Sutpen himself, civilizations, such as Greece and Rome, come and go, so why not the South and its Sutpens? Quentin knows that he cannot forge an identity out of a heroic past as precarious as common everyday life, even if he could or desired to do it.

Quentin's negativity, both stated and implied, pervades the novel. In early chapters, Quentin responds to questions with a "yes" that conceals a diffident "no" and later with a "no" that conceals a panicked "yes." "Better that he were dead," Grandfather said of Charles Bon's son, "better that he had never lived."[5] Quentin, Faulkner implies, would apply that comment to himself, the Quentin who says of himself, "I am older than many people who have died" (301). Miss Rosa will not "reconcile herself to letting him [Sutpen's son] lie dead in peace" (289), Shreve says to Quentin, who, the reader may infer, has already "become" Henry, wanting to lie dead in peace himself. "So now I shall have to go in" (294), thinks Quentin, invading Henry Sutpen's hiding place to satisfy Miss Rosa's craving for an answer to the mystery of "a ghost" in the old mansion, Miss Rosa who has refused to remain a ghost herself, and so Quentin moves out of storytelling into reality, to witness the suicide by fire of Clytie and Henry (and to commit his own suicide by water in *The Sound and the Fury*). The reader might wonder whether Charles Bon, recently revealed to be Thomas Sutpen's mixed blood son, forced Henry to kill him to avoid marrying their sister and fathering another mixed breed child, but the context of Quentin's listening might well imply that Quentin would conclude that he did, because, unable to respond to any positives intended by the storytellers, Quentin is deeply affected by all the suicides and suicidal behavior in the novel.

Faulkner implies that as each storyteller tells a story, earlier storytellers are remembered, so that Quentin's grandfather is a dominant figure hovering over Jason's telling about how his father helped Judith, and the reader feels his presence also, and so does Quentin, even more intensely. The reader must imagine, then, that as he listens specifically to Rosa, then to his father, then to Shreve, Quentin feels the urgent speaking presence of many other storytellers. Quentin is never of one mind. As early as the first few pages, Faulkner tells the reader that there are "two separate Quentins now talking to one another in the long silence of notpeople in notlanguage" (4–5), and that a third Quentin is listening to those two voices. "The eagerness of the listener," says Jane Eyre, in Bronte's novel, "quickens the tongue of a narrator," but unlike his father and Shreve, Quentin is not an eager listener, so the storytellers strive harder to capture and keep his attention and stimulate his interest, with the effect that he is all the more tormented, giving rise to the relentlessly implied questions, "Why *me*? What do you want me to *do*?" Early in the novel and then again halfway through, Quentin thinks, "Yes, I have had to listen too long" (102, 157). To what? To the implied pleas that he forge his identity out of these stories, but even more to the implications of the stories as they apply to who he really is, a potential suicide. Near the end, when Shreve's telling the story back to Quentin reaches a high pitch of intensity, Quentin yells, "Wait!" and thinks, "I am going to have to hear it all over again . . . I shall have to never listen to anything else but this again forever" (222). Influenced by the vigor and pace of Shreve's own enthralled retelling, Quentin takes up parts of the tale yet again, compulsive, obsessed, manic (225).

Sutpen's saga is unimaginative, in itself uninteresting; it is simple, operatic melodrama (not tragedy, as some have argued, not even near-tragedy), and, as such, it is *one* major expression of the South's and the world's conception of life in the South before, during, and after the Civil War. Sutpen's motive for telling his story to Grandfather Compson is self-justification and self-aggrandizement, a simple continuation of all his other actions. The men, women, and children, white and slave, who witness Sutpen's life, create his legend by telling his story in fragments that promote mystery and suspense, fragments embellished by imagination and repeated from generation to generation until they torment Quentin's ears. Exhorted to listen, Quentin is the principal listener in the novel. As Nick Carraway, not Gatsby, is the protagonist of *The Great Gatsby*, as Jack Burden, not Willie Stark, is the protagonist of *All the King's Men*, as the narrator, not Roderick Usher, is the protagonist of "The Fall of the House of Usher," an even more apt example—because the true protagonist of all first person narratives is the narrator—so Quentin, not Sutpen, is the protagonist of *Absalom*. The major difference is that Quentin the listener is not the sole storyteller in the novel. That some critics mistakenly identify Quentin as the sole narrator (as opposed to storyteller) testifies to the strength of the impression one gets of the pervasiveness of his consciousness, an effect toward which all Faulkner's techniques are deliberately working.[6]

Had he intended Sutpen to be the protagonist, Faulkner was in command of an array of techniques that he could have adroitly employed to tell Sutpen's simple, melodramatic story, to delineate its complex implications about the South, much more effectively. For instance, he could have used the omniscient point of view, getting into the perspectives of all the major characters; or he could have used third person, central intelligence point of view technique from Judith's or Henry's perspective; or he could have imagined a first person narration, with Judith or Henry as narrator, with one of Bon's descendants as listener.

Who *does* tell the story and to whom? Faulkner uses the omniscient point of view, from which he tells the reader that Miss Rosa and Quentin's father told Sutpen's story to Quentin, who tells it to Shreve, who tells it back to Quentin. Why does Faulkner create Rosa and Quentin's father as storytellers, since neither knows enough to tell the whole story? And why is Quentin necessary as a listener-storyteller since he knows only what they tell him and especially since his verbal responses seldom exceed "yes" and "no" and his mental responses do not directly express the effects of their storytelling upon his consciousness? The blunt question Faulkner deliberately poses for readers is this: *What is Quentin doing in this novel?*

We know that Faulkner had already told Sutpen's story with two narrators like Quentin and Shreve in the short story "Evangeline," written five years before *Absalom*. Both the basic "I" narrator and his friend who tells him parts of the story are keenly interested listeners who are motivated to seek answers to mysteries. Very little narrative evidence in the novel but all of the fiction techniques point to Quentin as Faulkner's primary interest. There are two Faulkners in this novel, one the artist at work, the other Faulkner's alter ego, given the name "Quentin."

Faulkner implies that before chapter 2 begins, Quentin has told his father the story Miss Rosa told him, and he implies that before chapter 6, Quentin has told Shreve the story of Miss Rosa. Faulkner renders Quentin's telling a story only once, when he and Shreve are retelling Sutpen's story together. The effect of this use of context and implication is to *suggest* that Quentin is ostensibly the major storyteller, while providing the reader's basic experience with Quentin as the Quentin who listens to stories.

The most pertinent way to show not only *that* Quentin is the protagonist but *how* he is the protagonist is to examine the techniques of the art of fiction that Faulkner employs in this novel and their effect on the reader. The techniques fiction writers use are in themselves expressions of meaning and conveyors to the reader of experience; that is true especially of innovative writers, and truest of Faulkner the innovator in this novel. One may see in Faulkner's careful and full revisions the stress he placed on the use of innovative techniques that in themselves would express the emotional, imaginative, and intellectual meaning of the novel.[7] This novel is a veritable encyclopedia of innovative techniques and innovative use of conventional techniques. Gathering all the Quentin fiction around *Absalom, Absalom!* will enable readers not only to understand Quentin and the works in which he figures, but to understand Faulkner's innovative techniques as well, and that understanding would most probably make all his works far more accessible.

Faulkner's overall technique is to combine innovative literary techniques with the dynamics of oral storytelling techniques to achieve the overall effect of a complex meditation, which the reader responding to implication must attribute to Quentin. The unique passiveness in Quentin's character enables, perhaps forces Faulkner to achieve technical effects not otherwise possible, effects that constitute much of his greatness as an innovative literary artist.

The ideal reader for this novel will examine Faulkner's use of the techniques of fiction to express his intentions. Just as readers may be aware of Faulkner's literary techniques, even Quentin and the storytellers themselves are conscious of the techniques of storytelling that they use to affect their listeners. Quentin tells Shreve, "I reckon Grandfather was saying [to Sutpen] 'Wait wait for God's sake wait' about like you are until he [Sutpen] finally did stop and back up and start over again with at least some regard for cause and effect even if none for logical sequence and continuity . . . telling it all over and still it was not absolutely clear" (199). By his use of techniques, such as metaphor, Faulkner teaches the reader how to read *Absalom*. "Maybe nothing ever happens once and is finished," meditates Quentin. "Maybe happen is never once but like ripples maybe on water after the pebble sinks, the ripples moving on, spreading . . ." (210). Quentin's metaphor alerts the reader to expect that the narrative events and other elements in this novel will not happen only once, but will be repeated in other forms, enhanced by Faulkner's patterned and controlled repetition of motifs, metaphors, and phrases.

Only through an awareness of Faulkner's artistry can the general reader feel the full impact and respond to the myriad implications of Quentin's drama of consciousness. Faulkner's ideal reader for this novel will become aware not just of narrative strategy but of his use of the technique of point of view, a complicated mixture of omniscient, third person central intelligence, to use Henry James's term, interior monologue, and *four* quoted first person narrations, with variations in style; his manipulation of shifting contexts to make simultaneous implications about Sutpen's story and Quentin's responses; his use of allusions to enrich the contexts; his use of transitions and lack of transitions in time and space, to disorient and reorient the reader and Quentin; his deliberately ambiguous and tormenting use of pronouns, especially "he," "they," and "it"; his use of the devices of incremental repetition, questions, digressions, interruptions, odd punctuation, long, complex parentheticals, long convoluted sentences, paragraphs as long as eight pages, juxtapositions, expressionistic effects, irony, parallels, symbolism, and startling imagery.

All those techniques achieve a sense of simultaneity and inevitability that result in a unity so complex many readers and some critics do not fully comprehend it, partly because the techniques I have listed cause disorientation and dismay, as his first vital reader, his editor, lamented to Faulkner.[8] While all of his techniques serve the Sutpen story, they simultaneously serve the more important characterization, created mostly by context and implication, of Quentin, whose responses are often similar to the frustrated, irritated, gasping reader's. Readers have asked, Why does Faulkner use such a vast array of techniques? Faulkner strives to create shifting, complex contexts within which to stimulate the reader's mind with implications that express what cannot be directly expressed—as he knew from the limited effect of Quentin's first person testimony in *The Sound and the Fury* and in "That Evening Sun," published two years later—and simultaneously to explore, perhaps subconsciously, his own (Faulkner's) psyche indirectly through Quentin's implied psyche.

The ostensible Antebellum, Civil War, Reconstruction generic narrative of the stock character Sutpen becomes meaningful as a paradigm of the decline of the South not in itself, but mainly as fragmented and embedded in the neurotic, probably psychotic consciousness of Quentin. Sutpen's story is an objective correlative of Quentin's ineffable state of consciousness.

Faulkner's achievement in this novel, as in all his best work, lies not in his having imagined the story of Thomas Sutpen but in his having imagined the techniques that innovatively render that story and its implications; and a unique achievement of this novel alone is that it is not mainly Faulkner's character-narrative based imagination but his techniques that create Quentin Compson. The medium *is* the message.

Faulkner is interested in each of the characters, especially in listeners who become storytellers, but his identification with Quentin was essential to his being. Faulkner is Quentin, but he takes a major step further than focus on Quentin by delineating each of three other character's immersion in Sutpen's story, with the effect that the novel is more about each of the characters and about the process of their storytelling than it is about Sutpen himself.[9] But when we compare the centrality of Quentin as listener and storyteller with the other characters, we find that no potential for further development is active at the heart of Rosa's story, because it is static and always was; Mr. Compson's narrative is impersonal—he has no motive beyond a pure compulsion to tell stories, except for the weak inference that he aims to affect and teach Quentin; Shreve's involvement is transitory. Southerners tell stories to teach and to create identity, especially as a postwar, Lost Cause ritual. Rosa and Quentin's father say, in effect, "Quentin! Listen! So you can transmit it to our own kind, to your children!" But Quentin will have no children. Staring at his father's letter about Rosa's death, as if in a trance, he tells the story to a sardonic,

Northern foreigner, Shreve, as if to be overheard telling it to himself, a dramatic monologue that is simultaneously a soliloquy. He tells it to take possession of the story, to give himself a sense that he exists, that he is not himself a ghost born of the ghosts of the past, but finally, he tells it to rid himself of the burden of Southern history, which as one of the last of the Compson line, he feels, but by mere torpor does not accept. Nor does he accept the implied obligation to pass it on through the representative story of Sutpen. Quentin starts with no ostensible motive to tell, and ends with none, but the reader must infer his existential dilemma from the innovative techniques Faulkner employs.

As omniscient narrator unusual in the infrequency of his speaking, Faulkner meshes his own narration with all the storytellers, who also have a kind of omniscience through overreaching imaginations, and Faulkner's complex consciousness finally meshes with Quentin's. Faulkner, a master of point of view technique, creates the most complex pattern in this novel. There are three elements: Faulkner's omniscient voices, voices telling "old tales and talking" (243), and Quentin's meditation voice. Within Faulkner's omniscient point of view, the various storytellers tell their stories. As Faulkner moves from one to another, sometimes within only a few sentences, the very juxtaposition of one storyteller to another expresses some aspect of Quentin's consciousness of storytellers and of times and places. Near the end of chapter 8, for instance, three storytellers intersect and interact on a single page: Clytie, like a messenger in a Greek tragedy, describing Wash Jones's slaughter of his granddaughter and his great-granddaughter, and Sutpen, as retold by Quentin's father, who imagines the missing parts, retold again by Quentin to Shreve, who interrupts, as told by Faulkner (233–34). Faulkner's own infrequent narration almost always relates to Quentin, with the effect that the reader is always aware of the presence of the Faulkner-Quentin consciousness even as Miss Rosa, Jason, and Shreve are telling stories. The precept that the protagonist of every first person narrative is the narrator applies to each storyteller in this novel. Faulkner modifies that aesthetic so that the novel becomes essentially more about Quentin as the major listener than as storyteller.

"So they will have told you doubtless already" (107) is a kind of phrase repeated to Quentin often. Subconsciously, Quentin is acutely aware of not just the listener-tellers Faulkner quotes, but of those people who are listeners only and even of tellers and listeners who are only implied in the novel: Charles Bon has told stories to his roommate Henry, Clytie has told Grandfather Compson a story, Grandfather Compson has told his son Jason a story—all those tellings are paraphrased by Miss Rosa and Jason, who tell the stories to Quentin, the all-encompassing listener. The reader must pay attention to Quentin and imagine the conscious and subconscious effects on Quentin of Shreve's sardonic retelling of the Sutpen story. As these listener-storytellers talk, readers should be ever mindful, as Quentin is, of the always-hovering presence of those characters to whom Faulkner does not give a storytelling voice: Sutpen's children, Judith and Henry, and those with black blood, Clytie and Bon, and that ever-present representative of the poor white trash from which Sutpen also sprang—Wash Jones. Faulkner does not directly give them storytelling voices because the technique of context and implication enables him to evoke their voices without quoting them.

Faulkner stresses the fact that each of the tellers of the Sutpen tale dwells upon fragments that reflect needs in their own lives: Rosa's love for Sutpen, Quentin's grandfather's friendship with Sutpen, Sutpen's own egocentric story of himself as told to Grandfather Compson, Jason Compson's desire to exhibit to his son Quentin his intellectual analysis of the Sutpen-Rosa story, and even the wise-cracking Northerner Shreve's exhilaration in retelling to Quentin the saga Quentin has just told him. The narrative logic of the Sutpen story as told by Rosa and Quentin's father calls for a listener who can and does respond fully, interactively, and meaningfully as the telling progresses. But Quentin is as far from being that kind of listener as any Southern twenty year old could be. Through Quentin's responses, and lack of responses, to the telling and the tale, Faulkner suggests to the reader the negative nature of the values of the world Sutpen and his witnesses represent. At no time does Quentin even hint that he derives any value on an exemplary level from what is being transmitted to him; he responds on a personal, subjective level to the stories he is told, affected most by parallels in his own life, mainly the relationship between himself and his sister Caddy, as seen in the brother-sister relationship of Henry Sutpen and Judith Sutpen, and, far less important, by parallels between the friendship of Henry and Charles Bon and the roommate relationship of Quentin and Shreve. Faulkner was once asked, "how much can a reader feel that this is the Quentin, the same Quentin, who appeared in *The Sound and the Fury*—that is, a man thinking about his own Compson family, his own sister?" Faulkner replied, "To me he's consistent. That he approached the Sutpen family with the same ophthalmia that he appreciated his own troubles."[10]

The legacy of the Civil War and Reconstruction in the South today is expressed in the varied responses of individuals. Quentin Compson, the most passive of Sutpen's vicarious witnesses, *is* the protagonist. The consciousness of Quentin Compson is the most trenchant expression of the legacy of the Civil War at the deepest existential level. The vigor of the transmission of the values of the Southern way of life, symbolized in Faulkner by high potency sexuality, mostly perverse in various ways, from generation to generation ends in Quentin's implied impotence, which is not only sexual but intellectual. Faulkner dramatizes the fact that while the conventional Southern values, which coalesced in the issues and the warrior mentality of the Civil War, fail to produce creative acts in the lives of individual descendants, the legends do stimulate each individual listener's imaginative participation, a value that transcends the ritual teaching function of the South's past. For them the unvicarious life is not worth living; at least they have *that* much of a life.

Storytelling inflames the imagination of the listener. Jason demonstrates that effect, saying often, "I imagine" (82, 85–87). But Quentin goes further and imaginatively becomes one of the characters with whom he most unconsciously identifies: Henry Sutpen. The image of Henry and Charles Bon "facing one another at the gate" triggers Quentin's own vicarious response: "It seemed to Quentin that he could actually see them" (105). A paradox in the power of the imagination is suggested when Faulkner as author says that Quentin "could see it; he might even have been there," as Henry kissed his sister Judith before returning to war, but Quentin contradicts his creator, thinking, "*No. If I had been there I could not have seen it this plain*" (155). Even though he knows he has listened too long and too much, until he is not listening anymore, and has no desire to be a storyteller (280), Quentin responds to his Canadian roommate, Shreve, when he exhorts him to "tell about the South" (142). Quentin infects Shreve with "the virus of suggestion" (Henry James's phrase). Shreve's imagination is so activated that he reimagines the story of Henry and Charles Bon, exploring possibilities, rendering the story even more ironic, that, for instance, Charles Bon saves the life of his brother Henry who later kills Charles Bon *because* he is his brother and Judith's (237–38, 254, 275). Quentin tells the story to Shreve only to get rid of it by telling it as an act of betrayal to a cynical listener, who tells it back to him, ironically, in an empathy so profound, Quentin and Shreve together not only retell it in two voices as one voice, but imagine their counterparts, Henry Sutpen and Charles Bon, so vividly that Quentin and Shreve feel they have become one, then they become Henry and Bon, "in the cold room . . . there was now not two of them but four," so that Quentin and Shreve and Henry and *his* roommate Bon are "riding the two horses through the iron darkness" (236–37).

The inflamed imagination leaps into vicarious experience. Sutpen, Bon, and Henry enact a story—and Wash Jones violently ends it. Rosa, Jason, Quentin, Shreve, and Faulkner do not act—they listen to the story and retell it. Vicarious experience is a major motif in the novel. All the storytellers to whom he listens are people whose lives are intensely vicarious, so that Quentin the listener is a captive of the vicariousness of others.

The South that Quentin knows through storytellers has, ever since defeat in the Civil War, been living vicariously at a level that threatens sanity, and Quentin symbolizes the product of that quality in the South—the inflamed imagination in an action vacuum. "But you were not listening," Quentin tells himself, in one of his meditation passages, "because you knew it all already, had ... absorbed it already without the medium of speech somehow from having been born and living beside it, with it" (172). But in the telling, the lives of others seem, compared with his own, very compelling: the lives of Henry and Judith, especially, but even Miss Rosa's and his father's. Jason tells Quentin that Judith and Henry were a "single personality with two bodies both of which had been seduced almost simultaneously by a man [Charles Bon] whom at the time Judith had never even seen" (73), only heard her brother tell stories about. Judith communes with her dead lover Bon through his son by another woman, taking care of him, and when Judith dies, Clytie lives vicariously through the same boy, raising him. From the same class as Sutpen, Wash Jones vicariously lives the dream of wealth through Sutpen. After the war, Wash meets the returning hero at the gate, "Well, Kernel, they kilt us but they aint whupped us yit, air they?" (150). Unlike Quentin and the others, Wash Jones, who has lived vicariously through his hero Sutpen, finally commits a real act, but out of the kind of past he has vicariously lived, he can act only in violence.

Every nonreality quality in the other nonactive characters is paralleled in Quentin, usually to a greater degree: meditation, imagination, passivity, accede (torpor, inaction). As he listens to stories about Sutpen and other men of action all his life told by numerous people, Quentin becomes aware that he has no life of action. The kind of storytelling and listening process Faulkner presents is a form of meditation, but the only literal mediation to which he gives the reader access is Quentin's.[11] Faulkner is interested less in the drama of action than in the drama of human consciousness. By the end, Quentin has turned even more inward (and will finally turn against himself). Even his imagination and his meditations are limited, narrow in scope, and fail to result in a compulsion to tell stories as a means of perpetuating the past and maintaining a sense of community.

Myriad voices speak obsessively to Quentin about his legacy, the epic story of the settling of his home region, and the lingering effects of the war fought to preserve that way of life. But Quentin brings to his reluctant listening to those voices his own private sexual feelings about Caddy, delineated in *The Sound and the Fury* and, as a submerged psychological process, in "That Evening Sun," in which again Quentin, not Nancy, is the protagonist. Joseph Blotner quotes Faulkner as saying that Quentin in *Absalom, Absalom!* listens to the story of the brother and sister, Henry and Judith Sutpen, as a bitter parallel to his own incestuous longings for his sister Caddy and his own bitter failure to protect his sister's honor.[12] Similarly, in "That Evening Sun," Quentin, who does not act, who only listens, is listening most attentively to Caddy's questions that relate to sex. The effect of Faulkner's technique of implication from shifting contexts in the various works featuring Quentin may culminate in the general implication that Quentin kills himself in *The Sound and the Fury* not so much out of guilt for merely desiring his own sister as out of a profound apprehending of the fact that he exists intensely only when he responds in amazement and bewilderment to the tales people tell him about people who are, compared with himself, very much alive. His is a purely existential dilemma, as posed by Kierkegaard in *The Sickness unto Death*, Martin Heidegger in *Existence and Being*, Rollo May in *The Meaning of Anxiety*, Jean-Paul Sartre in *Being and Nothingness* and in *Nausea*, Albert Camus in *The Stranger*, and Katherine Ann Porter in "Flowering Judas." Quentin is far less active, less questing than even the narrators in the Sartre and Camus novels and his accede, a mortal sin in the Catholic Church, is more severe than Laura's in Katherine Anne Porter's "Flowering Judas."

We know that the storyteller's need to identify a personal parallel among the characters in the stories is most acute in Quentin (who "becomes" Henry) because Faulkner *implies* the need, rather than letting Quentin directly state it, but his need is so great that the vicarious imagination can not save him. Quentin's need is the basic need to *be*, and his basic dilemma the anxiety that emanates from the inability to *be*. If existence precedes essence, Quentin's sense of his own existence is such that essence can hardly flow from it. Existential psychologist Rollo May defines anxiety as "the experience of the threat of imminent non-being. Anxiety is the subjective state of the individual's becoming aware that his existence can become destroyed, that he can lose himself and his world, that he can become 'nothing' . . . anxiety overwhelms the person's awareness of existence, blots out the sense of time, dulls the memory of the past, and erases the future . . . it attacks the center of one's being. . . . Anxiety is ontological, fear is not. Anxiety always involves inner conflict. . . . Ontological guilt 'arises' from forfeiting one's own potentialities."[13] Miss Rosa, his father, and others fervently tell Quentin stories about people who have lived fervently on a level of action; Quentin, even considering that he is young, has no life of action himself about which anybody could fervently tell a story. Even fervently telling a story is an action, but Quentin himself tells the Rosa-Sutpen story to Shreve in a kind of bewildered, impotent, static voice that Faulkner gives us in a controlled series of fragments. Far from motivating him to live a life of action that might embody the values of the Old South, both the tellers and the tales only make Quentin aware of how empty his own life and consciousness are. Quentin is passionate only in the last line, as Meursault is passionate, yelling at the priest, only at the end of *The Stranger*. When Shreve asks Quentin, "Why do you hate the South?" Quentin's hysterically anguished denial, "I dont hate it!" is true. His existential dilemma is that, having a self so famished, he doesn't even hate himself.

In *Absalom*, his father, Miss Rosa, and others offer family and public history for their own varied reasons, but they provide a way for Quentin to transcend his subjective sexual impotence and his emotional, imaginative, and intellectual paralysis. Given Quentin's inability to respond as an active receiver of the legacy, Faulkner implies that Quentin's dilemma is deeper than incestuous longing, that it is the existential dilemma of being and nothingness. Quentin is now and always has been a shadow verging on nothingness, amazed and anguished at the spectacle of richer lives of action or of active preservers of the lives of more active people. Quentin, who ends in suicide, helps us see why Faulkner himself, who in life merely posed as a warrior and man of action, who *may* have considered suicide, turned to creative re-creation, with war and its aftermath as the human action with the greatest range of possibilities in life and in literature. Meditating on Quentin, my student Melissa Wilkinson, in a moment of intellectual ecstasy, exclaimed, "It's wonderful that Faulkner could make so much out of nothing."

Many critics see Quentin as Faulkner's alter ego, his most autobiographical character.[14] Quentin was one of his favorite characters. He might have said, "*Quentin c'est moi!*" If a writer's life is most truly expressed in the act of creation, rather than in a recital of actual events, *Absalom, Absalom!* is Faulkner's autobiography as a person via Quentin and as an artist at work creating Quentin. Paradoxically, Quentin's narrow, single-minded consciousness is at the center of Faulkner's myriad-minded consciousness.

Quentin is listening, subconsciously, on the deepest level, deeper than the Henry-Judith incest implication, listening to the basic meaning of Sutpen's design, which is a calculated effort by the boy Sutpen to exist by having the mansion and all that went with a plantation way of life, because turned away from the front door of the mansion, the boy had an intuition of existential anxiety, the fear of nonbeing. Sutpen's design ends in catastrophe, maybe a suicidal overreaching. As both reader and Quentin listen to the Sutpen stories, Faulkner enables us to imagine Quentin's thoughts and emotions.

Faulkner, I imagine, and Sutpen felt the same anxiety but Sutpen distracted himself by building an empire, which failed him and his community; Faulkner distracted himself from anxiety by creating his Yoknapawtapha saga which, as a work of art that triumphs like Keats's urn, did not fail him and will not fail his readers, if they work with him as his collaborators by responding not only to the surface complications but to the implications that the shifting contexts generate. Faulkner's ideal reader will then feel unbearable pathos for Quentin in ways no other novel can stimulate.

Poem X in Faulkner's *A Green Bough* has been referred to as "Twilight," an apt title for Faulkner's meditation on the Quentin beneath the line by line surface of the novel:

> A terrific figure on an urn—
> ... caught between his two horizons,
> Forgetting that he cant return.[15]

This an allusion to the town emptied of its folk in Keats's "Ode on a Grecian Urn."

And Edgar Allan Poe's poem "Alone" evokes a sense of Quentin's life:

> From childhood's hour I have not been
> As others were—I have not seen
> As others saw—I could not bring
> My passion from a common spring ...
> And all I loved, *I* loved alone.
> Then—in my childhood ... was drawn ...
> The mystery which binds me still. ...
> From ... the cloud that took the form ...
> Of a demon in my view.[16]

For Quentin, the demon is not Sutpen, whom others called demon, but the spot of grease on the road where Quentin merely wished he could have more fully existed.

NOTES

1. Ernest Hemingway, *Green Hills of Africa* (New York: Charles Scribner's Sons, 1935), 22.

2. *Faulkner in the University*, ed. Frederick L. Gwynn and Joseph L. Blotner (Charlottesville: University Press of Virginia, 1959), 6, 263. Faulkner describes Caddy and her relationship with Quentin.

3. Faulkner disagrees, while stressing Quentin's importance. The argument may proceed not only from the author's intent in the novel but from its effect. *Faulkner in the University*, 71, 274–75.

4. One of the most recent examples is Dirk Kuyk, Jr., *Sutpen's Design: Interpreting Faulkner's "Absalom, Absalom!"* (Charlottesville: University Press of Virginia, 1990). Cleanth Brooks is an earlier, salient example, even though he understood, as a New Critic, how point of view expresses essence in a work of fiction: *William Faulkner: The Yoknapatawpha Country* (New Haven: Yale University Press, 1963), 295–324. See also his "Appendix B: Notes to *Absalom, Absalom!*" in *Twentieth Century Interpretations of "Absalom, Absalom!,"* ed. Arnold Goldman (Englewood Cliffs, N. J.: Prentice-Hall, Inc., 1971), 107–13. In most of the essays in that collection, the emphasis is upon the importance of the Sutpen story, with no stress on its effect upon Quentin.

5. William Faulkner, *Absalom, Absalom!* (1936; New York: Vintage International, 1986), 166.

6. Cleanth Brooks is again a major example: "All the information the reader has comes through Quentin directly or through Quentin's conversations." Brooks fails to call attention to the omniscient narrator of the entire novel, Faulkner himself. *Twentieth Century Interpretations of "Absalom, Absalom!,"* 107. In the same volume, Thomas E. Connolly instructs us that "Quentin" is "the principal narrator." Also in that volume, Richard Poirier says much the same thing (12–13). This misunderstanding is frequently repeated elsewhere. Ambiguity may be the culprit. To distinguish between Faulkner as authorial narrator and the characters he quotes telling old tales and talking, one should use the term "storyteller" for Quentin and others.

7. Gerald Langford, *Faulkner's Revision of "Absalom, Absalom!"* (Austin: University of Texas Press, 1971). See his introduction.

8. Joseph Blotner, *Faulkner: A Biography*, 1 vol. (New York: Random House, 1984), 348.

9. Langford, 3.

10. *Faulkner in the University*, 274.

11. *Absalom, Absalom!* A good example begins on 148.

12. Blotner, 348–49.

13. *Existence: A New Dimension in Psychiatry and Psychology* (New York: Basic Books, 1958), ed. Rollo May, Ernest Angel, and Henri F. Ellenberger, 50–54.

14. Among those critics who deal extensively with this question are John T. Irwin, *Doubling and Incest: Repetition and Revenge: A Speculative Reading of Faulkner* (Baltimore: Johns Hopkins University Press, 1975); Estella Schoenberg, *Old Tales and Talking: Quentin Compson in William Faulkner's* Absalom, Absalom! *and Related Works* (Jackson: University Press of Mississippi, 1977); Michael Grimwood, *Heart in Conflict: Faulkner's Struggles with Vocation* (Athens: University of Georgia Press, 1987). In *Critical Essays on William Faulkner: The Compson Family* (Boston: G. K. Hall and Company, 1982), ed. Arthur F. Kinney, several of the contributors take up the question. An interesting revelation of Faulkner's identification with Quentin is the fact that "he told Joan [Williams] to send her letters to Quentin Compson, General Delivery, in Oxford." Blotner, 520.

15. *The Marble Faun and A Green Bough* (New York: Random House, nd.) facsimile reprint, 30.

16. *The Portable Poe* (New York: The Viking Press, 1945), 637–38.

Imagining the Abstract: Faulkner's Treatment of War and Values in *A Fable*

Lothar Hönnighausen

The issue of war and the debate of values involved, above all their artistic rendering in such a complex work as *A Fable*, have attracted Faulknerians again and again not least because the author's treatment of these themes shows an astonishing range of forms and styles.[1] A good example is section 4 of *Collected Stories*, entitled "Waste Land" in homage to his modernist master T. S. Eliot and containing such diverse short stories as "Crevasse" and "Ad Astra." "Crevasse" is such an intense short story that some readers have erroneously taken it as personal experience, but the story also possesses an eschatological suggestiveness that transforms the battlefield into a symbolic landscape. In contrast, the political and philosophical reflexions, in the story of the Indian subadar and the German prisoner of war ("Ad Astra") anticipate the discursiveness of *A Fable*, while the malaise of the fliers in "Death Drag" expresses, as in Donald Mahon's war wound in *Soldiers' Pay* and Bayard Sartoris's trauma in *Flags in the Dust*, the sensibility of the lost generation.

Faulkner's first novel, *Soldiers' Pay*, seems a forerunner of his late work, *A Fable*, in that it relates war and its repercussions to a mythological framework. Donald Mahon is a mutilated World War One veteran as well as a "wounded faun," and Mrs. Powers appears not only as a war widow, but also as a Proserpina-figure with Beardsleyesque features and with a mouth "like a red scar," which reminds us of the hero's wound. *Flags in the Dust* juxtaposes the ever more glamorous retelling of the Civil War by Aunt Jenny with the raw impact of World War I on Bayard Sartoris. But the novel also presents Bayard's memories of his brother Johnny's death in an air battle as a psychic confrontation with an unintegrated and threatening counter-self. However, what distinguishes the treatment of war in both *Soldiers' Pay* and *Flags in the Dust* from that in *A Fable* is that, in the early novels, war appears above all as an arena of psychological projections. In contrast, the theme of war in *A Fable* has much wider philosophical and anthropological ramifications which the author seeks to enhance by employing a particular typological structure.

This means that the storylines and the major events of *A Fable*, like those in James Joyce's *Ulysses*, are typologically prefigured by grand old narratives. Nevertheless, there is a considerable difference in their use of narrative prototypes, which, in his famous review of Joyce's novel, Eliot called "the mythic method": That the biblical story of Christ's Passion has religious and moral connotations in American and European culture that are much more closely defined than those of Homer's epic is one of the circumstances troubling the reception of *A Fable*. As it is, many readers have not taken sufficient notice of the considerable differences in meaning between the orthodox Christian and Faulkner's satiric distortion of the biblical episodes which prefigure his story of the pacifist corporal in the French city of Chaulnesmont during World War I.[2]

The external structure of *A Fable* is typologically related to major events of Christ's Passion story but this does not mean that it is a Christian novel. What type of novel then is *A Fable*? In view of the fact that it deals with World War I, one might term it a war novel. But even a brief comparative look at distinguished specimens of that genre such as Erich Maria Remarque's *All Quiet on the Western Front* or Norman Mailer's *The Naked and the Dead* makes one realize that *A Fable* is rather different. The linchpin in its plot is not military action but the refusal to engage in such action. However, the corporal's mutiny does not make *A Fable* a pacifist utopia either, nor does the grotesque picture of a self-sufficient military apparatus reduce the book to an anti-utopia or satire in the manner of Joseph Heller's *Catch-22*. The fact that two key figures undergo a moral development, which in the case of the runner takes a positive course and in that of General Gragnon proves abortive, might make one consider the term *Bildungsroman*. However, as both characters are part of a comprehensive system of oppositions and analogies, in turn centered around the moral antagonism between the corporal and the old general, it seems preferable to speak of *A Fable* as a philosophical novel or—since that term suggests an abstract and systematic quality fortunately not dominant in the book—as a novel of ideas.

A Fable is Faulkner's only novel that, by its very title, draws attention to a literary genre that has been defined as "moral tale highlighting human faults and virtues." However, the morality of Faulkner's novel lacks the straightforwardness of traditional fables. In this regard, novels such as Thomas Mann's *Magic Mountain* or *Doktor Faustus* offer a more congenial frame of reference than either fables or traditional war novels. *A Fable*, although dealing with war, does so by making it the subject of far-ranging moral reflections: on power and order, on war and peace, on hierarchical authority and the freedom of the individual, and on death and life as moral goods. Like Thomas Mann, Faulkner presents these themes not *in abstracto*, but rather embodies them through plotting and character. However, this in itself is hardly a guarantee that the outcome will be a masterpiece. In fact, Faulkner would have ended up with wooden allegories and cheap moral propaganda if he had not been able to create a new language which, reconciling the abstract and the concrete, allowed him to convincingly embody his far-flung theme. It is this peculiar mode of *metaphorical thinking*, indigenous to *A Fable* but also to some of the great writing in *Absalom, Absalom!* and *The Hamlet*, that the phrase *imagining the abstract* in my title seeks to foreground.

We first have the opportunity to explore Faulkner's peculiar genius of *imagining the abstract* in the several mass scenes of the book. The mass scenes in chapters 1, 5, 7, 9, and 10, arguably among the best parts of *A Fable*, reflect the spirit of an age, witnessing to a hitherto unprecedented degree the phenomenon of anonymous, malleable masses and of gigantic sociopolitical structures with isolated all-powerful leader-figures at the helm. The mass scenes in *A Fable* do not only reveal what Faulkner had learned about the staging of mass scenes in Hollywood. They also show how he shared with other contemporary artists such as fellow novelist John Dos Passos, film director Sergei Eisenstein,[3] and theatrical producer Erwin Piscator, as well as with the socialist muralists Siqueiros, Orozco, and Rivera, the urge to artistically capture the masses that were at the same time targeted by politicians in the Soviet Union and Nazi Germany, in fascist Italy and Spain, but also in F. D. Roosevelt's and Huey Long's America.

The first sentence of *A Fable* appears as an anticipatory image of the thematic polarity between the military and the masses: "Long before the first bugles" (representing the military ritual regulating all life in the garrison city of Chaulnemont) "sounded . . . most of the people in the city were already awake" (669). The movement of the masses towards the city hall, the seat of government of the commander-in-chief, as well as the immediately following countermovement of the military against the people is presented from a bird's-eye view and through imagery remindful of prose poetry. It is striking that here, and in other parts of the novel, Faulkner uses organicist imagery for the masses and mechanistic metaphors for the military. Moreover, he employs a complex series of water images to express the force of the people overwhelming the cavalry and the metaphor of the snowplow to render the counterattack by the infantry and tank:

> trickles became streams and the streams became rivers . . . flowing like an unrecoiling wave . . . like a . . . flood . . . the people advancing on the cavalry . . . the crowd had underswept the military, irresistible in that passive and invincible

humility, carrying its fragile bones and flesh into the iron orbit of the hooves and sabres with an almost inattentive, a humbly and passively contemptuous disregard, like martyrs entering an arena of lions. . . . Accelerating now, the crowd poured into the boulevard. It flung the cavalry aside and poured on, blotting the intersecting streets as it passed them as a river in flood blots up its tributary creeks, until at last that boulevard too was one dense seething voiceless lake. (670–71)

[the tank] parted the crowd like a snowplow, thrusting the divided parting back from either curb like the snowplow's jumbled. . . . (672)

What is important here, with regard to the problem of *imagining the abstract*, is the synergic effect of the metaphoric flood vividly illustrating the power of the people and the moral qualification of this power as "irresistible in that passive and invincible humility." In this prose, contours tend to dissolve due to the length of the sentences, the expansion of the imagery beyond individual sentences, and the verbal and acoustic repetitions. In the present instance, the fusion of the concrete and the abstract is enhanced by an immediately following new imaginative impulse, which produces the dramatic picture of "carrying its fragile bones and flesh into the iron orbit of the hooves and sabres" and by reiterated abstract references to humility as the spiritual strength of the people: "a humbly and passively contemptuous disregard, like martyrs entering an arena of lions." Faulkner's greatness in *imagining the abstract* manifests itself in a manneristic detailing of his imagery, far beyond its illustrative function as when the cavalry horses and riders are lifted by the masses "like the martial effigies out of a gutted palace or mansion or museum being swept along on the flood."[4]

Seemingly opposed to this manneristic exuberance in style but actually growing from the same goal of combining the abstract and the concrete is a peculiar fascination with types rather than "round" characters. All figures, whether we think of the corporal and the old general or of Gragnon and the runner, represent some aspect of the novel's thematics, and the fact that most are identified not by their name but by their military rank makes them appear distant. They share this trait with the several minor characters who, as particles of the masses, are only identified as "a young woman, a girl, thin and poorly dressed" (672), as "the sergeant" (674), or as "the tall man" (676). What is surprising, though, is that the behavior of these anonymous characters is given in detail and at some length, for instance in the account of the young woman's acceptance of the bread and her refusal to eat it. Combined with this detailing is a peculiar insistence on word repetition, which fascinated Faulkner as it had fascinated Gertrude Stein and Ernest Hemingway. However, in contrast to Hemingway, Faulkner was not content with verbal patterning alone but strove for a peculiar symbolist heightening as in the case of the reiteration of the religiously loaded word *bread*. "But she refused again, repudiating the *bread*, not the gift of it but the *bread* itself, and not to whoever had offered it, but to herself. It was as if she were trying to keep her eyes from looking at the *bread*, and knew that she could not.... Her eyes, her whole body, denied her mouth's refusal, her eyes already devouring the *bread* before her hand reached to take it, snatching it . . ." (673).

Apparently, what is important is not any individual complexity of "the young woman" but, as in the sculptures and drawings of Ernst Barlach or Käthe Kollwitz, the detailed expression of her moral status, her hunger, her loneliness, her suffering. Adding to this effect is the staging of this and other comparable figures. "The young woman, a girl" attracts the reader's attention by reemerging like a musical leitmotif several times in the chapter and by appearing in close-up scenes that contrast with the panoramic or bird's-eye scenes of the masses and the military. The inventiveness of Faulkner's *imagining of the abstract* manifests itself in a close-up of the young woman ("her chewing face between her slender dirt-stained hands" [675]) with the soldier in the blue uniform. The hungry woman reveals to him in an epiphany how his military status has alienated him from humanity. The scene, characteristic of the novel's combination of the concrete and the reflective in rendering the thematic polarity "masses and military," drives home to him that it is not "the kinless and nameless girl," but he himself who is morally an alien.

> But now something had happened. Looking about the waiting faces (all except the young woman's, she alone was not watching him, the end of the heel of bread still cupped against her chewing face between her slender dirt-stained hands, so that it was not he alone, but the two of them, himself and the kinless and nameless girl, who seemed to stand in a narrow well of unbreathing), *it seemed to him with a kind of terror that it was himself who was the alien, and not just alien but obsolete*; that on that day twenty years ago, in return for the right and the chance to wear on the battle-soiled breast of his coat the battle-grimed symbolical *candy-stripes of valor and endurance and fidelity and physical anguish and sacrifice*, he had sold his birthright in the race of man. (675 [my emphasis])

The text, juxtaposing valor and birthright in the human race, military and humane claims, demonstrates that the novel, in dealing with war, seeks to affirm more profound and more comprehensive values which the shattering of the *American dream* in 1929 and in the hungry thirties had put in doubt.

The first chapter of *A Fable* ends with the masses and the military gone and the young woman in a haunting freeze "wringing her hands" (683) alone on the *Place de Ville*. The attentive reader will have noticed that she

Faulkner's Treatment of War and Values in *A Fable* 125

runs after the lorry in which the corporal is travelling, but the fact that she is his wife can only be surmised on a second reading of the book. The result of this technique of character presentation is a peculiar thematic suggestiveness. As readers we cannot say what, in the sense of a conventional allegory, the "woman" stands for, but we feel that she *embodies* major aspects of the conflict between the masses and the military, between power and individual freedom, between the citizens of Chaulnesmont and the foreigners, and between the corporal and the old general.

These two protagonists are also introduced in this first chapter, which is not only a great prose poem, but also a very effective exposition of the novel. In contrast to the floodlike emerging and spreading masses, the military is presented in carefully contrived tableaux, rituals and parades. However, these *performances* are always witnessed by the masses who are "parents and kin ... fathers and mothers and sisters and wives and sweethearts of the soldiers" (669) of the doomed regiment from Chaulnesmont and who have spent the night "huddled in one vast tongueless brotherhood of dread and anxiety." Thus the arrival of the generalissimo with the other allied commanders and the lorries with the mutinous regiment, which General Gragnon wishes to see executed, is heralded and accompanied by the carefully elaborated sound motif. Against this musically structured imagery evolves the counterpoint of the military leitmotif of "clashing and crashing arms" as the car of the generalissmo approaches the city hall:

> Then they all heard *it* ... the *sound* now coming up the boulevard from the old city gate like a wind beginning ... the *sound was not voices* yet so much as a *sigh, an exhalation*, travelling from breast to breast up the boulevard. It was as if the night's anxiety, quiescent for a time beneath the simple weight of waiting ... was gathering itself *to flow* over them like the new day itself in one great blinding *wave*, as the first car entered the city. (677-78 [my emphasis])

> It came fast, so fast that the *shouts* of the section leaders and the *clash of rifles* as each section presented arms and then *clashed back* to 'at ease,' were not only continuous but overlapping, so that the car seemed to *progress on one prolonged crash of iron* as on invisible *wings with steel feathers* ... *flashing* across that terrified and aghast amazement and then gone ... and the boots and the *rifles crashed back* to simple alert. (678 [my emphasis])

The pomp and circumstance of the military is effectively displayed (the repetition of the number three: "the three generals of the three allied armies amid a rigid glitter of aides" [678] has a structuring effect), but the generalissimo himself is seen only for a moment ("*flashing* across that terrified and aghast amazement and then gone" [678]). However, this moment is sufficient for revealing his position within the thematic polarity of the novel: "the slight gray man with a face wise, intelligent, and unbelieving, who no longer believed in anything but his disillusion and his intelligence and his limitless power" (678). Then follow the trucks with the prisoners, with the sound of the overwhelmed people remaining first only "indefinite" (11), then shaping into a concerted sound (12), and finally erupting into single and then widespread yelling. While the prisoners on the trucks appear "packed like cattle, bareheaded, disarmed, stained from the front lines . . . unshaven and sleepless faces . . . like the faces of sleepwalkers . . . and curiously identical" (12), the power of the military is satirically represented by the generals: "three gaudy panoplied old men . . . identified not merely by their juxtaposition to the three flags but by their isolation on the balcony" (680).

The carefully postponed climax in the military procession comes with the truck on which the corporal's thirteen companions ride. Their difference from the other prisoners of the regiment is very pronounced: "like wild beasts . . . like creatures of another race . . . alien, bizarre, and strange" (681). However, in a carefully built-up process of intensification, yet a more exotic core group of four foreigners is set off from the thirteen, with the corporal appearing as the most foreign of all:

> four of the thirteen were really foreigners, alien not only by their gyves and isolation to the rest of the regiment, but against the whole panorama of city and soil . . . the faces of the four mountain men in a country which had no mountains, of peasants in a land which no longer had a peasantry. . . . (681)

> now the crowd itself had discovered that the fourth one was alien still somehow even to the other three, if only in being the sole object of its vituperation and terror and fury. Because it was to—against—this one man that the crowd was raising its voices and its clenched hands. (681)

Faulkner's narrator explains the foreignness of the corporal's companions in geographical and sociological terms, but he lets the crowd itself recognize that the corporal's foreignness is greater because it coincides with his moral foreignness. While the people's resentment of the corporal's companions results from ordinary chauvinism, "its vituperation, and terror and fury" (681) against the corporal himself are caused by its fear of his courageous rebellion against the absolute authority of the military system. Obviously, Faulkner has no rousseauist or socialist sentiments about *homo sapiens* in the aggregate. In assessing the rendering of the novel's theme, we have to pay attention not only to the tension between the military and the masses, but also to the corporal's conflict with both. Even his brief appearance here indicates that he has little in common with Christ the Redeemer: "a face merely interested, attentive, and calm, with something else in it which none of the others had: a comprehension, understanding, utterly free of compassion" (682). The momentary glances that he and the old general exchange prepare the reader for their eventual debate which is about moral, not religious values.

After the exposition in chapter 1, chapter 2 focuses on the military. At the center is division commander General Gragnon: "It seemed to him that he had been intended by fate itself to be the perfect soldier, pastless, unhampered and complete" (684). The mutiny causes a crisis in his life, but also a brief epiphanic flashback to the peace of his childhood in an orphanage in the Pyrenees (local leitmotif: "the unbearable golden silence . . . lark . . . the same cicada" [699]), before he resumes his lifelong military rigidity ("chopstriding, bull-chested, virile, in appearance impervious and indestructible, starred and exalted" [699]), to be eventually murdered as victim of the military machinery. Gragnon's memories of his sophisticated and decadent aide (of doubtful sexual proclivities, a couturier, a role-player who, ironically, is killed when he pretends to be brave [707]) reveal his inner uncertainties and his potential of change and opening up. Further, his calls on the corps and army commanders show how the tough front-line division commander is lost in the sophisticated and cynical world of the higher military echelons. The corps commander holds a view of the role of the military that is closer to Carlyle's cult of Napoleon and military dictatorship than to the function of the military in a modern mass democracy. The group commander sees wars and the military as unavoidable manifestations of the human condition, that is, as something that cannot be removed by the corporal's pacifist rebellion. The true enemies are not other nations, but the masses of one's own, who threaten the absolute authority of the military class:

> It is man who is our enemy: the vast seething moiling spiritless mass of him. Once to each period of his inglorious history, one of us appears with the stature of a giant, suddenly and without warning in the middle of a nation as a dairy maid enters a buttery, and with his sword for paddle he heaps and pounds and stiffens the malleable mass and even holds it cohered and purposeful for a time. (693)

> It wasn't we who invented war . . . it was war which created us. From the loins of man's ineradicable greed sprang the captains and the colonels to his [man's] necessity. We are his responsibility; he shall not shirk it. . . . [The rank and file soldiers] may stop war . . . ours merely to guard them from the knowledge that it was actually they who accomplished that act. (715)

Faulkner caricatures the group commander by letting him hold a ludicrous theory of the army as "a digestive machine . . . no army was better than its anus" [713]) and enjoys the grotesque tension between the elevated rank and the personal life style of General Bidet who "with night cap and flannel night shirt" drops Gragnon's heroic resignation hissing in a chamberpot and pulls the covers over his head, murmuring ironically: "It will be glorious." (716).

After the military elite in chapter 2, chapters 3 and 4 feature junior officers and simple soldiers. In chapter 3, an officer full of hatred against man and hope dissociates himself from the doubtful goals of the military leadership to rejoin the army as a runner and to emerge, in the end, as representing Faulkner's philosophy of *living as enduring*. He and the juvenile flying officer David Levine (in chapter 4), who commits suicide because the armistice destroys his hope for military glory, are thematically functional figures, serving as foils for the pacifist idealism and the martyrdom of the corporal. Chapter 5 returns to the setting of the garrison town of Chaulnesmont, and the leitmotives of flood and sound accompany again, as in the tableau of chapter 1, the dominant constellation of "military vs. masses." The realization of the people that the generalissimo may or may not order the regiment to be executed leads to an other example of Faulkner's *imagining the abstract*: a poetic prose passage, in which through repetition and cramming the word *grief* and related abstracts but also terms denoting collectivity, or as counterpoint, expressing the generalissimo's absolute power, gain a peculiar iconic concreteness that is quite independent of their actual meaning.

> out of the villages and farms and into the city by simple *grief to grief, since grief and anxiety*, like poverty, take care of their own; to *crowd into the already crowded city* with no other will and desire except to relinquish their *grief and anxiety into the city's vast conglomerate* of all the *passions and forces—fear, and grief, and despair, and impotence, and unchallengeable power and terror and invincible will*; to *partake of and share in all by breathing the same air breathed* by all, and therefore both: by the *grieving and the begrieved* on one hand, and on the other the lone gray man *supreme, omnipotent and inaccessible behind the carved stone door and the sentries and the three symbolical flags of the Hotel de Ville, who dealt wholesale in death*.... (780–81 [my emphasis])

In this tableau-scene, Faulkner gives his theme of "military vs. masses" a new satiric turn by freeing the military from the embarassing task of a mass execution and by letting the crowd "learn" that it is not the regiment that is to blame but a core group of foreigners that have instigated the mutiny. As a consequence, an orgy of chauvinism erupts and, ironically, covers up the tension between the masses and the military.

The introduction, in chapter 6, of the totally different, *tall tale* plot of the race-horse and the grotesque quartet—"horse, groom, old negro and black child jockey"—has upset many readers, but it has also reminded some of the two very different plots in Faulkner's novel *If I Forget Thee, Jerusalem (The Wild Palms)*. Although Faulkner has made every effort to integrate the alien race-horse plot into the World War I plot (for instance through the American foundation to support French ambulance units *Les Amis Myriades et Anonymes à la France de Tout le Monde* and through establishing a connection between the old negro and the runner in chapter 8), the two heterogeneous plots are "violently yoked together," as Dr. Johnson said of the manneristic linkages in the poetry of the *Metaphysical Poets*, and they work by contrast more than by affinity. However, this type of linkage is characteristic of the courage and the risk-taking that Faulkner considered the hallmark of artistic greatness and that he had missed in Hemingway and other contemporaries.

The connection in *A Fable* between the two plots exists above all on the thematic level: the moral achievement of the groom and his quartet is their brave and determined fight against hopeless odds and corresponds with that of the corporal and his group. In both cases, the courageous actions of the few have a great impact on the many because they upset the *status quo* and the routine of the established powers. In both cases, the actions are extraordinary, the achievements of the horse-racing quartet even bordering on the miraculous. The parodic allusions to proto-typical mythic relationships of humans and animals ("Eve and the Snake and Mary and the Lamb and Ahab and the Whale" [814] and all the "celestial zoology" [814]) in the race-horse plot ironically echo and correspond with the typological use of Christ's Passion in the World War I main plot. Above all, the actions in both plots are morally motivated: the corporal challenging the authority and self-sufficiency of the military apparatus, the horse-racing quartet frustrating the money-making millionaire-owners. Both stories end heroically and tragically. The corporal dies a martyr's death, and the groom, rather than tolerating the stallion's "abuse" as a money-procuring breeding machine ("geared by machinery to the rhythm of ejaculation ... a skillful pander with a tin cup and a rubber glove" [816]), kills the horse with whom he, like Ike and the cow in *The Hamlet*, has a mysterious and mythic affinity.

The greatest difference between the two plots concerns their underlying sociopolitical systems. While the main plot is dominated by the absolutism of military rule, the race-horse chapter (6) features the American democratic system and, although its foibles are humorously displayed (the lawyer's sectionalist and chauvinistic speech [836], for instance, comes fairly close to those of Bilbo, Vardaman, Huey Long, and their ilk), the basic rightness and humaneness of the Southern version of the American system is never in doubt. In fact, Faulkner, the sardonic humorist, has the star attorney envision himself and his clients, the horse-thieves, enthusiastically as part of the great American tradition of westward expansionism "where nothing save the vast unmoral sky limited what a man could try to do" (821),

> as a—perhaps *the*—figure in a pageant which in reality would be the affirmation of a creed, a belief, the declaration of an undying faith, the postulation of an invincible way of life: the loud strong voice of America itself out of the westward roar of the tremendous and battered and yet indomitably virgin continent,

where nothing save the vast unmoral sky limited what a man could try to do, nor even the sky limit his success and the adulation of his fellow man. . . . (820–21)

That Faulkner's irony did not preclude his own adherence to this rather robust and very un-European concept of democracy is shown by his vitriolic criticism of F. D. Roosevelt's faith in a much empowered state. A suitable subtext in this regard is the passage from *The Mansion* (1959) in which Mink Snopes, returning home after forty-four years in Parchman penitentiary, is puzzled by the blessings and the total control of the welfare state:

> So that was another part of the new laws they had been passing; come to remember, he had heard about that in Parchman too; they called it Relief or W P and A: the same government that wouldn't let you raise cotton on your own land would turn right around and give you a mattress or groceries or even cash money, only first you had to swear you didn't own any property of your own and even had to prove it by giving your house or land or even your wagon and team to your wife or children or any kinfolks you could count on, depend on, trust.[5]

Chapter 6 opens with another mass scene in Chaulnesmont in which the growing hatred against the corporal and his foreign family (his sisters Marthe, Marya and his wife) erupts in the hate-speech of blind old Angélique. But this scene is soon replaced by the elaborate parodic tableau[6] in which General Gragnon submits (unsuccessfully) his sweeping execution plan to the generalissimo and the allied military hierarchy. The tableau receives its satiric edge from the incongruity between military pomp and rococo circumstance (it takes place in "a boudoir back in the time of its dead duchess or marquise . . . its valanced alcoves and pilastered medallioned ceiling and crystal chandeliers and sconces and mirrors" [876]). The military regime's dependence on the superannuated culture of the *ancien régime* and its lack of any genuine culture of its own is further illustrated by the frugality of the generalissimo's lonely meal and by his mysteriously reduced appearance ("he resembled a boy, a child, crouching amid the golden debris" [885]). In contrast to the spirit of communality in the crowd scenes of the American race-horse story, the generalissimo in his European setting appears aloof from "the whole meek mist of men" (887): "Now the old general stood above the city which, already immune to man's endurance, was now even free of his tumult" (887). Further, Faulkner consistently emphasizes the venerable age of the city of Chaulnesmont which, crowned by its Roman citadel, serves as counterpoint to the vacillations of its inhabitants.

The old general's prehistory, revealed in the ensuing flashback, is that of an industrialist-politician-aristocrat, carefully bred for his omnipotent leadership. As one of its highpoints, it contains the quartermaster general's ironic as well as appreciative prose-poem on the cultural productivity of rapacity, or more radically put, on rapacity as the basis of culture. The text illustrates the essential contradictoriness of human nature as well as the anthropological range of *A Fable*, which only a superficial reader will reduce to a book on Christian pacifism. Moreover, the passage coupling, in the service of this amalgam of rapacity and culture, "Michelangelo and Phidias . . . Archimedes and Krupp" as "priests and popes and bishops" (906) gives proof of the satiric impulse that is a more essential part of Faulkner's genius than is generally realized:

> Rapacity does not fail, else all man must deny he breathes. Not rapacity: its whole vast glorious history repudiates that. . . . Not just one family in one nation privileged to soar cometlike into splendid zenith through and because of it, not just one nation among all the nations selected as heir to that vast splendid heritage; not just France, but all governments and nations which ever rose and endured long enough to leave their mark as such, had sprung from it and in and upon and by means of it . . . civilization itself is its password and Christianity its masterpiece, Chartres and the Sistine Chapel, the pyramids and the rock-wombed powder-magazines under the Gates of Hercules its altars and monuments, Michelangelo and Phidias and Newton and Ericsson and Archimedes and Krupp its priests and popes and bishops. . . . (906)

Returning the reader from the novel's past to its present, chapter 7, in a parodic as well as mythicizing setup, shows the generalissimo gleefully listening to the contradictory attempts of a British Colonel, French major, and an American captain to identify the corporal. That the corporal is the generalissimo's natural son, that he is the result of a liaison between the generalissimo and the mother of the foreign women (reminding one of Jove's affairs with mortal women), and that like Jesus Christ he was born in a cow-byre, is all revealed in the ensuing scene with the generalissimo and the three foreign women. After the peculiar mix of stylization and neorealism, intimacy and distance of this meeting, the reader is catapulted into a ludicrous state scene in which the sibylline generalissimo and a caricature of a German general negotiate the armistice.

After this packed and intense chapter, the following chapter 8 is rather subdued and deals with the evolving subplots. The runner's pacifist activities are contrasted with Levine's, the military idealist's, suicide because to him the end of war means the end of military glory. In view of the generalissimo's handling of the corporal's case and the related crisis, the quartermaster general, who had mythicized the generalissimo as a redeemer of mankind, has come to reject his former friend as a Machiavellian manipulator of the military and as an enemy of "the simple unified hope and dream of simple man" (972). The repetition of the value-charged term *simple* is of some importance because it dominates the rural subplot of the corporal's sisters Marya and Marthe. Moreover, the quartermaster general's identification of "the simple unified hope and dream of simple man" (972) with the revolutionary corporal is characteristic of the spirit of the thirties and forties. It was an age that in the effort to rediscover human roots and assess basic values fell prey to right-wing and left-wing radicalisms, not only in Europe but also to some extent in the USA (see Sinclair Lewis's novel *It Can't Happen Here*, 1935).

In chapter 8, "Thursday. Thursday Night," the thirteen prisoners are served their last supper. However, Faulkner does not subject the corporal to Christ's Gethsemane, but rather exposes him to the generalissimo's, his father's, temptation to renounce his pacifist rebellion and choose life instead of martyrdom. While in Christian theology God the Father is one with his Son and supportive of his redemptive mission on earth, Faulkner satirically inverts the biblical prefiguration of Christ's temptation in the desert by casting the old general in the role of the devil. In tempting the corporal with a vision of limitless power, the old general's idea of man is not the responsible christian individual, but the demagogue and the gullible cipher of mass society: "You will be God, holding him forever through a far stronger ingredient than his simple lusts and appetites: by his triumphant and ineradicable folly, his deathless passion for being led, mystified, and deceived" (989).

After the temptation of power the old general seeks to seduce his son by offering him life and telling him of a Mississippi murderer who, after he had already confessed, rescinds his confession when a bird on a bough evokes the overwhelming appeal of life for him: "[He] cast away heaven, salvation, immortal soul and all . . . all because one bird, one weightless and ephemeral creature which hawk might stoop at or snare of lime or random pellet of some idle boy destroy before the sun set" (991). Clearly, the values making the old general in his enthusiam adopt a Shakespearean tone can hardly be termed "Christian."

Furthermore, his ironic remark that the masses will not appreciate the corporal's heroic pacifism and blood sacrifice, but are enraged against him because the Chaulnesmont regiment may be executed for mutiny because of him, is obviously to the point. Nevertheless, the old general adduces a weightier philosophical argument against the corporal's pacifism in that he defines war as an ineradicable human vice, the perverseness of which he defines satirically as *hermaphroditism*: "the phenomenon of war is its hermaphroditism: the principles of victory and of defeat inhabit the same body" (985). Even the Germans, whom Faulkner characterizes as obsessively warlike (984)—in this sardonic view—will experience the relativizing of victory and defeat in regard to the distribution of resources: "a nation insolvent from overpopulation will declare war on whatever richest and most sentimental opponent it can persuade to defeat it quickest, in order to feed its people out of the conqueror's quartermaster stores" (985). No less interesting and timely (in view of American Star Wars-projects) than the generalissimo's economic view of war is his opinion that future wars will be technologically so advanced that they "out-distance" man: "his simple frail physique will be no longer able to keep up, bear them, attend them, be present" (993).

It is noteworthy that Faulkner has the old general, whom many readers consider the master of the evil empire, finally proclaim his own peculiar eschatological optimism. It should also be noted that Faulkner has the old general announce his own belief in human survival in a context showing his concern for the irrepressible human urge to conduct wars as well as for the total technologization of human beings and their environment. Even when man has given in to his last and worst vice, that is, to become totally technology-dependent, in our lingo, a cyborg, will he "endure and prevail" (994):

> I know that he has that in him which will enable him to outlast even his wars; that [there is in him something] more durable than all his vices, even *that last and most fearsome one* . . . *his enslavement to the demonic progeny of his own mechanical curiosity* . . . and that other one which is no vice at all but instead is the quality mark of and warrant of man's immortality: his deathless folly . . . *he wont dismount from his automobile at all because he wont need to: the entire earth one unbroken machined de-mountained dis-rivered expanse of concrete paving protuberanceless by tree or bush or house* . . . with *pipes and hoses* leading upward from underground reservoirs to charge him with one composite squirt . . . to die at last *at the click of an automatic circuitbreaker on a speedometer dial*, and, long since freed of bone and organ and gut, leaving nothing for communal scavenging but a *rusting and odorless shell.* (992–93)

> It will be his own frankenstein which roasts him alive with heat, asphyxiates him with speed . . . when he will crawl shivering out of his cooling burrow to crouch among *the delicate stalks of his dead antennae like a fairy geometry, beneath a clangorous rain of dials and meters and switches and bloodless fragments of metal epidermis* . . . to watch the final two *mechanical voices* bellowing at each other polysyllabic and verbless patriotic nonsense. (994 [my emphases])

The ludicrous vision of two robots shouting "at each other polysyllabic and verbless patriotic nonsense" shows Faulkner's environmental concern as much as his waning patriotic fervor.

With regard to the rendering of war, it is important to underline that Faulkner made the scene between the old general and his son, the corporal, the occasion of an affirmation of his humanistic philosophy closely resembling the one expressed in his Nobel Prize speech. What should also be considered is the fact that the style of his affirmation of man's survival does not bespeak a quiet, sure confidence in man. Rather, it has a traditional promethean ring about it as well as a peculiar air of pathos, eschatology, and melodrama, as if he had to shout down a deeply worried, skeptical, suicidal inner voice. Further, the values associated with eschatological man ("more efficient and louder and faster" [994]) reminds us that Faulkner is not, after all, an ironic decadent European, but a positive and self-assertive American.

The dialogue between the old general and his son, the corporal, rather resembles Plato's dialogues in which one person does all the talking. However, with regard to the opposition between the military and the masses, between authoritative order and the freedom of the individual, it is rather striking that the old general's arguments fail to make the corporal give up his position. On the other hand, one feels that the corporal's idealistic death for peace and individual freedom has less weight than the old general's Machiavellian philosophy. In fact, there are indications that Faulkner's sympathy lay more with the cold pragmatic power broker since he makes him voice his own endurance philosophy and almost verbatim repeat his Nobel Prize speech. In *imagining the abstract*, Faulkner makes the old general and the corporal the embodiments of two opposed but, to the author, equally important views, that is, the pragmatic and the idealistic, evolving in a dialectic process: "We are two articulations . . . [which] can even exist side by side" (988). They conclude this exercise by dialogistically proclaiming Faulkner's creed that man will "endure and even prevail":

> he has that in him which will endure even beyond the ultimate worthless tideless rock freezing slowly in the last red and heatless sunset because already the next star in the blue immensity of space will be already clamorous with the uproar of his debarkation, his puny and inexhaustible voice still talking, still planning; and there too after the last ding dong of doom had rung and died there will still be one sound more: his voice, planning still to build something higher and faster and louder; more efficient and louder and faster. . . . I dont fear man. I do better: I respect and admire him. . . . Because man and his folly—
> "Will endure," the corporal said.
> "They will do more," the old general said proudly. "They will prevail." (994)

This reassuring message is satirically offset by the priest's suicide (after unsuccessfully repeating the old general's temptation effort) and by the masterful if sinister story in which three American soldiers, representatives of the mother-country of democracy and humanity's progress, volunteer to carry out General Gragnon's murder in such a way that it looks like a hero's death and he becomes eligible for the state funeral that is to bolster the military regime. The black humor of this story, which concludes chapter 8, finds its match in the grotesque episode opening chapter 10 in which drunken soldiers have to transport a body from the national ossary in St. Mihiel to the grave of the unknown soldier in Paris. The two black humor stories frame chapter 9, in which the corporal is executed like Christ with the two thieves.

The scene in the country, in which the corporal's sisters Marthe and Marya receive two very different but equally strange visitors, is of some relevance in connection with the issue of values and the theme of war. The corporal's family comes from a faraway mountainous country—they have the telling name Dumont—and they are farmers. Both their life as farmers and their foreign origin set them off from the military as well as from the urban masses ("in their hive-dense tenements" in Chaulnesmont [669]). The closeness of both sisters to the land and to nature is particularly emphasized: the phrasing of Marthe's description as sower ("like a ritual, the second oldest of man's immemorial gestures or acts" [1061]) suggests that we are to appreciate the symbolic suggestiveness of her pose: "the sister herself moving across the land's panorama like a ritual, her hand and arm plunging into the sack slung from her shoulder, to emerge in that long sweep which is the second oldest of man's immemorial gestures or acts" (1061). Her sister Marya belongs—like Benjy Compson and Ike Snopes—with Faulkner's feeble-minded characters in whom he seems to take a special interest because they allow him thematically and stylistically to explore the border area between humans and animals. Marya is no Leda, but her scene with the geese is remindful of the erotic and mythic overtones of the Ike and the cow episode in *The Hamlet*:

> They [the geese] surrounded and enclosed her as though with a tender and eager yearning; two of them on either side, kept absolute pace with her, pressed against her skirts, their long undulant necks laid flat against her moving flanks, their heads tilted upward, the hard yellow beaks open slightly like mouths, the hard insentient eyes filmed over as with a sort of ecstasy. (1060)

As in so many texts of the time, *the land*, to which the corporal's family has close ties, is meant as a potential counterworld to the battlefields of the novel. However, Faulkner does not preach a chauvinistic agrarian (*bluboistic*) gospel, as is shown by his insistence that the corporal and his family are immigrants, that they have only a temporary lease of the farm, and that the farm land is scarred by war. Nevertheless the simplicity and naturalness of the Dumonts' life is a counterweight to the mechanistic complexity and artificiality of the military apparatus. That Marya and Marthe's life on the farm is not meant as an idyllic pipe dream is further shown by the visit of two grotesque shadows of war and disaster, the mutilated runner ("not quite like a human being . . . like some kind of giant insect. . . . one furious saffron scar beginning at the ruined homburg hat" [1061]) and the money-obsessed Judas-figure Polchek ("sick, a tall thin cadaver of a man . . . a filthy hat . . . raking feather . . . as though suspended from the ceiling" [1062]). In accordance with Faulkner's effort *to imagine the abstract*, the two characters embody two opposite moral attitudes, the grotesquely mutilated runner, who stands for the indefatigable effort of humans to remain human, and Polchek, who represents human greed that ends in suicidal despair. The juxtaposition of different approaches, the coincidence of opposites and, above all, the inversion of the grand tableaux reflects the ambiguity of such central values as social order and individual freedom in *A Fable* to the very end.

The last scene of the book, the old general's state funeral ("from the Place de la Concorde to the Arch [Arc de Triomphe]" [1068]) confirms this. Father and son have both been awarded public burial places since the corporal, as a consequence of a grotesque accident, rests in the grave of the Unknown Soldier. However, this strange coincidence is symbolic of the more profound coincidence of opposites in the novel: as we have seen, at the end of the temptation scene, father and son express their common belief that "man will not only endure but will prevail" (994). The state funeral taking place in Paris—the phrase "gray and grieving sky" (1069) serves as a local leitmotif—may be read *straight* as glorifying the old French general as savior of western culture and also as an occasion for the solemn self-celebration of France as a nation-state. However, it may also be taken ironically as celebrating the self-sufficient power of the industrial-military complex.

In any case, Faulkner does not allow the old general's funeral to remain the final scene of *A Fable*. Instead, he has the runner and his "indomitable laughter" (1071) interrupt the funeral splendor of the military in a farcical interlude. Caricaturing French nationalism by his British outcry "My country right or wrong. Here is a spot which is forever England" (1071), the runner's rebellious laughter causes a turmoil and the speedy end of the solemn show ("rite and solemnity gone for good now . . . the rest of the cortege huddling without order" [1071]). As a consequence, the runner is badly manhandled by police and outraged French nationalists. But when he regains consciousness, he laughs again at the ring of faces enclosing him: "Tremble. I'm not going to die. Never" (1072). The runner's gesture of defiance is matched by the quartermaster general's gesture of human sympathy and regret.

In the stylized configurations of *A Fable*, Faulkner, thinking metaphorically, *imagining the abstract*, embodies central philosophical conflicts of his time. In the course of it, he lets the quartermaster general, who, after admiring and mythicizing the generalissimo, has come to reject his inhumane military regime, change sides and reorient his values. Cradling the runner in his arms, the quartermaster general assures the book's most impressive champion of "enduring and prevailing" that he is not laughing at him, but weeping at the *comédie humaine*.

NOTES

1. For an overview of Faulkner's treatment of the theme, see my "The Military as Metaphor," *The Faulkner Journal* 2.2 (Spring 1987): 12–22. See also the dissertations of Keen Butterworth, *A Critical and Textual Study of Faulkner's "A Fable"* (Ann Arbor: UMI Research Press, 1983) and Thomas Nordanberg, *Cataclysm as Catalyst: The Theme of War in William Faulkner's Fiction* (Uppsala: Acta Universitatis Upsaliensis, 1983). See also Joseph Urgo, *Faulkner's Apocrypha: "A Fable, Snopes," and the Spirit of Human Rebellion* (Jackson: University Press of Mississippi, 1989), 94–125. For a new and original approach, see Noel Polk, "Woman and the Feminine in *A Fable*," in his *Children of the Dark House: Text and Context in Faulkner* (Jackson: University Press of Mississippi, 1996), 196–218. Quotations from *A Fable* are from *William Faulkner, Novels 1942–1954*, Joseph Blotner and Noel Polk, eds. (New York: Library of America, 1994).

2. For a recent discussion of the problem, see Noel Polk, "The Trouble with Christianity": *Faulkner, Jesus, and the Word Made Flesh* (Marie Fletcher Lecture in American Literature Series, Thibodaux, Louisiana: Nicholls State University, 2000). For a discussion of the several forms and functions of the imagery in *A Fable*, see my "The Imagery in Faulkner's *A Fable*," in *Faulkner: After the Nobel Prize*, ed. Michel Gresset and Kenzaburo Ohashi (Kyoto: Yamaguchi, 1987), 147–71.

3. *The Battleship Potemkin*, 1925; *Alexander Nevsky*, 1938; *Ivan the Terrible*, 1944, 1958.

4. On Faulkner and the tradition of manneristic art, see my "A Masterpiece of Mannerism: On the Style of Faulkner's *Absalom, Absalom!*," in *William Faulkner in Venice*, Rosella Mamoli Zorzi and Pia Masiero Marcolin, eds. (Venice: Marsilio Editori, 2000), 37–53.

5. *The Mansion*, in *William Faulkner, Novels 1957–1962*, Joseph Blotner and Noel Polk, eds. (New York: Library of America, 1999), 589.

6. See my interpretation of this and related scenes in *Faulkner: Masks and Metaphors* (Jackson: University Press of Mississippi, 1997), 151–56.

Scar

Noel Polk

A nation is a community organized for war.
—League of Nations
quoted by Huxley[1]

The least bloody battle of the Civil War occurred at Harrykin Creek, on the Sartoris farm just outside Jefferson, Mississippi, on 28 April 1862, just after the fall of Memphis. According to Bedford Forrest's official written report of this battle, the only victim was Lieutenant P. S. Backhouse.

Perhaps "battle" is too grandiose a name for what actually happened. "Skirmish" might be more apt. Some days earlier, a band of a half dozen Yankee scavengers had shown up to steal the family silver. With all the skill and discipline of a general herself, Granny Rosa Millard, every night almost for the duration of the war, had made the family practice burying the silver in a spot in back of the house, to protect it against such scavenging. All her plans, however, depend on her having sufficient warning of the Yankees' advent to have time to get the heavy chest from its hiding place behind Granny's bed upstairs, to drag it down the stairs and out to the burying spot, and finally put into the ground and covered over. Of course the crisis comes without sufficient warning, as crises always do, and the best they can manage is to get the chest to the outhouse and to have Cousin Melisandre sit on it, draping her large skirt over it. The Yankees, on to this trick, however, have brought with them a huge log pole, carried on braces between their paired and yoked horses. They dismount and, carrying the log, ram the flimsy backhouse, which "explode[s],"[2] and exposes Cousin Melisandre sitting there, screaming. She is of course not doing anything we should not be privy to, but she is humiliated nevertheless—guilt by association, one might say—so that even though Lieutenant Backhouse falls instantly in love with her, she steadfastly refuses to have anything to do with him because of his name—more guilt by association!

The rejected and dejected Lieutenant Backhouse takes out his frustrations on Yankees, adopting Bedford Forrest's own guerila tactics to disrupt Yankee plans throughout the region. He becomes such a loose cannon that even Forrest knows he must be reined in, if only so that he himself can become once again the sole author of chaos for the Yankees. But he can't harness Backhouse's energy until he gets the lieutenant's raging libido under control. Melisandre, however, is adamant: she will not become Mrs. "Backhouse." So Forrest and Granny Millard conspire to have Backhouse killed off, and to replace him with a very similar Lieutenant named Backus. Granny writes out and Forrest signs a citation that notes simultaneously the death in battle of Lieutenant Philip St.-Just Backhouse and the appointment of Philip St.-Just Backus to the rank of Lieutenant. Forrest then tells Granny to get another sheet of paper because he's "got to have a battle." "A battle?" Granny asks. "To give Johnston," he replies. "Confound it, Miss Rosie, can't you understand either that I'm just a fallible mortal man trying to run a military command according to certain fixed and inviolable rules, no matter how foolish the business looks to superior outside folks?" He proposes to call it the "Battle of Sartoris," but Granny refuses, primly: "Not at my house," she says, perhaps for the same reasons Melisandre refuses to be Mrs. Backhouse. The narrator, the young Bayard Sartoris, pipes up to remind them that the only shots during the battle had been fired "down at the creek" (696–97).

The Battle of Harrykin Creek, then, is not purely of whole cloth, but almost. Forrest's insistence on having something written to perpetrate his well-intended and bureaucratically essential fraud, on having a paper to show his general, a bureaucratic paper for the bureaucratic files, reminds me irresistibly of the passage in *A Fable* which describes how the "bizarre convulsion of that military metabolism . . . does everything to a man but lose him, [it] learns nothing and forgets nothing and loses nothing at all whatever and forever—no scrap of paper, no unfinished record or uncompleted memorandum no matter how inconsequential or trivial."[3]

I'm completely charmed with the notion of Bedford Forrest as bureaucrat, a soldier best known for his disregard of traditional rules of warfare, his brilliant and resourceful and usually spontaneous battle tactics that caught his opponents off guard and rendered them vulnerable precisely because they, the Yankees, continued to expect their enemies to play by the traditional rules of combat. That even he, Nathan Bedford Forrest, should be so concerned with rules and regulations of any kind takes us several steps toward what I really want to talk about here. My epigraph holds that the very definition of "nation" is based in its degree of "organization for war," its arrangement of systems for recruiting and distributing soldiers and supplies, of the means to control information, and of hierarchies of authority; each rank, as it exists on the next rung up, positions itself farther and farther from the actual fighting, the eminent danger, so that those at the top are, of course, completely exempt from the grime and sweat and danger of the battlefield.

I want to talk about the structure of that system, the upper part of which feeds upon the bottom parts, the upper part of which, indeed, *requires* the expendability of a certain number of the bottom parts. I want to focus on those at the bottom, *mostly* from the point of view of those who are *not* expendable (or at least who do not consider themselves so), who thrive upon the others' expendability. I am not here, as on other occasions I have been, and will on other occasions continue to be, concerned with the pathologies of the martyr's death wish or the ideological certitude of the super patriot—which makes citizens willing, even eager, to die for a cause: willing to lead the charge across the open field directly into enemy fire, to be the first over the wall, the first up the high bluff, the first out of the landing craft. I am more interested in the workings of the national apparatuses, political and cultural, which create and nurture a national state of mind which will insure that enough young people will be willing to die to promote the nation's purposes, whatever they may be, however they may be redefined from generation to generation, from administration to administration. In so using its expendables, a nation is neither moral nor immoral, not even amoral, no more than digestion or breathing are, but like digestion and breathing simply necessary, and it is sentimental to think otherwise.

In fact, I want to caution us against sentimentality in thinking about such matters, against anger and indignation about the condition of our own fathers and brothers and sisters and children, who are and have ever been the expendables, the mud- and blood-fouled grunts who shoot the rifles, man the barricades, stop the bullet or the shrapnel, and bear the scar that writes the word "grunt" on their bodies. It is easy enough to weep over the body counts, over the coldly, perfectly aligned rows of crosses and the crisply green manicured lawns at cemeteries at Normandy, Vicksburg, and Arlington, and many other such cemeteries, or over the bones in ossuaries at Verdun and, indeed, all over Europe, where lie the bones, the shattered and fragmented chaotically jumbled and desiccated remains of nameless millions who have given their lives for reasons patriotic and religious and personal, for reasons heroic and trivial, virtually since time began; easy enough to weep reading accounts of Civil War battles which ended with the bodies of the dead and the wounded so thick and so entangled that observers could not see the ground for acres around, battles which had to be recessed because bodies, rotting and stinking in the July sun, were piled so high where they fell that the attacking armies could not step over them to advance.

I ask us also not to think patriotically, since patriotism is a peculiarly virulent form of sentimentality, the more virulent because it cannot recognize itself as sentimentality. To put it very unsentimentally, a nation—a community organized for war—very unsentimentally *requires* such "ultimate sacrifices" of its young people, traditionally men, of course, but of women too now, *as a condition of its existence as a nation*, whether the sacrifice is for a nation's aggression or its defense. Whether its cause is just or unjust, no nation can live unless it plans for the slaughter of some of its young. To think sentimentally about this condition of nationality would blunt our edges and so thwart my purposes here, by exciting our anger and cynicism, which would lead to quick and easy condemnations of war and of governments. To think patriotically is to excite us to an equally mindless defense of war and governments, and to be patriotic is in fact to perform our parts in the national script of war, to do what we are told and expected to do. To understand the real monstrousness of war, we must not even think of it as monstrous, if only because that is too damned easy: we must instead focus on the cool bloodless dispassionate and completely unillusioned bureaucratic maneuvers a nation must make to sacrifice its young to whatever ends its leaders discover to be the national interest. Nations use patriotism to blunt our anger and our rage over our losses; it finds the bones and bodies of their dead, brings home what remains it finds, reassembles their shattered parts if possible, builds huge cemeteries and monuments to the gallant dead, and grants us our grief in an orgasm of patriotic weeping. Thus we become a Grateful Nation. We put names on the crosses if we know the names, if enough parts are left to own a name. We even designate one grander monument to honor the *unknown* soldier, the body which stands for all bodies, the unnamed apotheosis of all the named and unnamed lost. So please: we cannot afford to be sentimental here, for sentimentality is the grease that oils the wheels of war. And besides, Steven Spielberg is sentimental enough for us all. *Saving Private Ryan* is a sop to the heroic dead, which never questions—apparently never even notices—the economy of sacrificing a whole platoon of soldiers to save one soldier's life: it's the heroism that counts, the death for something noble—several deaths to save a mother's heart. Saving mama's baby is a good thing: but what of the mothers of those who die that he might live?

Part of any nation's necessary business, then, is to prepare its young to be willing to offer their individual bodies for the common good and, not less necessary, to prepare those who are *not* called upon to die to be willing to offer their fathers and mothers and children and grandchildren and brothers and sisters and cousins to the good of the nation. Nations do this by creating and sustaining by infinite repetition a national narrative, a history that glorifies the sacrifices others have made for us, the unselfish sacrifices of our ancestors, whom we celebrate through daily pledges to flags and the singing of national anthems at sporting and other public events. When such rituals fail to produce the necessary sheep for slaughter, nations resort to conscription, for sheep for slaughter it must have. I do not forget that a nation also demands that its expendables kill and maim the expendables of other nations and trains them to do so, and that promise, the promise of adventure or aggression may motivate considerable numbers to join any military—war is legal murder: we not only give them a license to kill, we insist that they will be heroic in proportion to the numbers they do kill. I am not, however, concerned with the aggressives or the martyrs, but with those good-hearted, patriotic, even gentle apples of their mothers' eyes, who go to battle knowing that there is a very fine chance they will not return at all, or if they return, will do so dismembered. They leave in groups, amid the gaiety and swirl of civic panoply; they return alone, no matter how many they return with.

Few things are more chilling than the willingness of a nation's young to pledge their lives to its Führer, no matter which country he leads, which country he invades, which peoples he defeats, no matter what reasons he gives. Recall the tens of thousands, North and South, who eagerly enlisted during the Civil War, and who marched off to their deaths, the many who returned minus a limb or an eye, or sporting a scar; and the thousands of others during World War I, like Faulkner himself, who longed for war so intensely that they lied about their ages or went to Canada to enlist, and when they did not fight returned with lies, canes, and stories about metal plates in their heads. Or recall Mr. Compson's description of the north Mississippi young marching off to the Civil War:

> fathers and mothers and sisters and kin and sweethearts of those young men—were coming to Oxford from further away than Jefferson—families with food and bedding and servants, to bivouac among the families, the houses, of Oxford itself, to watch the gallant mimic marching and countermarching of the sons and the brothers, drawn all of them, rich and poor, aristocrat and redneck, by what is probably the most moving mass-sight of all human mass-experience, far more so than the spectacle of so many virgins going to be sacrificed to some heathen Principle, some Priapus—the sight of young men, the light quick bones, the bright gallant deluded blood and flesh dressed in a martial glitter of brass and plumes, marching away to a battle.[4]

Why Mr. Compson finds the sacrifice of soldiers more moving than the sacrifice of virgins is a question we should save for another occasion, but the implied comparison is apt because the connection suggests the atavistic nature of the blood sacrifice of war, a practice held over from ancient worlds long after the sacrifice of virgins had been abandoned by most civilizations. *A nation is a community organized for war.*

The Battle of Harrykin Creek, as Forrest and Granny Millard write it, is thus fought by one for the benefit of another; one dies that another might live. The battle report, the history of that battle, is written by a third party for his own purposes—that is, to benefit his nation. That the sacrificer and the sacrificee are one and the same is also to the point, since the cause of the willingness to die in battle is the complete identification of the one with the other, of the dead with the living and the living with the dead. To put it another, more relevant way, the nation's need, the group's, subsumes the needs of the individual. Though bullets or grenades from another nation do the maiming and the killing, it is our own people who put us in front of the wall, blindfolded and ready for the executioner's bullet (and, until recently, gave us free cigarettes to smoke while we waited, at least hoping we would live long enough to smoke enough to repay the investment). We die for those we love, who watch us leave with lumps in their throats if not actual tears in their eyes, who love us even more when we die for them, who are to be sure grieved that we die but happy enough to accept our sacrifice so that they can live and continue to grieve and be grateful and, the nation would say, free. If these words sound vaguely religious, that is by design: little wonder that Faulkner embodied, then disembodied, the full meaning of his *Fable* in the person of a Christ figure in World War I, a figure named Stefan, for Steven the Martyr, but nearly always called "the corporal," to emphasize his body, his flesh-bound corpo-reality, which yields itself passively to and who dies literally for his Father's land, for its and his purposes, for in him father and land unite.

A death is one thing, a scar is another, but closely related. The scar, the stump, are the visible signs of a soldier's brush with annihilation: not so much a badge of courage, as Stephen Crane's Henry Fleming would have it, but rather a marker of chaos, a site where death has tapped him on the shoulder in grim reminder.

A scar has multiple significations. It is a symbol of a rupture and a sign of the rupture's necessity. If it marks a healing in the smooth surface of the skin, it also marks the rupture too and is thus a visible marker of the violence which caused the rupture, and so a sign of the reasons for the violence which caused the rupture which left the scar. A scar is thus a constant, inescapable memento mori, a reminder of flesh's vulnerability, of flesh's all too feeble hold on its own cohesion. Human scars have counterparts in the body of the nation: graves and monuments are scars, too: graves are the essence of the trench: monuments heal them over, anneal the national rupture. A scar is a carapace; tougher and uglier and deader than the flesh it has replaced; monuments, too, no matter how magnificently marbled, are invariably uglier and deader than the flesh they replace and stand for: they signify national resiliency and steadfastness of purpose while proclaiming the nation's vulnerability. War is, in this way, literally written on the bodies of a nation's most expendable citizens. A scar is the sign of the death each owes his country, a flag to which each nation pledges allegiance.

Faulkner's fiction is littered with scars and stumps, the residue of wars. Indeed, at the metaphorical center of *Soldiers' Pay* sits Donald Mahon's vividly undescribed scar across his brow. His scar is the mirror into which all the characters look, seeing themselves in pity and revulsion and even pride; it is a text in which they read their own narratives. The very young Cadet Lowe, like Faulkner—they "stopped the war on him"[5]— with no experience of war, sees it as "dreadful" (SP 21), but longs for it: "To have been him!" he moans. "Just to be him. Let him take this sound body of mine! Let him take it. To have got wings on my breast, to have wings; and to have got his scar, too, I would take death to-morrow. . . . to be him, to have gotten wings, but to have got his scar too!" (SP 45–46). Cecily's younger brother Robert makes a peep show of sorts out of the scar, bringing his buddies by to show off his personal access to the war-scarred hero; but they come and "go away fretted because he [Donald] wouldn't tell them any war stories" (SP 145). Neighbors of Donald's father, the rector, chat about Donald's "scarred, oblivious brow"; former girlfriends come "to look once upon his face, and then quickly aside in hushed nausea, not coming any more unless his face happened to be hidden on the first visit (upon which they finally found opportunity to see it)" (SP 145). Mrs. Powers, herself a war widow, believes that "the man that was wounded is dead and this is another person, a grown child. It's his apathy, his detachment, that's so terrible. He doesn't seem to care where he is or what he does. He must have been passed from hand to hand, like a child" (SP 114). Cecily Saunders, Mahon's fiancée, is frantic, torn between her engagement and her simple revulsion: "How can I [marry him] with that scar? How can I?" (SP 127). "Donald, Donald!" she cries. "I will try to get used to it, I will try! Oh, Donald, Donald! Your poor face! But I will, I will" (SP 133). Donald's father believes that Cecily "is the best medicine he can have," that she can "make a new man of him in a short time" (SP 100–10). Januarius Jones sees "death in his face" (SP 63), and the doctor believes he is "practically a dead man now. More than that, he should have been dead these three months were it not for the fact that he seems to be waiting for something. Something he has begun, but has not completed, something he has carried from his former life that he does not remember consciously. That is his only hold on life that I can see" (SP 150–51).

Other scars and stumps, bodies and disembodiments: Ab Snopes's limp. The German prisoner in "Ad Astra," has a bandage around his head (CS 409) and under it a "high, sick face" (CS 423); a French officer has a "gaunt, tragic face," bearing one glass eye, an eye "motionless, rigid in a face that looked even deader than the spurious eye" (CS 422); even the whole characters feel their flesh separated from their bones (CS 427). In "Crevasse" two of a party of soldiers carry a third whose "head is bound in a bloody rag," who "stumbles his aimless legs along" (CS 465). They pass through a wasteland of "old healed scars of trees" whose leaves are "neither green nor dead" (CS 469). "Pallid grass bayonets saber at their legs" (CS 468) until the grass bayonets become real ones, and the land becomes filled with "chalky knobs thrusting up through the soil" (CS 469–70) which when turned over reveal themselves to be skulls, turning upward their "earth-stained eyesockets and ... unbottomed grin[s]" (CS 470). This soil opens up and they smell an upward explosion of "rotted flesh," then drop into the darkness where other skeletons of soldiers killed by gas await them. Faulkner no doubt had in mind the famous Trench of Bayonets at Verdun, a memorial marking the spot where the earth did in fact cave in on several soldiers, enclosing them in dirt, while leaving their bayonets sticking up straight out of the ground. The narrator of "All the Dead Pilots" has a mechanical leg (CS 512), as the narrator of "The Leg" has a wooden one. Weddel Saucier in "Mountain Victory" is missing an arm. This list speaks nothing of the corpses, broken, decayed, and stinking, among which the drunken detail finds a complete corpse to offer the French nation as the Unknown Soldier. Nor do I forget the fabulous scar that envelopes half of the runner's body in *A Fable*.

Monuments write war, too, as I say, but do so on the home front. The problem with the nation's necessary and ongoing sacrifice of its young to the maw of war is that each missing body or body part leaves a gap, a wound—a grief, a terror—back home, creates a fissure in, a disruption of, local lives, local histories, local emotional economies—fissures that can be healed over only by the ideological soundness, the prevailing moral "rightness" that public monuments to dead soldiers so massively represent: the monumental cultural scar that both conceals the bloody wound and reveals it in glaring marble effigy: the promise that the sacrificial lambs have died in the service of something larger, more magnificent, than any local need, something larger and more important than any mere local grief. A grieving parent or spouse or sibling or child becomes, through the scar, part of the Grateful Nation. *And a nation is a community organized for war.*

Thus division commander Gragnon, in *A Fable*, believes himself to be the "perfect soldier: pastless, unhampered, and complete." He is an orphan, raised in a "Pyrenean orphanage run by a Catholic sisterhood, where there was no record of his parentage whatever, even to be concealed" (AF 684). Though he longs for Mother, for family, he has none to grieve him if he dies or is maimed; that's why he is the perfect soldier: with no Mother, he gives himself to Fatherland. In the same manner, the nameless, faceless, sergeant who feeds the hungry woman in the crowd in the novel's opening scene, thinks of the military as the

> vocation and livelihood to which twenty years ago he had not merely dedicated but relinquished too, not just his life but his bones and flesh . . . relinquishing volition and the fear of hunger and decision to the extent of even being paid a few sure sous a day for the privilege and right, at no other cost than obedience and the exposure and risk of his tender and brittle bones and flesh, of immunity forever for his natural appetites." (AF 674–75)

By resigning themselves to their own expendability, Gragnon and this sergeant have absolved themselves of what the runner calls "that sort of masturbation about the human race people call hoping" (AF 722).

Those who hope—that is, those grunts for whom hope is the only defense against their expendability—become vulnerable to prophets and visionaries such as the runner, who leads them to their deaths. They are also vulnerable to the financial dealings of the foulmouthed cockney groom, the partner of Tooleyman in the horsethief episode. You will recall that he advances the members of his society, the masons, 10 bob, or 120 pence, which they repay at a usurious rate of 6 pence a day or 180 pence a month before they can get another advance. The groom thus gets a 150 percent return on his money, *if* his clients live long enough to repay. Perhaps he is the ultimate cynic, exploiting their need to make the most of each day they have left; but since in fact he is gambling that they will live and they are gambling that they won't, he may be instilling in them that hope the runner despises them for. The groom is thus the only one in the novel who gambles that more soldiers will live than will die; at *worst* his clients get to enjoy their last few days alive with whatever pleasures and satisfactions money can bring.

The farther removed from the citizens and the grunts a soldier is, that is, the higher up the ranking ladder, the more contempt he has for the grunts. That sergeant in the novel's opening pages feels that his dedication to his "vocation and livelihood" places an "insuperable barrier" between him and the masses (AF 674); he gives the hungry woman bread: "Here," he says, "harshly, with that roughness which was not unkindness but just impatience" (AF 763). He helps her to her feet "not roughly, just impatient at the stupidly complicating ineptitude of civilians at all times" (AF672). The runner, made an officer by virtue of his valor in battle, tries to resign his commission because he hates the grunts for being so helpless:

> When I, knowing what I have been, and am now, and will continue to be . . . can, by the simple coincidence of wearing this little badge on my coat, have not

only the power, with a whole militarised government to back me up, to tell vast herds of man what to do, but the impunitive right to shoot him with my own hand when he doesn't do it, then I realise how worthy of any fear and abhorrence and hatred he is. (AF 722)

He claims to despise humanity because it *hopes*, but he despises their odor too; "the stench too, the smell, the soilure, the stink of simple usage: not the dead bones and flesh rotting in the mud, but because the live bones and flesh had used the same mud so long to sleep and eat in" (AF 721). Even so, he wants to be decommissioned and to return to the ranks because he does not want official power, the power of life and death, over them. When he won't shoot himself in the foot—and so inflict his own crippling wound—he arranges to flout the military's rules so flagrantly that the higher-ups bust him back to the ranks. His commanding officer persuades him not to return to the trenches, and he asks to be made a runner, a fluid and mobile and so dehierarchized position which gives him freedom to move horizontally from trench to trench, from battleground to Paris, and vertically up and down the chain of command, from grunt to officer, even to general. He thus refuses to be part of the system that takes the lives of its own young—refuses with impunity, he thinks. It's only the more savagely ironic, then, that he pursues his idealistic goal of peace by murdering three, perhaps five or six guards, including the cockney groom, and causes the deaths of thousands who follow him, unarmed, into that No-Man's-Land, where they are greeted by barrages from both sides, from both nations, enemies, who have teamed together, as they have throughout the novel, to keep the war going.

Division Commander Gragnon, whose division's mutiny initiates the action of *A Fable*, is a Company Man if ever there was one. Unlike the runner, Gragnon actually *insists* on his right, as commander, to pull the trigger on his disobedient troops. He is frustrated by his own superiors' refusal to allow him to, and will himself be murdered by three newly arrived American privates, at the behest and in the pay of his own nation, precisely because he insists that the system's rules must be obeyed. He has not learned, apparently, that a nation is bound by its "rules" only when the rules are useful, and that expedience may well dictate an abrogation or at least a reinterpretation of the rules. All organizations are conservative, and the first thing any organization must conserve is itself, even if it has to break its own rules to do so. Gragnon's conversation with the notorious general, his group commander, known as Mama Bidet, to whom he goes to request permission to shoot his mutinying troops, is instructive about the system's attitude toward the masses.

Mama Bidet has no use for humanity *except* its military uses. For him, for all the officers to some extent, "human being" and "individual" are value-laden terms completely useless, even antithetical, to a community organized for war; individuals have value only when their individual fingers can pull individual triggers, stop individual bullets. Mama Bidet is very clinical about "humanity": he has

> a pitiless preoccupation with man, not as an imperial implement, least of all as that gallant and puny creature bearing undismayed on his frail bones and flesh the vast burden of his long inexplicable incomprehensible tradition and journey, not even in fact as a functioning animal but as a functioning machine in the same sense that the earthworm is: alive purely and simply for the purpose of transporting, without itself actually moving, for the distance of its corporeal length, the medium in which it lives, which, given time, would shift the whole earth that infinitesimal inch, leaving at last its own blind insatiate jaws chewing nothing above the spinning abyss: that cold, scathing, contemptuous preoccupation with body vents and orifices and mucous membrane as though he himself owned neither, who declared that no army was any better than its anus, since even without feet it could still crawl forward and fight. (AF 713)

Gragnon hands his resignation to Bidet, who sets fire to it and drops it, flaming, into his own waste-filled chamberpot, to show his contempt for Gragnon's inability to recognize military reality. Gragnon insists that "there are rules.... Our rules" (AF 715); we must enforce them, he argues, or we—the officers, the military—will die. But Bidet disagrees; we, officers, didn't invent war, he argues, war created us, at mankind's need and behest, its simple inability to behave itself: "From the loins of man's furious ineradicable greed sprang the captains and colonels to his necessity. We are his responsibility," he concludes; "he shall not shirk it." That is, officers, the entire military establishment, emerged as an orderly, systemic response to the chaos which the masses both fear and cause, their "furious ineradicable greed." They thus created us, Mama Bidet argues, and we shall hold them responsible, even though they inevitably let us down on occasion: "They may even stop the wars, as they have done before and will again; ours merely to guard them from the knowledge that it was actually they who accomplished that act. Let the whole vast moil and seethe of man confederate in stopping wars if they wish, so long as we can prevent them learning that they have done so." Breaking the rules won't destroy the system, he says; what *will* destroy it is the "simple effacement from man's memory of a single word." When Gragnon doesn't know which word, Bidet supplies it: "Fatherland." He then concludes, "let them believe that they can stop it, so long as they dont suspect that they have.... Let them believe that tomorrow they will end it; then they wont begin to ponder if perhaps today they can. Tomorrow. And still tomorrow. And again tomorrow. That's the hope you will vest them in" (AF 715–16). He knows that that masturbation called hoping is what keeps the war going.

At a later point in the novel, the old general himself undertakes a deeper, more comprehensive meditation on the hierarchy at the summit of which he sits; though measurably more humane than Mama Bidet's sense of humanity as good for little more than to supply fingers to pull triggers with, the old general is no less certain of the implacability of the national hierarchy, no less certain that the structure is in the nature of things and not constructed, and that it is the only alternative to chaos.

On Wednesday evening at sunset, he takes a moment standing at the open window of his quarters to contemplate the two different crowds below. The first is the crowd of civilians gathered in the *Place de Ville*, awaiting the verdict to be given about their relatives in the mutinous regiment. They hate the corporal because he has led their soldier-kin to forsake their lives in advance of victory or defeat in order to stop the war; they do not realize that their own nationalism, their commitment to Fatherland, has already pledged those deaths; being nationalistic, of course, being a community organized for war, they can think only in the binary terms of victory and defeat, submission and dominance, of being Number One or the national humiliation of being anything less than Number One, not of compromise or, more simply, of peace, of peaceful coexistence with enemies or inferiors or just plain Otherness. Their hatred and fear of the corporal is all the more bitter because he is an alien, a foreigner, and so unknown, an other, and necessarily antagonistic to the national good. As Keen Butterworth long ago showed,[6] these folks are constrained by those structures of civilization symbolized by the walls of the ancient walled city of Chaulnesmont, which give them shape, even if only the constantly malleable shape of water, to which they are frequently compared. That is, the city's shape gives the crowd what shape and coherence it has; when once they follow the lorries carrying the prisoners out of the city, they lose their coherence and dissipate out into the plain.

The other crowd the old general contemplates is that one formed by the jailed mutineers, the three thousand. Like the civilians, they too seek coherence in the old forms: released into the open yard of the abandoned factory where they are being held, they

> coalesce without command into the old sheeplike molds of platoons and companies.... [They] shuffle and grope for the old familiar alignments, blinking a little after the dark barracks, in the glare of sunset. Then it began to move. There were no commands from anywhere; the squads and sections simply fell in between the old file-markers and -closers and began to flow, drift as though by some gentle and even unheeded gravitation, into companies in the barracks streets, into battalions onto the parade ground, and stopped. It was not a regiment yet but rather a shapeless mass in which only the squads and platoons had any unity, as the coherence of an evicted city obtains only in the household

groups which stick together not because the members are kin in blood but because they have eaten together and slept together and grieved and hoped and fought among themselves so long. . . . (AF 873)

As the old general contemplates these two faceless, nameless, voiceless, shapeless masses of humanity from his second-storey window, watching the three allied national flags furl and listening to the three allied national bugles blow colors simultaneously, together but in discord, he meditates on these people's relationship to the civilization at whose apex he stands. The meditation is actually, finally, about *their*, the mass's, capacity to endure, but "endurance" in his thinking is barely a step or two above vegetating, if that far; the city, the nation, the civilization, is "immune to man's enduring," he thinks. It doesn't have to care if any individual survives or not, for there will always be billions more. His confidence lies in the city itself, one of the central structures and symbols of his nation. He notes that the city of Chaulnesmont, at evening, is

> already immune to man's enduring, was even now free of his tumult. Or rather, the evening effaced not man from the *Place de Ville* so much as it effaced the *Place de Ville* back into man's enduring anguish and his invincible dust, the city itself not really free of either [the anguish or the dust] but simply taller than both. Because they endured, as only endurance can, firmer than rock, more invincible than folly, longer than grief, the darkling and silent city rising out of the darkling and empty twilight to lower like a tumescent thunderclap, since it was the effigy and the power, rising tier on inviolate tier out of that mazed chiaroscuro like a tremendous beehive whose crown challenged by day the sun and stemmed aside by night the celestial smore. (AF 887)

"First and topmost," at the apex of civilization's hierarchy, the old general muses, are such as himself: "the three flags and the three supreme generals who served them: a triumvirate consecrated and anointed, a constellation remote as planets in their immutability, powerful as archbishops in their trinity, splendid as cardinals in their retinues and myriad as Brahmins in their blind followers" (AF 887). First, indeed, are the three flags, the symbols of the nations, the immutable signs of their immutable ideological values, their national narratives and their national cohesion, standing first, above and apart from the generals themselves, but identified with them and, indeed, investing them with their power. The generals are "a triumvirate consecrated and anointed." The general does not bother to ask *by whom* he has been consecrated and anointed; we can only wonder whether he even thinks of these terms as problematic—terms usually reserved for popes and kings—or whether he questions his fitness to be the Big Boss Man. Perhaps he does, since we know that for the first many years after his graduation at the top of his class at St. Cyr, the French West Point, he did everything he could to escape his "doom"; he volunteered for a post in the deepest of Saharan Africa, then retreated, in escape, to the high Himalayas, where he fathered the corporal, who has returned to him as surely as the repressed, and whose life and death he now holds immediately in his hand—has, in effect, so held it since the day he, the general, was born, and in more ways than one. It simply may not occur to him to wonder the *why* of his placement, but he finally accepts it as his birthright, his fate, since he is, as he tells his corporeal corporal son, the scion of one of the wealthiest and most powerful families in Europe: he was "born heir to that power as it stood then," holding that "inheritance in escrow to become unchallenged and unchallengeable chief of that confederation" (AF 989). He is, as Faulkner describes Flem Snopes in *The Mansion*, "a pillar, rock-fixed, of things as they are."[7]

Next in the hierarchy, just under him, are the

> three thousand lesser generals who were [the three supreme generals'] deacons and priests and the hierarchate of their households, their acolytes and bearers of monstrance and host and censer: the colonels and majors who were in charge of the portfolios and maps and memoranda, the captains and subalterns who were in charge of the communications and errands which kept the portfolios and maps up to date, and the sergeants and corporals who actually carried the portfolios and mapcases and protected them with their lives and answered the telephone and ran the errands, and the privates who sat at the flickering switchboards at two and three and four oclock in the morning and rode the motorcycles in the rain and snow and drove the starred and pennoned cars and cooked the food for the generals and colonels and majors and captains and subalterns and made their beds and shaved them and cut their hair and polished their boots and brass.... (AF 887–88)

Because of the mutiny, Chaulnesmont is now so crowded with generals "of high rank" that there develop ranks within the ranks of officers, at the bottom of which are the wounded: the outcasts and untouchables: the

> men who had actually been in, come out of, the battle zone, as high in rank as majors and even colonels sometimes, strayed into the glittering and gunless city through nobody knew what bizarre convulsion of that military metabolism...; a few of them were always there, not many but enough: platoon or section leaders and company commanders and battalion seconds stained with the filth of front lines who amid that thronged pomp and glitter of stars and crossed batons and braid and brass and scarlet tabs moved diffident and bewildered and ignored with the lost air of oafish peasants smelling of field and stable summoned to the castle, the Great House, for an accounting or a punishment: a wounded man armless legless or eyeless was stared at with the same aghast distasteful refusive pity and shock and outrage as a man in an epileptic seizure at high noon on a busy downtown corner. (AF 888)

Not only is the military rigidly organized: civilian structures parallel and support the military's, in lockstep with it, with mutual goals, and, like the military, operating always in its own best interests:

> Antipas his friends and their friends, merchant and prince and bishop, administrator and clacquer and absolver to ministrate the attempt and applaud the intention and absolve the failed result, and all the nephews and godsons of Tiberius in far Rome and their friends and the friends of the wives and husbands of their friends come to dine with the generals and sell to the generals' governments the shells and guns and aircraft and beef and shoes for the generals to expend against the enemy ... mayor and burgher, doctor attorney director inspector and judge who held no particular letter from Tiberius in Rome yet whose contacts were still among generals and colonels and not captains and subalterns.... (AF 888–89)

The list goes on until it reaches the least of these their brethren, the people of the city, the lowest rung of civilization's people, the bees, the workers, that teeming class who supply the soldiers who fight the wars that keep the structure in place, the point toward which the old general's powerful meditation has been aiming:

> and last even anonymity's absolute whose nameless faceless mass cluttered old Jerusalem and old Rome too while from time to time governor and caesar flung them bread or a circus as in the old snowy pantomime the fleeing shepherd casts back to the pursuing wolves fragments of his lunch, a garment, and as a last resort the lamb itself—the laborers who owned today only the spending of what they earned yesterday, the beggars and thieves who did not always understand that what they did was beggary and theft, the lepers beneath city gate and temple door who did not even know they were not whole, who belonged neither to the military nor to the merchants and princes and bishops, who neither derived nor hoped for any benefit from army contracts nor battened by simply existing, breathing coeval with the prodigality and waste concomitant with a nation's mortal agony, that strange and constant few who each time are denied any opportunity whatever to share in the rich carnival of their country's wasting lifeblood, whose luck is out always with no kin nor friends who have kin or friends who have powerful kin or friends or patrons....

He thinks of those

> who owned nothing in fact save a reversion in endurance without hope of betterment nor any spur of pride—a capacity for endurance which even after four years of existence as tolerated and rightless aliens on their own land and in their own city still enabled them without hope or pride even in the endurance to endure, asking or expecting no more than permission to exercise it, like a sort of immortality. (AF 889–90)

These "tolerated and rightless aliens . . . in their own city" have, the old general knows, no shape or coherence other than that he gives them, as he will claim in his dialogue with the corporal and demonstrate when he orders the corporal's execution. Doubtless he is thinking of these "tolerated and rightless aliens" when toward the end of that dialogue with the corporal, he foresees the day when wars will be fought not by people at all but by machines—tanks—in which case a nation, a community organized for war, would have nothing to do with its billions and billions of constantly reproducing individual human beings. The conclusion is thus inescapable that one of the reasons for war is to prevent the burden of overpopulation.

And then, ratcheting his meditation's intensity up a notch or two, the old general articulates a considerably more poetic version, a magnificent version, of Mama Bidet's belief that humanity had created the military, had created the city, had created the church, the inextricably interlocked principal structures of civilization which converge here in the general's powerful imaging:

> Out of that enduring and anguished dust [the people, the city] rose, out of the dark Gothic dream, carrying the Gothic dream, arch- and buttress-winged, by knight and bishop, angels and saints and cherubim groined and pilastered upward into soaring spire and pinnacle where goblin and demon, gryphon and gargoyle and hermaphrodite yelped in icy soundless stone against the fading zenith. (AF 890)

Division Commander Gragnon works through a related sort of system, though his is the horizontal one of history, not, like the old general's vertical one of hierarchy and privilege. But these two systems are intimately related in ways that demonstrate the relationship between history and the structure of a community perpetually organized and organizing for war. Gragnon stands before the three supreme generals to make his case for executing the mutinying regiment, which is simply that the rules demand that he do so. Having been turned down at the lower levels, he knows that his appeal to this ultimate triumvirate will fail, too, and he plans to commit suicide when they refuse him. He understands the system's needs, however, and so knows that they will not permit him a suicide, will not permit him that much control over his own life, especially if that life can be useful; he knows that they will in fact execute him and, for the nation's purposes, advertise his death as a heroic one, a glorious death in battle. He delivers the speech to the three top generals, a speech arguing the efficacy, the necessity, of the rules. Faulkner blanks out the actual speech, however, since it is essentially the same one he gave to Mama Bidet, in favor of Gragnon's thought while he delivers it; his meditation is thus a counter-narrative to the speech. He knows that both the speech and his need to give it are "much older than that moment two days ago in the observation post when he discovered that he was going to have to make it. Its conception"—that is, his acceptance of the principle that orders must be obeyed—"was the moment he found he was to be posted to officers' school, its birth the day he received the commission, so that it had become, along with the pistol and sabre and the sublieutenant's badges, a part of the equipment with which he would follow and serve his destiny with his life as long as life lasted." The speech, he knows, is deadly, and in fact he connects the speech to the bullet with which, out of honor to his profession, he plans to take his life. The bullet is the speech's

> analogous coeval . . . that one of the live cartridges constant through the pistol's revolving cylinder, against the moment when he would discharge the voluntary lien he had given on his honor by expiating what a civilian would call bad luck and only a soldier disgrace, the—any—bad luck in it being merely this moment now, when the need compelled the speech yet at the same time denied the bullet. In fact, it seemed to him now that the two of them, speech and bullet, were analogous and coeval even in more than birth: analogous in the very incongruity of the origins from which they moved, not even shaped yet, toward their mutual end [i.e., his death on principle]:—a lump of dross exhumed from the earth and become, under heat, brass, and under fierce and cunning pressure, a cartridge case; from a laboratory, a pinch, a spoonful, a dust, precipitate of earth's and air's primordial motion, the two condensed and combined behind a tiny locked grooved slug and all micrometered to a servant breech and bore not even within its cognizance yet, like a footman engaged from an employment agency over the telephone. (AF 879–80).

The analogy with the bullet connects national history with his personal history, he now understands, as a designated sacrifice for his country.

But Gragnon's meditation doesn't stop there. Bullet and speech are both part of a design much grander, larger, more terrifying:

> half Europe went to war with the other half and finally succeeded in dragging half the western hemisphere along: a plan, a design vast in scope, exalted in conception, in implication (and hope) terrifying, not even conceived here at Grand Headquarters by the three old generals and their trained experts and advisers in orderly conference, but conceived out of the mutual rage and fear of the three ocean-dividing nations themselves, simultaneously at Washington and London and Paris by some immaculate pollenization like earth's simultaneous leafage, and come to birth at a council not even held at Grand Headquarters but behind locked and guarded doors in the Quai d'Orsay—a council where trained military experts, dedicated as irrevocably to war as nuns are married to God, were outnumbered by those who were not only not trained for war, they were not even braided and panoplied for it—

He means the civilians, the politicians and bankers and merchants who drive the military:

> the Prime Ministers and Premiers and Secretaries, the cabinet members and senators and chancellors; and those who outnumbered even them; the board chairmen of the vast establishments which produced the munitions and shoes and tinned foods, and the modest unsung omnipotent ones who were the priests of simple money; and the others still who outnumbered even these: the politicians, the lobbyists, the owners and publishers of newspapers and the ordained ministers of churches, and all the other accredited travelling representatives of the vast solvent organizations and fraternities and movements which control by coercion or cajolery man's morals and actions and all his mass-value for affirmation. (AF 880–81)

Gragnon's vision of the structure of civilization is far more complex, far more demonic, at any rate, than the old general's. Whereas the old general and Mama Bidet, beneficiaries of the system, believe the human moil, the sheep, the bees, have created the military, Gragnon understands that the powerful establishment figures of church, state, and opinion have combined in deviously intricate ways to serve themselves at the expense of the grunts and such as he who must die that they might live not just more abundantly but very abundantly indeed. Gragnon thinks of

> all that vast powerful terror-inspiring representation which, running all democracy's affairs in peace, come indeed into their own in war, finding their true apotheosis then, in iron conclave now decreeing for half the earth a design vast in its intention to demolish a frontier, and vaster still in its furious intent to obliterate a people; all in conclave so single that the old gray inscrutable supreme general with the face of one who long ago had won the right to believe in nothing whatever save man's deathless folly, didn't need to vote at all but simply to preside, and so presiding, contemplated the plan's birth and then watched it, not even needing to control it as it took its ordained undeviable course, descending from nations confederated to nations selected, to forces to army groups to armies to corps; all that gigantic long complex chronicle, at the end reduced to a simple regimental attack against a simple elevation of earth too small to show on a map, known only to its own neighborhood and even that by a number and a nickname dating back less than four years to the moment when someone had realised that you could see perhaps a quarter-mile further from its summit than its foot. (AF 881)

The old general envisions civilization as a pyramid, with him and the other military leaders at the top and the teeming sheeplike masses at the bottom, creating together a structure with the strength and durability and majesty of a Gothic Cathedral. Gragnon sees an inverted pyramid, the old general's turned upside down and depending for its very existence, survival, on the strength of its smallest unit, the human individual, on whose back the pyramid's upturned point rests, and he believes that the structure therefore is as fragile as an eggshell—*unless* the individuals, alone or in groups, abide by the laws which keep the fragile structure in place.

Gragnon and the old general at least agree on this: a community cannot organize itself for war without the willingness of its expendable citizens to die for it or to give up its young: a community organized for war must write its wars with and on the flesh of its young. The individual who refuses to die or at least who refuses to die for culturally sanctioned reasons thus confounds the system, clogs it up so that it must huff and puff, readjust its methods and its own laws, evict or co-opt the foreign, refusive body, so that it can function smoothly again, be a community organized for war again. Rejected by the nation whose laws he had faithfully served, Gragnon too becomes, or at least threatens to become, a clog in that smooth functioning. But one has only to consider the chaos that would follow if *all* human beings refused to play their class-determined role; civilization depends on order, so it must insist that the vast majority obey all the rules, give up their individuality—even that individuality that Faulkner spoke of so often in his public statements in the fifties—so that they—we—can all live reasonably in an orderly world.

The generals co-opt Gragnon by executing him, for their own purposes: they plan to have him shot full in the face and then to advertise his death as a glorious heroic one. According to the war they will write, he will have died a hero, in the name and for the glory of France. To his credit, however, Gragnon resists his executioners' clumsy methods and twists his head away just as the gun goes off, so that the bullet hits him behind the ear instead of in the face (AF 1019); the executioners repair the damage with wax from a candle they are looking for when the scene ends. He thus fights his own Battle of Harrykin Creek, though this time the battle is very bloody indeed.

Thus Gragnon becomes my hero in this novel, a fact I didn't realize until the moment I wrote the previous paragraph. Unlike Levine, who commits suicide because his nation betrays his high patriotic idealism, Gragnon, equally betrayed by his country, disengages himself from the nation, refuses to be used as its hero, as the poor corporal is to be used. He, Gragnon, is also more heroic than the idealistic runner if only because his own sacrifice doesn't require the lives of *any* soldier. He and the runner essentially trade ideological positions as regards the value of the rules, the value of the lives of the grunts. That is, Gragnon begins by wanting to follow the rule that says he can execute his disobedient troops; the runner doesn't want that responsibility, so he defaults from his position as officer to his position as runner. But in his eagerness to save humankind from war, he is more than willing both to personally kill three or more guards, and to sacrifice the lives almost literally of every soldier who will follow him. Indeed, all he needs to do is to provide the sign, he thinks—the Masonic sign which he gets from the cockney groom and from Tooleyman—to get all soldiers to embrace in the middle of No-Man's-Land and just refuse to fight. And he is willing to sacrifice them all to that end. Unlike Gragnon, who imagines a single bullet predestined for him alone, the runner constructs a system which will fail precisely because he thinks that there simply aren't enough officers or bullets to execute an entire army of mutineers, envisioning with a sort of grim, sardonic glee, a parody of Gragnon's and the old general's systems, his own a fantastic system which would simply wear itself out trying to execute all the guilty peaceniks:

> it would not matter whether Authority knew about it or not, since even ruthless and all-powerful and unchallengeable Authority would be impotent before that massed unresisting undemanding passivity. He thought: *They could execute only so many of us before they will have worn out the last rifle and pistol and expended the last live shell*, visualizing it: first, the anonymous fringe of subalterns and junior clerks to which he had once belonged, relegated to the lathes and wheels to keep them in motion rifling barrels and filling shell-cases; then, the frenzy and the terror mounting, the next layer: the captains and majors and secretaries and attachés with their martial harness and ribbons and striped trousers and briefcases among the oilcans and the flying shafts; then the field officers: colonels and senators and members; then, last and ultimate, the ambassadors and ministers and lesser generals themselves frantic and inept among the slowing wheels and melting bearings, while the old men, the last handful of kings and presidents and field marshals and spoiled-beef and shoe-peg barons, their backs to the last crumbling rampart of their real, their credible, their believable world, wearied, spent, not with blood-glut at all but with the eye-strain of aiming and the muscle-tension of pointing and the finger-cramp of squeezing, fired the last puny scattered and markless fusillade as into the face of the sea itself. (AF 728)

There are simply *too many* such citizens to be controlled if they refuse to obey orders. But their refusal can only be effective against the system if they act as a group. Thus the runner would have them refuse to be one group, subservient to the state, only to become another group, subservient to the high idealism of his own leadership and the sign of authority that he offers them.

The runner led them, wrongly following the "sign" he wrongly gives them, into the middle of No-Man's-Land, where they are bombarded from both sides. We don't in fact know how many of them are killed or injured; we know only that the runner himself receives his own scar, in a "soundless rush of flame which enveloped half his body neatly from heel through navel through chin" (AF 964), creating the "vermilion" scar that is so terrible and so symbolic.

A *Fable* ends as it began, in a crowd scene. This one, though, is some years after the war's end, in Paris, and the Grateful Nation honors the old general at his death by his burial at the Arc de Triomphe, along with the body of the unknown soldier whom we know to be the body of his son, whom he, like other parents in a Grateful Nation, sacrificed to the national good. That is, when he orders his son's execution, he does no more than other fathers and mothers do who think *dulce et decorum est pro patria mori*. Their burial here, together, is a continuation of the dialogue begun that evening before the corporal's execution, the always ongoing dialogue between the one and the many, the specific body of the individual and the abstract body of the state; between a system which insists and the body, the corporeality the system insists upon, whose death, whose scars, are essential to the nation's life.

The runner disrupts this solemn occasion. He is now "not a man but a mobile and upright scar, on crutches, he had one arm and one leg, one entire side of his hatless head was one hairless eyeless and earless sear, he wore a filthy dinner jacket from the left breast of which depended on their barber-pole ribbons a British Military Cross and Distinguished Conduct Medal, and a French *Médaille Militaire*" (AF 1070). His medals for bravery hang ironically on his tattered coat and body, but give him passage through the crowd to the center, where he rips the medals off his coat and flings them at the caisson on which the old general's body lies, shouting at him the clichés of nationalism, of Fatherland, of patriotism, which had gotten the nation into and then out of the war: "You too helped carry the torch of man into that twilight where he shall be no more; these are his epitaphs: They shall not pass. My country right or wrong. Here is a spot which is forever England—" (AF 1071). The crowd, the police, finally grab him to shut him up. The walking scar, the ugly national wound and symbol of all their pain and anguish, which they all want to forget, is thus cast off out of sight, thrown literally into the gutter, its bearer untouchable because he reminds them that wars are dirty, ugly affairs fought not by generals in their safe clean headquarters or by Führers in Berchtesgadens or Presidents in Oval Offices, but by the corporealities of their own individual families, the vulnerable issue of their own flesh, and they cannot afford to let themselves think of that now that this war is over, now that this pain is gone.

The marble Arc de Triomphe accepts the bodies of the general and the corporal, father and son, conservative and anarchist, have and have not. The marble arch, declaring triumph, stands solemn there at ground zero of Western Civilization, presiding solid powerful and profound, absorbing and returning the adoration from the proud throbbing hearts and glistening eyes of the Grateful Nation, a community, still and always, organized for war.

NOTES

1. Aldous Huxley, *An Encyclopaedia of Pacifism* (London: Chatto & Windus, 1937), 76.
2. William Faulkner, "My Grandmother Millard and General Bedford Forrest and the Battle of Harrykin Creek," *Collected Stories of William Faulkner* (New York: Random House, 1950), 667. Other stories in this volume hereafter cited in the text as CS.
3. William Faulkner, *A Fable*, in Joseph Blotner and Noel Polk, eds., *William Faulkner: Novels 1942–1954* (New York: Library of America, 1994), 888. Hereafter cited in the text as AF.
4. William Faulkner, *Absalom, Absalom!: The Corrected Text* (New York: Random House, 1986), 97. Hereafter cited in the text as AA.
5. William Faulkner, *Soldiers' Pay* (New York: Boni & Liveright, 1926), 3. Hereafter cited in the text as SP.
6. Keen Butterworth, *A Critical and Textual Study of Faulkner's "A Fable"* (Ann Arbor, Mich.: UMI Research Press, 1983).
7. William Faulkner, *The Mansion*, in Joseph Blotner and Noel Polk, eds., *William Faulkner Novels 1957–1962* (New York: Library of America, 1999), 530.

Contributors

Don H. Doyle, professor of History at Vanderbilt University, is the author of five books, including *New Men, New Cities, New South: Atlanta, Nashville, Charleston, Mobile, 1860–1910* and, most recently, *Faulkner's County: The Historical Roots of Yoknapatawpha, 1540–1962*. His study *Nations Divided: American Nationalism and Separatism in Comparative Perspective* was published by the University of Georgia Press in 2002.

Lothar Hönnighausen is director of the North American Program at the University of Bonn and author or editor of six volumes of literary criticism, including *William Faulkner: The Art of Stylization* and, most recently, *William Faulkner: Masks and Metaphors*.

John Limon is professor of English and American Studies at Williams College. He is the author of three volumes: *The Place of Fiction in the Time of Science: A Disciplinary History of American Writing*, *Writing after War: American War Fiction from Realism to Postmodernism*, and, most recently, *Stand-Up Comedy in Theory, Or, Abjection in America*.

John Lowe, professor of English at Louisiana State University, is the author of over fifty essays, the bulk of them on Southern literature and culture. He has also written the volume *Jump at the Sun: Zora Neale Hurston's Cosmic Comedy*, edited *Conversations with Ernest Gaines* and *Redefining Southern Culture*, and coedited *The Future of Southern Letters*.

David Madden is founding director of the United States Civil War Center and Donald and Velvia Crumbley Professor of Creative Writing at Louisiana State University. He is the author of over a dozen works of fiction and criticism, including *The Suicide's Wife*; two of his novels have been nominated for the Pulitzer Prize. His new novel, *London Bridge Is Falling Down*, is set in London in 1666 in plague and fire.

Paula Elyseu Mesquita teaches Portuguese in the Department of Hispanic Studies, University of Birmingham, UK. She is also a Ph.D. candidate in the Program in American Studies at the University of Coimbra, Portugal. The title of her doctoral dissertation is "William Faulkner, Willa Cather, and Modernity."

Noel Polk, professor of English at the University of Southern Mississippi, is the author or editor of over a dozen volumes, including, most recently, *Outside the Southern Myth*, *Children of the Dark House*, *Eudora Welty: A Bibliography of Her Work*, and *Reading Faulkner*: The Sound and the Fury.

James G. Watson is professor of English and former department chair at the University of Tulsa. He has written three books on Faulkner, most recently, *William Faulkner, Self-Presentation and Performance*, and is the editor of a collection of Faulkner letters, *Thinking of Home: William Faulkner's Letters to His Mother and Father, 1918–1925*.

Index

Absalom, Absalom! (Faulkner), 29–30, 55–68, 71–72, 102–18
"Ad Astra" (Faulkner), viii–x, 28, 95, 120, 144
Adams, Timothy Dow, 78–79
Adler, Alfred, 84
Aldington, Richard, 41
All Quiet on the Western Front (Remarque), 41, 121
"All the Dead Pilots" (Faulkner), viii–ix, 45, 86, 91
American Boy, 77
Ames, Dalton, 30–32
Anderson, Sherwood, 21, 81
As I Lay Dying (Faulkner), 29, 36–49, 52–53, 71

Baird, Helen, 22, 80
Barr, Caroline, 4, 77, 97
Barthes, Roland, 98
Beauchamp, Terrel (Tomey's Turl), 73, 93
Benbow, Horace, 104
Benbow, Narcissa, 46–47
Berlin, Irving, 94
Bidet, Mama, 147–49, 153, 155
Black Reconstruction (Du Bois), 5
Blight, David, 17
Bloom, Harold, 50
Blotner, Joseph, 78
Bon, Charles, 72, 99, 105–7, 114–15
Borges, Jorge Luis, 38
Born to Rebel: Birth Order, Family Dynamics, and Creative Lives (Sulloway), 83, 85
Boyd, Thomas, 27
Broderick, Carlfred B., 84
Bronte, Charlotte, 107
Brooks, Cleanth, 118–19
Brown, Maud Morrow, 4
Bundren, Addie, 37–38, 41–45, 49, 53
Bundren, Anse, 42–43
Bundren, Cash, 38, 39
Bundren, Darl, 36–39, 49

Bundren, Dewey Dell, 41–42, 49
Bundren, Jewel, 38–39
Butler, Burlina, 14–15

Camus, Albert, 116–17
Caspey, 92–93
Catch-22 (Heller), 121
Cather, Willa, 94
Clytemnestra (Clytie), 56, 58, 63–68, 112
Cofield, J. R., 59–60
Coldfield, Rosa, 56–67, 106–7, 111–13, 116–17
Cole, Arthur, 4–5
Colonel Dick, 7
Compson, Benjy (Benjamin), 104
Compson, Caddy, 104, 115–16
Compson, General Jason Lycurgus, II, 106, 112, 142
Compson, Jason Lycurgus, III, 55, 106–7, 112
Compson, Quentin, 30, 62, 102–18
Cowley, Malcolm, 23, 83
Crane, Stephen, 102, 143
"Crevasse" (Faulkner), 41, 93, 120, 145
Curtis, Susan, 77

Darwin, Charles, 83–84
Death of a Hero (Aldington), 41
Dos Passos, John, 94, 122
Douglas, Mary, 40–41
"Dry September" (Faulkner), 29
Du Bois, W. E. B., 5
Dumont, Marthe and Marya, 135–36

Eisenstein, Sergei, 122
Ekstein, Modris, 36, 50
Eliot, T. S., 88, 89, 120
"Evangeline" (Faulkner), 109

Fable, A (Faulkner), vii–viii, 25, 53, 120–37, 143, 145–58
Falkner, Dean Swift, 72, 75–77, 85–86, 90
Falkner, J. W. T., III (John), 71–78, 81–83, 88, 91, 96, 98

Index

Falkner, John Wesley Thompson (Young Colonel), 20, 76–77
Falkner, Maud Butler, 21, 23, 73, 83, 96
Falkner, Murry Charles, Jr. (Jack), 22, 26–27, 71–78, 80–81, 85–88, 98
Falkner, Sally Murry, 16
Falkner, William C. (Old Colonel), 4, 12, 76, 82, 90, 97
Faulkner, Estelle Oldham, 26, 78, 81, 88
Faulkner, Jill, 81, 91
Faulkner, Jimmy, 22, 81–83, 86, 91, 98–99
Faulkner, William: on Civil War, 4; as historian, 4; on his own war record, 22–23
Fitzgerald, F. Scott, 49–50
Flags in the Dust (Faulkner), 45–48, 53, 57, 71, 89–93, 97, 120
Forrest, Nathan Bedford, 14, 138–39, 142
Fowler, Doreen, 84, 96
Freud, Sigmund, 84–85
Frye, Northrup, 97
Fussell, Paul, 22–23, 39, 43

Go Down, Moses (Faulkner), 73, 92–93
Gone with the Wind (Mitchell), 5, 16
Gragnon, General, 123, 125, 127, 130, 134, 145–57
Grant, Ulysses S., 8
Gray, Richard, 84
Great Gatsby, The (Fitzgerald), 49
Great War and Modern Memory, The (Fussell), 22–23, 39
Green Bough, A (Faulkner), 29
Gresset, Michel, 88

Hamlet, The (Faulkner), 129, 135
Hart, Liddell, 48
Hawk, Drusilla, 11
Hawks, Howard, 29
Heart Is a Lonely Hunter, The (McCullers), 103
Heller, Joseph, 121
Hemingway, Ernest, 43, 88, 94, 98, 102, 123–24, 129
"Home" (Faulkner), 21
Homer, 48, 50–51

If I forget thee, Jerusalem (Faulkner), 128
Illiad, The (Homer), 48, 50–51
Irrepressible Conflict, The (Cole), 4–5

Irving, Washington, 50
Irwin, John, 103
It Can't Happen Here (Lewis), 132

James, Henry, 110
James, William, 52
Jameson, Frederic, 76
Jane Eyre (Bronte), 107
Johnson, Samuel, 129
Jones, Januarius, 46–47, 88, 144
Jones, Wash, 112–15
Joyce, James, 121

Keats, John, 117–18
Keegan, John, and Richard Holmes, 51

"Landing in Luck" (Faulkner), 26
Leed, Eric, 40–41, 44
Lewis, Sinclair, 132
Lie Down in Darkness (Styron), 103
Light in August (Faulkner), 29
"Lilacs" (Faulkner), 22, 26
Lincoln, Abraham, 6
Loosh, 7, 9
Lowe, Julian, 26, 77, 86–88, 144

Mahon, Donald, 26, 45–46, 77, 86–88, 120, 144
Mailer, Norman, 121
Mann, Thomas, 121–22
Mansion, The (Faulkner), 130, 151
Marble Faun, The (Faulkner), 26
May, Rollo, 116
McCannon, Shreve, 107–14
McCullers, Carson, 103
Millard, Granny, 7–9, 11–12, 138–39, 142
Miller, Douglas, 3
Millgate, Michael, 20
"Mississippi" (Faulkner), 31
Mitchell, Margaret, 5
Moral Equivalent of War, The (James), 52
Mosquitoes (Faulkner), 21, 81, 89
My Brother Bill (John Falkner), 73–75
Murry, Dr. John Y., 76–77

Naked and the Dead, The (Mailer), 121
Natural, The (Malamud), 50
No Man's Land (Leed), 40

Old General, 132–34, 136, 149–50, 153, 155–56

Page, Thomas Nelson, 73
Plato, 134
Poe, Edgar Allan, 118
Polk, Noel, 84, 103
Portable Faulkner, The (Cowley), 23
Pylon (Faulkner), 29, 82

Race and Reunion (Blight), 17
R.A.F., 20–21, 23–26, 78–79, 86
Railey, Kevin, 76
Red Badge of Courage, The (Crane), 102, 143
Reich, Wilhelm, 44
Remarque, Erich Maria, 41, 121
Ringo, 7, 11, 93
"Rip Van Winkle" (Irving), 50
Rites of Spring (Ekstein), 36
Roosevelt, Franklin D., 130
"Rose for Emily, A" (Faulkner), 104
Rowan Oak, 82

Sanctuary (Faulkner), 29
Sartoris (Faulkner), 29, 31
Sartoris, Bayard, 7, 10, 45–48, 89–93, 95, 97, 120
Sartoris, Bayard (Old), 47–48, 89–93
Sartoris, John, 47–48, 86, 89, 91–94, 97
Sartoris, Virginia (Aunt Jenny), 46, 57, 89–90, 120
Saunders, Cecily, 26–27
Saving Private Ryan (Spielberg), 141
Scarry, Elaine, 52–53
Schoenburg, Elaine, 103
Scott, Sir Walter, 106
Sherman, William Tecumseh, 7–8
Shreve. *See* McCannon, Shreve
Sigma Alpha Epsilon, 80
Slavery in Mississippi (Sydnor), 5
Smith, General Andrew Jackson, 14–15
Snopes, Flem, 151
Snopes, Ike, 135
Snopes, Mink, 130

Soldier's Pay (Faulkner), 21–22, 26–27, 45, 77, 81, 86–89, 94, 120, 144
Sound and the Fury, The (Faulkner), 30–32, 41–42, 55–56, 71, 86, 104, 111–13, 115–16
Spielberg, Steven, 141
Stein, Gertrude, 37
Stevens, Gavin, 29
Stevens, Wallace, 28–29
Stone, Phil, 4, 29, 76–77
Stranger, The (Camus), 116–17
Styron, William, 103
Sulloway, Frank J., 83–85
Sun Also Rises, The (Hemingway), 49
Sutpen, Henry, 30, 63–65, 72, 105–9, 114–15, 117
Sutpen, Judith, 13, 56, 58, 63–65, 67–68, 114–15, 117
Sutpen, Thomas, 102, 104–6, 111
Sydnor, Charles S., 5

Tennie's Turl. *See* Beauchamp, Terrel
"That Evening Sun" (Faulkner), 111, 115–16
Thompson, Jacob, 14
Through the Wheat (Boyd), 27
Tomey's Turl. *See* Beauchamp, Terrel
"Town, The" (Faulkner), 29
"Turnabout" (Faulkner), 93–94
Two Little Confederates (Page), 73

Ulysses (Joyce), 121
University of Mississippi, 5, 13, 80, 94
Unvanquished, The (Faulkner), 4–5, 7–12, 31, 72, 93

Van Dorn, General, 8
"Victory" (Faulkner), 27–28, 39–40, 93, 95

Westrum, Dexter, 92
Wild Palms, The (Faulkner), 128
Williams, John S., 92
Wolfe, Thomas, 103

www.ingramcontent.com/pod-product-compliance
Lightning Source LLC
Chambersburg PA
CBHW030344240426
43661CB00052B/1741